Recent Research in Psychology

Hans Westmeyer (Ed.)

Psychological Theories from a Structuralist Point of View

Springer-Verlag
Berlin Heidelberg New York
London Paris Tokyo Hong Kong

Editor

Hans Westmeyer
Institute of Psychology, Free University of Berlin
Habelschwerdter Allee 45, D-1000 Berlin 33, FRG

ISBN 3-540-51904-1 Springer-Verlag Berlin Heidelberg New York
ISBN 0-387-51904-1 Springer-Verlag New York Berlin Heidelberg

Printed in Germany

Printing and binding: Druckhaus Beltz, Hemsbach/Bergstr.
2126/3140-543210 – Printed on acid-free paper

Preface

Metatheoretical and, more generally, methodological analyses of psychological problems and theories have a long tradition; however, their impact on scientific practice, especially on the clarification and testing of existing psychological theories and the formulation of new ones, has so far been less than spectacular. The increased interest in theoretical psychology visible during the past ten or twenty years is associated with the hope that a change of this situation will gradually be effected. Thus, in their preface to the proceedings of the founding conference of *The International Society for Theoretical Psychology*, Baker et al. (1987, pp. Vf)[1] take up once more the objectives of a theoretical psychology formulated by Koch[2] already in 1951:

(a) Education in the methodology and logic of science.

(b) Analysis of methodological or foundational problems that are more or less unique to psychology. ...

(c) Internal systematization of suggestive, but formally defective, theoretical formulations.

(d) Intertranslation and differential analysis of conflicting theoretical formulations.

(e) Construction of new theory.

Reflecting on possible reasons for the relative inefficacy so far of methodological and metatheoretical analyses in psychology, it seems to me that the following two have been of prime importance:

(1) Many of the existing analyses are at best tenuously connected to concrete existing psychological theories, i.e., they deal with their subject matter in a too abstract, detached way. This detracts from the persuasive power which their results might otherwise have, and impedes the realization of these results within scientific practice.

(2) Theoretical psychology, as a metatheoretical discipline, is itself in need of an adequate methodology. Those who assume that e.g. informal logic and set theory play a comparable role in theoretical psychology as does statistics in empirical psychology, will find their

[1] Baker, W.J., Hyland, M.E., Van Rappard, H., & Staats, A.W. (Eds.) (1987). *Current issues in theoretical psychology.* Amsterdam: North-Holland.

[2] Koch, S. (1951). Theoretical psychology 1950: An overview. *Psychological Review*, **58**, 295-301.

expectations disappointed. Instead, analyses of psychological theories are usually conducted in an informal, narrative manner; as a consequence, the efforts to systematically study and compare psychological theories are frequently incompatible with one another and are guided by criteria separately conceived of by every new author. Obviously, this state of affairs does not promote the reliability of the results of theoretical psychology.

The present book is intended as a remedy for these two problems and to thereby contribute to the attainment of the objectives of theoretical psychology as originally formulated by Koch. Concrete psychological theories are reconstructed in a precise way and submitted to a thorough-going analysis by using the conceptual apparatus provided by the *structuralist approach* to scientific theories (see chapter 1 for an introduction to this new approach in the philosophy of science). While it must be ultimately left to the reader to decide whether the insights and outlooks emanating from this research represent true progress for theoretical psychology, progress which is associated with implications for scientific practice, the research presented in this book demonstrates that the structuralist approach is suited both for the precise reconstruction of existing psychological theories, and the construction of new ones.

After a brief introduction into the central ideas and concepts of the structuralist program (chapter 1), this book presents structuralist *reconstructions* of five psychological theory-nets (chapters 2 - 6), and structuralist *constructions* of two further ones (chapters 7 and 8). On the basis of these constructions and reconstructions, a first assessment of the current state of efforts to apply the structuralist approach to psychology is possible.

With one exception (chapter 6), the reconstructions of psychological theories published in this book have been presented and discussed at least at one of the first three conferences on "Psychological theories from a structuralist point of view", which were held in 1987 and 1988 at the Werner-Reimers-Foundation, Bad Homburg. At these conferences, the reconstructions were checked by psychological experts with respect to their substantial adequacy, and by philosophers of science with regard to their exactness and syntactical correctness.

It is planned to hold two further conferences in 1989 and 1990, respectively, at which additional reconstructions and constructions of psychological theories will be presented; these will be published in a second volume. A third volume will contain comments by psychologists and philosophers of science on the reconstructs and constructs presented in the first two books. However, the interdisciplinary character of the present research in theoretical psychology, in which psychologists cooperated closely with exponents of other disciplines, especially from philosophy of science, is already reflected in this volume by the fact that two of the authors (W. Balzer and M. Kuokkanen) are philosophers of science. I am very glad that they were willing to participate in this project.

This book would not have come into existence without assistance from several sides. Most of all, I would like to thank the Werner-Reimers-Foundation and its director, Konrad von Krosigk, for having made possible our conferences both by providing financial support and a congenial setting for the meetings. Thanks are also due to the Free University of Berlin for a grant which permitted the preparation of a manuscript ready for press. Special thanks are due to two people: Uwe Czienskowski, who prepared, with visible success, the printer's copy of the book manuscript; and Rainer Reisenzein, who helped to render the English of my contributions more readable. Finally, I would like to express my gratitude to the Springer publishing house for its readiness to publish this volume.

Berlin, August, 1989 Hans Westmeyer

Contents

Notational Conventions

The authors have attempted to use the standard notation of set theory and, in some chapters, the standard symbols for connectives and quantifiers as used in symbolic logic. Besides these conventions, each chapter has its own "formal style".

$\{... : --\}$	the set of ... such that $--$
$... \in --$	... is an element of $--$
$... \cup --$	the union of ... and $--$
$... \cap --$	the intersection of ... and $--$
$... \subseteq --$	... is a subset of $--$
$... \subset --$	... is a proper subset of $--$
$... \times --$	the Cartesian product of ... and $--$
$Po(...)$	the power-set of ...
$\neg ...$	the complement/negation of ...
$,,, : ... \Longrightarrow --$	,,, is a function from ... into $--$
$D_I(...)$	*dom*(...), i.e. the domain of ...
$D_{II}(...)$	*ran*(...), i.e. the range of ...
$\|...\|$	the cardinality of ..., i.e., the number of elements of ...
$\emptyset$	the empty set
$\mathbb{R}$	the set of real numbers
$\mathbb{R}^+$	the set of positive real numbers
$\mathbb{N}$	the set of natural numbers
$... \wedge --$	... and $--$
$... \vee --$	... or $--$
$... \longrightarrow --$	... implies $--$
$... \longleftrightarrow --$	... is equivalent to $--$
$... :\longleftrightarrow --$	... is equivalent by definition to $--$
$\exists ...$	there exist ...
$\forall ...$	for all ...
$... = --$	... is identical to $--$
$... \neq --$	... is not identical to $--$
$... := --$	... is identical by definition to $--$
$... \cong --$	... is approximately identical to $--$
iff	if and only if

Chapter 1

Psychological Theories from a Structuralist Point of View

A First Introduction

Hans Westmeyer

Free University of Berlin

Abstract

The structuralist program in the philosophy of science offers a promising framework for theoretical investigations in psychology. It recommends as a scientific language the informal theory of sets, and provides powerful tools to handle many problems of interest in the analysis of psychological theories. This chapter gives a short introduction into the structuralist view of theories, and assesses the current state of attempts to reconstruct or construct psychological theories from a structuralist perspective.

When it comes to the design and analysis of empirical investigations, psychologists can draw on a differentiated and elaborated set of tools with which they become well acquainted already as students. In contrast, for the purpose of analyzing, reconstructing and developing theories, a comparable set of tools is nearly completely lacking. Not surprisingly, analyses of psychological theories are therefore usually conducted in an informal, narrative manner. As a consequence, the efforts to systematically study and compare psychological theories are frequently incompatible with one another and are guided by criteria separately conceived of by every new author.

Since the beginning of the seventies, however, with the advent of the structuralist conception of scientific theories, a new approach in the philosophy of science is under development which promises to allow a unified presentation of psychological theories, a precise formulation of intra- and intertheoretical relations, and the investigation of these relations for concrete psychological theories. Since the beginning of the eighties, this new approach in the philosophy of science has been increasingly utilized by psychologists.

So far, there are over 20 structuralist analyses of various psychological theories. For the most part, these analyses are concerned with *reconstructions* of already existing theories, but in a few cases, new theories were developed and formulated within the structuralist framework from the outset. In these instances, it is appropiate to speak of structuralist *constructions* of psychological theories.

What is Structuralism ?

"Structuralism" and "structure" are ambiguous terms. They designate a variety of concepts, many of which relate to the subject matter of psychology. This object-related use of the term "structure" is exemplified by such concepts as "cognitive structure", "propositional structure", "semantic structure", and "syntactic structure", concepts which are quite common in cognitive psychology as well as in linguistics. Indeed, psychological and linguistic theories and approaches dealing with these and similar kinds of structures are often called "structural" or "structuralist" (cf. Wilson, 1980).

Of course, this sort of structuralism is not the issue at stake in this paper. Here, "structuralism" refers to a certain view of scientific theories. It therefore denotes a *metatheoretical* position, and a structuralist view of psychological theories does in no way presuppose a structuralist position with regard to their subject matter. The kind of structuralism with which we are concerned here is a certain position within the philosophy of science, and its opponent is not - as in the case of the object-related kind of structuralism in psychology - functionalism, but the so-called *statement view* of scientific theories, which regards scientific theories as sets of propositions (cf. Stegmüller, 1973, 1976).

However, despite the differences in principle between the diverse forms of structuralism, they have also elements in common. Wilson (1980, p. 27) who has furnished a review and analysis of various versions of structuralism in psychology suggests that the following definition of "structure" captures the meaning of this term common to the various positions:

> A *structure* consists of elements, their relations and rules for the generation of new elements and relations from previous elements.

Given certain interpretations of the phrase "rules for the generation of ...", this formulation is certainly general enough to subsume even the structure concept as used by the proponents of the structuralist view of scientific theories.

As Wilson (1980) also points out, a further aspect common to many structuralist positions is "some attempt to formally describe the structures which are central to their theorizing" (p. 12). This is certainly true of the structuralist approach to scientific theories, which relies extensively on informal logic and informal set theory for the reconstruction (or construction) of scientific theories, thereby following a recommendation made already many years ago by Patrick Suppes (cf. 1957). Indeed, Suppes could be called a precursor of the structuralist approach.

To introduce the reader to the structuralist approach to theories, let us consider, as an example, a mathematical theory which we all know and use in our daily research, namely, the theory of probability. In accordance with Suppes (1957, p. 277), the basic concept of a finitely additive probability space can be defined in the following way:

Def-PS
x is a *finitely additive probability space* if and only if there are S, F, P such that
(1) $x = \langle S, F, P \rangle$;
(2) S is a finite, non-empty set (the sample space);
(3) F is a field (algebra) of sets on S, i.e. F is a non-empty family of subsets of S and for every A and B in F: (a) $A \cup B \in F$, (b) $\neg A \in F$;
(4) P is a real-valued function on F (the probability measure);
(5) for every A in F : $P(A) \geq 0$;
(6) $P(S) = 1$;
(7) for every A, B in F : if $A \cap B = \emptyset$, then $P(A \cup B) = P(A) + P(B)$.

Definition *Def-PS* fixes what counts as a finitely additive probability space: It has to be an entity consisting of three components, a base set S (cf. [2]), a family F of subsets of S (cf. [3]), and a function P with F as its domain and a set of real numbers as its range (cf. [4]). However, not all structures typified and characterized in this way are finitely additive probability spaces. In (5) - (7), certain restrictions are imposed on the structures defined by (1) - (4). Only those structures satisfying these restrictions count as finitely additive probability spaces, or, in other words, may be considered as models of the theory of finitely additive probability spaces.

We can express this somewhat differently by saying that the ***conceptual apparatus*** of the theory, so to speak, is delineated in (1) - (4) of *Def-PS*, whereas the ***theoretical assumptions*** are formulated in (5) - (7). With regard to Wilson's previously mentioned definition of the structure concept, the "elements" are, in the present case, the elements of the sample space and the elements of the family of its subsets, as well as the set of real numbers; their "relation" is given by the probability measure; and the "rules" are captured by the assumptions (5) - (7), especially by (7), which yields the probability of the disjunction of two mutually exclusive events, given their individual probabilities.

Of course, other exemplars of this Suppesian type of axiomatization of a theory by definition of a set-theoretic predicate could also have been given. Suppes himself defined, among others, such notions as "is a stimulus-response model", "is a rational subjective choice structure", and "is a linear response model" (see Suppes, 1969).

But although Suppes is a precursor of the structuralist program, its genuine founder is Joseph D. Sneed. In 1971, Sneed published a book on "The logical structure of mathematical physics". This book was the starting point of the developments known today as the structuralist approach in the philosophy of science. What Sneed did was to extend Suppes' approach in various ways to make it better suited to the analysis of empirical theories. Sneed's work was soon taken up by Wolfgang Stegmüller (cf. 1973, 1976) and further elaborated by him (cf. 1979, 1980, 1986) and his collaborators, especially Wolfgang Balzer (cf. 1982, 1985; Balzer & Heidelberger, 1983) and C. Ulises Moulines (cf. 1976, 1982). For the most recent presentation of the structuralist program, see the book "An architectonic for science" by Balzer, Moulines, and Sneed (1987).

This is not the place to describe in detail the differences which exist between the structuralist view of scientific theories and the earlier approach by Suppes (but see e.g. Stegmüller, 1979). Instead, by building on the material which has already been introduced, a brief survey of the most important concepts of the structuralist approach shall be presented. This presentation borrows heavily from Balzer et al. (1987) and Stegmüller (1979).

Central Concepts of the Structuralist Approach

According to the structuralist view, theories, including psychological theories, consist of (typically several) theory-elements. What, then, is a theory-element?

Def-TE
T is a *theory-element* iff (if and only if) there exist K and I such that
(1) $T = \langle K, I \rangle$;

(2) K is a theory-core;
(3) I is a domain of intended applications of K.

Def-TE says that a theory-element is a set-theoretical structure consisting of two components, a *theory-core* K and a set I of *intended applications* of K. The inclusion of this latter set I into the definition of a theory-element is characteristic of the structuralist approach. It is a fundamental tenet of structuralism that a theory is not universally applicable, but only to a certain set, range, or domain of intended applications. The specification of this open set is an important part of the formulation of a theory-element. In most cases, I is "anchored" in a paradigmatic subset I_0 containing those successful applications of the theory-core which the founder and/or influential proponents of the theory regard as exemplary of the theory.

Reverting to the theory of probability, the respective range of *intended* applications of *PS* would be the set of all entities for which it is reasonable to ask whether they are finitely additive probability spaces. *Successful* applications are those structures which satisfy the definition, i.e., which are models of *PS*.

However, *Def-PS* does not qualify as a definition of a theory-core, although it may be part of such a definition. What, then, is a theory-core?

Def-K(T)
$K(T)$ is a *theory-core* iff there exist $M_p(T), M(T), M_{pp}(T), GC(T), GL(T)$ such that
(1) $K(T) = \langle M_p(T), M(T), M_{pp}(T), GC(T), GL(T)\rangle$;
(2) $M_p(T)$ is a class of potential models;
(3) $M(T)$ is a class of models within $M_p(T)$;
(4) $M_{pp}(T)$ is the class of partial potential models given by $M_p(T)$ and $M(T)$;
(5) $GC(T)$ is the global constraint belonging to $M_p(T)$;
(6) $GL(T)$ is the global link belonging to $M_p(T)$.

As *Def-K(T)* shows, a theory-core is a rather complex set-theoretical structure consisting of, in all, five components. In $M_p(T)$, the class of potential models, the conceptual apparatus of the theory is introduced. The definition of $M_p(T)$ does not, however, include the theoretical assumptions made by the theory. Hence, to be an element of $M_p(T)$ it is only necessary to satisfy the typifications and characterizations given in the definition.

As concerns *Def-PS*, the proper definition of $M_p(PS)$ would be:

Def-Mp(PS)
x is a *potential model* of the theory of finitely additive probability spaces iff there are S, F, P such that
(1) $x = \langle S, F, P\rangle$;
(2) S is a finite, non-empty set (the sample space);
(3) F is a field (algebra) of sets on S, i.e. F is a non-empty family of subsets of S and for every A and B in F: (a) $A \cup B \in F$, (b) $\neg A \in F$;
(4) P is a real-valued function on F (the probability measure).

Those potential models of a theory which satisfy, in addition, the theoretical assumptions or laws of the theory, be they fundamental or special laws, are called actual models or simply *models* of the theory. To define $M(PS)$, only a slight reformulation of *Def-PS* is required:

Def-M(PS)
x is a *model* of the theory of finitely additive probability spaces iff

(1) x is an element of $M_p(PS)$;
(2) for every A in F : $P(A) \geq 0$;
(3) $P(S) = 1$;
(4) for every A, B in F : if $A \cap B = \emptyset$, then $P(A \cup B) = P(A) + P(B)$.

The reader may recall that, within the statement view of scientific theories, scientific terms are differentiated into theoretical versus observational ones. Hence, the distinction between theoretical and non-theoretical terms coincides with the non-observational vs. observational dichotomy, which is regarded as being relatively independent of concrete theories. In contrast, from the structuralist perspective, the problem of the *theoreticity* of scientific terms and the question of the *observability* of the entities to which they refer are separate issues. Their conflation is therefore seen as inadequate and as preventing a proper conception of theoretical terms.

According to the structuralist position, theoreticity must always be relativized, but not to a (theoretical in contrast to an observational) language, but to a scientific theory. "The exact denotation is, therefore, not 'theoretical' but 'T-theoretical"' (Stegmüller, 1979, p. 10). There are several criteria of T-theoreticity. A semiformal one is the following by Balzer et al. (1987, p. 55):

> A concept t is called *theoretical* relative to theory T (or just T-theoretical) iff every determination of t in any application of T presupposes the existence of at least one actual model of T.

Examples of T-theoretical concepts occuring in psychological theories are easy to find. For example, most theories containing latent variables treat these variables implicitly as T-theoretical, because they presuppose, in attempts to determine their specific parameter values for a concrete application, the validity of the theoretical assumptions which directly or indirectly connect latent and manifest variables. Intervening variables in psychological theories are another kind of concepts which are typically of a T-theoretical nature.

The distinction between T-theoretical and T-non-theoretical concepts forms the basis of the differentiation between *potential models* and *partial potential models* of a theory. Potential models are those structures which exemplify all of the concepts of the theory, i.e. both the theoretical and the non-theoretical ones. If we omit all theoretical terms from a potential model we are left with a partial potential model, i.e. a structure consisting of all and only the non-theoretical concepts of the theory.

If we assume, for the purpose of illustration, that the probability measure P in $Def-PS$ is a PS-theoretical term, $M_{pp}(PS)$ would be defined as follows:

Def-M$_{pp}$(PS)
x is a *partial potential model* of the theory of finitely additive probability spaces iff there exist S, F, P such that
(1) $x = \langle S, F \rangle$;
(2) $\langle S, F, P \rangle$ is an element of $M_p(PS)$;
(3) exactly P is PS-theoretical.

Besides the classes of potential, actual and partial potential models, a theory-core also comprises a global constraint and a global link. "Global" refers, in these cases, to the intersection of all constraints and links, respectively, which appear in the theory. Now, what are constraints and links more precisely?

Concerning first the concept of *constraints*, note that the definitions of M_p, M, and M_{pp} refer to *individual elements* of the set of intended applications. Every structure is considered by itself. But the elements of M_p may be connected in certain ways; in particular, they may in part overlap. For example, let us assume that a psychological theory analyzes the dependency of client behavior on personality traits of the therapist. A specific interacting client-therapist dyad, as described by the theoretical and non-theoretical concepts of the theory, would then constitute one of its potential models. A second analogously described client-therapist pair would be another potential model of the theory. However, it could easily be that these two potential models consist of two different clients which are treated by the same therapist. Thus, the two potential models of the theory are connected by the identity of one of the members of the dyad (the therapist), and it is perhaps possible to predict client behavior in one dyad on the basis of what is known about the other client-therapist pair.

These real, as well as conceptual connections between different applications of a theory are expressed by constraints. In set-theoretical terms, a *constraint* C for a class of potential models M_p is defined as a non-empty subset of the power-set of M_p which (a) does not contain the empty set, but (b) does contain, for each potential model of the theory, the respective singleton.

Let us now turn to the notion of a *link*. As mentioned before, T-theoretical terms are concepts specific to a theory T, whereas T-non-theoretical terms are not theory-specific. In part, these T-non-theoretical terms are base sets, relations, and functions which may occur in many theories but cannot be interpreted by concepts of other theories. In many cases, however, important T-non-theoretical concepts of a theory are interpretable by concepts of other theories. Such an interpretation is expressed by intertheoretical links which therefore, so to speak, serve to import concepts from one theory to another.

Links connect individual theory-elements and are important tools for the reconstruction of the global structure of science (cf. Balzer et al., 1987, p. 60f). They are of fundamental importance for the systematic treatment of intertheoretical relations in psychology and of the connections between a psychological theory and the structures we refer to in the course of its empirical investigation, which include the structures appealed to in the operationalization of psychological constructs. A simple definition of this concept is: L is an (abstract) *link* from M_p to M'_p iff L is a subset of the Cartesian product of M_p and M'_p.

All components of the concept of theory-core as defined in *Def-*$K(T)$ have now been introduced. Let us therefore turn to the second component of a theory-element, the domain of intended applications I. As can be seen from the following definition of $I(T)$, the theory-core K and the domain of intended applications I are not totally separate parts of a theory-element:

Def-I(T)
$I(T)$ is a *set of intended applications* for $K(T)$ only if
(1) $K(T) = \langle M_p(T), M(T), M_{pp}(T), GC(T), GL(T)\rangle$ is a theory-core;
(2) $I(T)$ is a subset of $M_{pp}(T)$.

Hence, the intended applications of T are partial potential models of T. The connections between $I(T)$ and the other components of $K(T)$ enter into the empirical claim of the theory-element T (cf. Balzer et al., 1987, pp. 91, 85).

Def-EC(T)
If $T = \langle K(T), I(T) \rangle$ is a theory-element then the (idealized) *empirical claim* of T is that $I(T)$ belongs to the content of $K(T)$.

$I(T)$ belongs to the *content* of $K(T)$ if the elements of $I(T)$ can be augmented by T-theoretical terms in such a way that the resulting subset $Y(T)$ of the set of potential models $M_p(T)$ fulfills the following conditions: (1) all elements of $Y(T)$ are actual models of the theory, i.e., $Y(T)$ is an element of the power-set of $M(T)$; (2) $Y(T)$ satisfies the global constraint, i.e., $Y(T)$ is an element of $GC(T)$; and (3) all elements of $Y(T)$ are correctly linked to the relevant other theory-elements, i.e., $Y(T)$ is an element of the power-set of $GL(T)$.

Many additional concepts introduced within the structuralist approach are of interest to the scientist concerned with the reconstruction or construction of psychological theories. To mention only a few, there is the concept of a *theory-net* as a set of theory-elements connected by the *specialization* relation; there are conceptual tools for the exact analysis of problems of *reduction* and *approximation*; historical developments of theories can be conceptualized as *theory-evolutions*; and the global structure of science can be dealt with by using the concept of a *theory-holon*, i.e. a set of linked theory-nets, and its graph-theoretical supplements (cf. Balzer et al., 1987).

However, in this introductory chapter, only the first-mentioned one of these further structuralist concepts shall be defined, i.e., the concept of a theory-net. This concept is indispensable for the reconstruction of even the simplest psychological theory. A theory-net is a set of theory-elements which are partially ordered by the specialization relation:

Def-TN
TN is a *theory-net* iff there exist ST and σ such that
(1) $TN = \langle ST, \sigma \rangle$;
(2) ST is a non-empty, finite set of theory-elements;
(3) $\sigma \subseteq ST \times ST$ is the specialization relation.

The binary relation σ is defined as follows:

Def-σ
If $T = \langle M_p(T), M(T), M_{pp}(T), GC(T), GL(T), I(T) \rangle$ and
$T' = \langle M_p(T'), M(T'), M_{pp}(T'), GC(T'), GL(T'), I(T') \rangle$ are theory-elements, then
T' is a *specialization* of T (abbreviated as $T' \sigma T$) iff
(1) $M_p(T') = M_p(T)$;
(2) $M_{pp}(T') = M_{pp}(T)$;
(3) $M(T') \subseteq M(T)$;
(4) $GC(T') \subseteq GC(T)$;
(5) $GL(T') \subseteq GL(T)$;
(6) $I(T') \subseteq I(T)$.

Thus, although the specialized theory-element T' has a more restricted scope than the original theory-element T, it has "the same conceptual structure, i.e. the same primitive concepts and the same distinction between the theoretical and the non-theoretical level" (Balzer et al., 1979, p. 169). Therefore, the differences which exist between T' and T concern only the classes of actual models, constraints, links, and intended applications, but not the sets of potential and partial potential models.

Applications of the Structuralist Program in Psychology

Table 1 summarizes, in chronological order, the efforts which exist to date to reconstruct or construct psychological theories from a structuralist point of view. In most cases, the listed items refer to reconstructions of previously existing theories, but a few theories have been developed and formulated from the outset in consideration of the structuralist conception of scientific theories, e.g. (6), (18), and (23). These theories may therefore be called structuralist constructions. An intermediate position, which combines constructive and reconstructive elements, is exemplified by (3) and (4).

Table 1 includes all attempts which I am aware of to reconstruct or construct a psychological theory within the structuralist framework. In some cases, the reconstructions and constructions exist only in preliminary, as yet unpublished versions (e.g. [20] - [23]), or have not yet been published in full length (e.g. [4] and [5]), but all constructions have at least been presented at a conference or symposium concerned with the application of the structuralist program to psychology.

It may be expected that the various reconstructions and constructions are of different quality. However, a systematic evaluation presupposes standards or conditions of adequacy: For a proposed reconstruction to be acceptable, it has to satisfy certain requirements. But what are reasonable standards for evaluating a structuralist reconstruction of a theory?

Balzer et al. (1987) suggest the following *primary criterion*: "The reconstruction of each particular piece of science should 'generate' in a systematic, standardized, and natural way the essential properties of that piece and the central claims associated to it by the average users of that piece" (p. XVIIf). Secondary criteria include *consistency, elegance, economy*, as well as *perspective* (Balzer et al., 1987, p. XVIII). These criteria are very similar to the requirements which Carnap (1962, p. 5ff) proposed for the explication of concepts. There are analogies between the primary criterion and Carnap's requirement that the explicatum should be similar to the explicandum; between consistency and Carnap's requirement of exactness; between elegance and economy and Carnap's requirement of simplicity; and between perspective and Carnap's requirement of fruitfulness.

Besides the consistency and exactness of a reconstructum, its *fruitfulness* is of particular importance. This requirement is satisfied if the reconstruction offers interesting, perhaps even surprising insights into the theory which were not previously evident. In particular, new intra- and intertheoretical relations may be revealed, and new or more stringent possibilities for testing the theory may be discovered.

One aspect of the primary criterion should be especially emphasized, namely, the *completeness* of a reconstructum. Psychological theories can usually be reconstructed only as complex theory-nets consisting of many theory-elements. In the case of theories with a large set of already established successful applications and an even larger domain of intended ones,

Table 1
Structuralist reconstructions and constructions of psychological theories

(1)	B.F.Skinner's theory of operant behavior (Kraiker, 1976, 1977, 1980)
(2)	S.Freud's theory of neurosis (Balzer, 1982; Stegmüller, 1986; Balzer & Marcou, 1987, 1989)
(3)	A theory of psychophysics (Wegener, 1982)
(4)	A general psychological action theory (Birkhan & Friedrichsen, 1982, 1983)
(5)	H.Lenk's theory of action (Birkhan & Friedrichsen, 1982, 1983)
(6)	H.Westmeyer's theory of behavior interaction (Westmeyer et al., 1982, 1987; Westmeyer & Nell, 1987; Westmeyer, 1987, 1989)
(7)	The theory of information processing (Ueckert, 1983)
(8)	L.Festinger's theory of cognitive dissonance (Kuokkanen, 1986; Westermann, 1987, 1988a, 1988b,1989)
(9)	B.Cohen's theory of social conformity (Kuokkanen, 1986; Stephan, 1988)
A net of psychological utility theories (Stephan, 1987, 1988, 1989a, 1989b)	
	(10) SEU-, (11) SEV-, (12) OEU-models
	(13) D.Kahneman and A.Tversky's prospect theory
	(14) K.Lewin's theory of resultant valence
	(15) J.W.Atkinson's risk-taking theory
	(16) A general theory of achievement motivation
(17)	F.Heider's balance theory (Stephan, 1988; Kuokkanen, 1989a)
(18)	H.Holling's theory of behavior interruption as a condition of stress (Holling, 1988a, 1988b, 1989)
(19)	J.R.Anderson's theory of cognitive architecture, ACT* (Heise & Westermann, 1988, 1989)
The theories of attribution by (20) E.E.Jones, (21) H.H.Kelley, and (22) B.Weiner (Debler, 1988)	
(23)	H. Ueckert's theory of action and action probing (Ueckert, 1988)
(24)	The theory of role conflict resolution proposed by N.Gross, W.S.Mason, and A.W.McEachern (Kuokkanen, 1989b)

a complete structuralist reconstruction amounts to a time consuming, laborious enterprise which cannot be accomplished in one piece. Therefore, reconstructive efforts are often restricted to the reconstruction of only the basic theory-element and/or a few theory-elements which refer to certain applications of special interest. Of course, this does not yield a complete reconstruction of the theory.

If we try to evaluate the structuralist reconstructions listed in Table 1 in terms of these intuitively sketched criteria, considerable differences with regard to their adequacy become apparent. (1), (4), and (7), for example, are only concerned with the basic elements of the respective theories, especially (1), which exist only as a rough draft. In contrast, (6), (8), and (18) are elaborated theory-nets, which even comprise structures appealed to in the course of attempts to test the respective theory-elements. (3), (9), and (10) - (16) have been likewise developed to a point where interesting conclusions concerning the testability of the theory-elements can be deduced. Particularly in these latter cases, the reconstructions have yielded a number of new and surprising insights into the respective psychological theories, as well as into the more global structure of science of which these theories are a part.

I hope that a closer examination of some of the mentioned reconstructions and constructions, which are presented in the following chapters of this book, will convince the reader that the structuralist program offers a promising framework for theoretical investigations in psychology. It recommends as a scientific language the informal theory of sets, a language which can be easily utilized by every scientist; and it provides a set of powerful tools to handle many problems of interest in the investigation of psychological theories.

References

Balzer,W. (1982). *Empirische Theorien: Modelle - Strukturen - Beispiele.* Braunschweig: Vieweg.

Balzer, W. (1985). *Theorie und Messung.* Berlin: Springer.

Balzer,W., & Heidelberger,M. (Eds.) (1983). *Zur Logik empirischer Theorien.* Berlin: Springer.

Balzer, W., & Marcou, Ph. (1987). *A reconstruction of Sigmund Freud's early theory of the unconscious.* Paper presented at the first conference "Psychological theories from a structuralist point of view", Werner-Reimers-Foundation, Bad Homburg.

Balzer, W., Moulines, C.U., & Sneed, J.D. (1987). *An architectonic for science: The structuralist program.* Dordrecht: Reidel.

Birkhan, G., & Friedrichsen, G. (1982). *Versuch einer strukturalistischen Rekonstruktion von psychologischen Handlungstheorien.* Unpublished paper, University of Hamburg.

Birkhan, G., & Friedrichsen, G. (1983). Handlungstheorien im Lichte der strukturalistischen Theorienauffassung. In G.Lüer (Ed.), *Bericht über den 33. Kongreß der Deutschen Gesellschaft für Psychologie in Mainz 1982.* Volume 1 (pp. 453-456). Göttingen: Hogrefe.

Carnap, R. (1962). *Logical foundations of probability.* Chicago: University of Chicago Press.

Debler, W. (1988). *Strukturalistische Rekonstruktion der Attributionstheorie: Ein Theoriennetz.* Paper presented at the third conference "Psychological theories from a structuralist point of view", Werner-Reimers-Foundation, Bad Homburg.
Abstract in W. Schönpflug (Ed.), *Bericht über den 36. Kongreß der Deutschen Gesellschaft für Psychologie in Berlin 1988.* Volume 1 (p. 400). Göttingen: Hogrefe.

Heise, E. & Westermann, R. (1988). *Erste Überlegungen zur strukturalistischen Rekonstruktion von Andersons Theorie der kognitiven Architektur ACT*.* Paper presented at the third conference "Psychological theories from a structuralist point of view", Werner-Reimers-Foundation, Bad Homburg.
Abstract in W. Schönpflug (Ed.), *Bericht über den 36. Kongreß der Deutschen Gesellschaft für Psychologie in Berlin 1988.* Volume 1 (p. 399). Göttingen: Hogrefe.

Heise, E. & Westermann, R. (1989). *Anderson's theory of cognitive architecture (ACT*): A structuralist reconstruction of some important theory-elements.* Paper presented at the First European Congress of Psychology in Amsterdam.

Holling, H. (1988). *Wahrscheinlichkeitsmodelle und empirische Analysen zur Beanspruchung durch Systemresponsezeiten.* Berlin: Springer. (a)

Holling, H. (1988). *Zur strukturalistischen Konstruktion einer Theorie zur Beanspruchung durch Handlungsunterbrechungen.* Paper presented at the third conference "Psychological theories from a structuralist point of view", Werner-Reimers-Foundation, Bad Homburg.
Abstract in W. Schönpflug (Ed.), *Bericht über den 36. Kongreß der Deutschen Gesellschaft für Psychologie in Berlin 1988.* Volume 1 (p. 400-401). Göttingen: Hogrefe. (b)

Holling, H. (1989). *Interruption of behavior and stress: A structuralist approach.* Paper presented at the First European Congress of Psychology in Amsterdam.

Kraiker, C. (1977). Zum Problem von Theorien und ihrer Anwendung in der Psychologie. In P. Gottwald, & C. Kraiker (Eds.), *Zum Verhältnis von Theorie und Praxis in der Psychologie* (pp. 33-46). München: GVT.

Kraiker, C. (1977). Behavioural analysis and the structural view of scientific theories. *European Journal of Behavioural Analysis and Modification*, **4**, 203-213.

Kraiker, C. (1980). *Psychoanalyse, Behaviorismus, Handlungstheorie.* München: Kindler.

Kuokkanen, M. (1986). Conceptual correlation: An example of two social psychological theories. *Theory and Decision*, **20**, 1-32.

Kuokkanen, M. (1989). *A generalization of social psychological balance theories.* Paper presented at the colloquium "Recent results of the formal philosophy of science", Institute of Philosophy, Free University of Berlin. (a)

Kuokkanen, M. (1989). *A generalization of the theory of role conflict resolution.* Unpublished paper, Department of Philosophy, University of Helsinki. (b)

Moulines, C.U. (1976). Approximate application of empirical theories: A general explication. *Erkenntnis*, **10**, 201-227.

Moulines, C.U. (1982). Exploraciones metacientificas. Madrid: Alianza.

Sneed, J.D. (1971). *The logical structure of mathematical physics.* Dordrecht: Reidel.

Stegmüller, W. (1973). *The structure and dynamics of theories.* New York: Springer. (German edition, 1973)

Stegmüller, W. (1979). *The structuralist view of theories.* New York: Springer.

Stegmüller, W. (1980). *Neue Wege der Wissenschaftsphilosophie.* Berlin: Springer.

Stegmüller, W. (1986). *Die Entwicklung des neuen Strukturalismus seit 1973.* Berlin: Springer.

Stephan, E. (1987). *Strukturalistische Rekonstruktion psychologischer Nutzentheorien.* Paper presented at the first conference "Psychological theories from a structuralist point of view", Werner-Reimers-Foundation, Bad Homburg.
Abstract in W. Schönpflug (Ed.)(1988), *Bericht über den 36. Kongreß der Deutschen Gesellschaft für Psychologie in Berlin 1988.* Volume 1 (p. 398). Göttingen: Hogrefe.

Stephan, E. (1989). *Zur logischen Struktur psychologischer Theorien. Eine Untersuchung im Rahmen der strukturalistischen Wissenschaftstheorie.* Berlin: Springer. (a)

Stephan, E. (1989). *A net of psychological utility theories.* Paper presented at the First European Congress of Psychology in Amsterdam. (b)

Suppes, P. (1957). *Introduction to logic.* Princeton, N.J.: Van Nostrand.

Suppes, P. (1969). *Studies in the methodology and foundations of science.* Dordrecht: Reidel.

Ueckert, H. (1983). Computer-Simulation. In J. Bredenkamp & H.Feger (Eds.), *Hypothesenprüfung* (pp. 530-616). Göttingen: Hogrefe.

Ueckert, H. (1988) *Strukturalistische Konstruktion einer Theorie des Handelns und Probehandelns.* Paper presented at the third conference "Psychological theories from a structuralist point of view", Werner-Reimers-Foundation, Bad Homburg.

Wegener, B. (1982). Outline of a structural taxonomy of sensory and social psychophysics. In B. Wegener (Ed.), *Social attitudes and psychophysical measurement* (pp. 1-40). Hillsdale, N.J.: Lawrence Erlbaum Associates.

Westermann, R. (1987). *Strukturalistische Theorienkonzeption und empirische Forschung in der Psychologie.* Berlin: Springer.

Westermann, R. (1988). Structuralist reconstruction of psychological research: Cognitive dissonance. *The German Journal of Psycholoy*, **12**, 218-231. (a)

Westermann, R. (1988). *Festingers Dissonanztheorie: Zur Präzisierung ihrer strukturalistischen Rekonstruktion als Theoriennetz.* Paper presented at the third conference "Psychological theories from a structuralist point of view", Werner-Reimers-Foundation, Bad Homburg.
Abstract in W. Schönpflug (Ed.), *Bericht über den 36. Kongreß der Deutschen Gesellschaft für Psychologie in Berlin 1988.* Volume 1 (p. 397-398). Göttingen: Hogrefe. (b)

Westermann, R. (1989) *Festinger's theory of cognitive dissonance: A revised structuralist reconstruction.* Paper presented at the First European Congress of Psychology in Amsterdam.

Westmeyer, H. (1987). *Strukturalistische Rekonstruktion einer Theorie der Verhaltensinteraktion.* Paper presented at the first conference "Psychological theories from a structuralist point of view", Werner-Reimers-Foundation, Bad Homburg.

Westmeyer, H. (1989). *A theory of behavior interaction: A structuralist construction.* Paper presented at the First European Congress of Psychology in Amsterdam.

Westmeyer, H., Eller, F., Winkelmann, K. & Nell, V. (1982). A theory of behavior interaction in dyads: A structuralist account. *Metamedicine*, **3**, 209-231.

Westmeyer, H., Hannemann, J., Nell, V., Völkel, U. & Winkelmann,K. (1987). Eine Monotheory-Multimethod Analyse: Plädoyer für einen deduktivistischen Multiplismus. *Diagnostica*, **33**, 227-242.

Westmeyer, H. & Nell, V. (1987). Psychologische Theorien aus strukturalistischer Sicht. In M.Amelang (Hrsg.), *Bericht über den 35. Kongreß der Deutschen Gesellschaft für Psychologie in Heidelberg 1986.* Volume 2 (pp. 179-190). Göttingen: Hogrefe.

Wilson, K.V. (1980). *From association to structure: The course of cognition.* Amsterdam: North-Holland.

Chapter 2

A Reconstruction of Sigmund Freud's Early Theory of the Unconscious

W.Balzer and P.Marcou
University of Munich

Abstract

A version of Freud's early theory of the unconscious — which is a completely qualitative theory — is reconstructed in precise terms. The important structuralist components: models, potential models, partial potential models, constraints, links, measuring models, intended applications are identified, and an explanation for neurosis is given. The theory's empirical claim and confirmation are considered. The particular position of therapeutically relevant theories is discussed and clarified. The reconstruction shows that Freud's early theory lends itself to a completely precise logical treatment and has all the features of empirical theories in the social sciences in general.

In this paper a version of Freud's early theory of the unconscious is presented in the format of an empirical theory which was developed in structuralist philosophy of science.[1] The present account emends our earlier treatment in Balzer (1982) which was already taken up in Stegmüller (1986). We concentrate on Freud's first writings from the years 1892-99 in which his theoretical ideas are expressed in few sentences dispersed in those texts. These sentences together with his descriptions of various cases (many of which occur in later works) form the "data" on which our reconstruction is based.[2] We want to show that Freud's ideas can be stated so as to form a consistent and (in a certain sense) complete picture which - though qualitative - allows for a precise description. By this, we hope to contribute constructively to the never ending debate about his writings. If it should turn out that our reconstruction misses some point this will come out by precisely locating that point; by so doing the reconstruction may be emended, and the controversy had some definite result.[3]

From the theory's exemplifying all important features of an empirical theory, and from the assumption that our reconstruction is adequate it follows that the theory satisfies the essential requirements empirical theories outside the realm of natural science are generally expected to satisfy. On the level of psychology this is a point in favour of "bold" theorizing (as contrasted to the dominant, operational attitude). On the meta-level we provide a further successful application of the structuralist view of theories.

Moreover, we take side on the issue of how to look at medical (or therapeutically relevant) theories in general: sickness (e.g. neurosis) is represented by specializing a respective model

[1]Compare Balzer, Moulines, & Sneed (1987) for a recent, comprehensive account of the structuralist meta-theory.

[2]We use Freud (1967) as main text. The works mentioned are found in volume 1, pp. 2-459. Further references always refer to this volume, if not stated otherwise.

[3]In fact, two such emendations of our original account have been induced by criticism of W.Stegmüller and M.Perrez (which we gratefully acknowledge), and are built in in the present version.

of health. In formalizing this picture a decisive difference emerges between medical theories on the one hand and theories from the natural sciences as well as from the social sciences on the other hand.

In order to avoid misunderstandings it may be useful also to state what we are not claiming. We are not claiming that our reconstruction is the only possible one. As the word indicates, any re"construction" involves some constructive element which may well go beyond the original or beyond what the original author wanted to express. We are not so much interested in what a particular author meant by writing his papers, the interesting point for a reconstruction is whether his theories have some content independent of his intentions. Other reconstructions of the same matter may look differently, and by comparison it may be possible to eliminate one in favour of another one (if they are equivalent, or if the former reduces to the latter, for instance).

This leads to a second point. We do not have independent, "absolute" criteria for a reconstruction being adequate. The business of reconstructing scientific theories is very recent, not much older than 50 years. No criteria ready for use have been put forward in this time. This situation is by no means exceptional, it also obtains in every other domain where scientific theories are applied to real systems. In physics, to mention the most admired case, 400 years of experimental application did not lead to rough and ready criteria of when the application of a theory to a system, or in an experiment, is adequate. The criteria for adequacy of a reconstruction, as well as those for successful application of a theory still are mainly those of performance in comparison with alternative attempts.

Third, we do not want to discuss in detail, and to put forward a kind of decision on, the issue of whether psychology is scientific or not.[4] We feel that the standards for "scientific" activities as put forward by logical empiricism or by Popper are too narrowly drawn from the theoretical branches of natural science. On these standards too many scientific activities (among them many firmly established at universities) fall off the board. We do not object to drawing distinctions but we fear great damage from eliminating psychology (together with most social sciences) from the realm of science by insisting on criteria mainly drawn from classical physics.

Fourth, we do not claim that our reconstruction covers the overwhelming richness present in Freud's writings. There are two aspects to this richness. First, there are many details, data, reported in the descriptions of real cases. These details are parts of the descriptions of intended applications of the theory, and do not occur in the following because for reasons of space we cannot state the intended applications in detail. Second, Freud states, or partially indicates a large number of hypotheses; far more than will be treated here. With respect to these the axiomatic method proves its force. It reduces a large number (infinitely many, to be sure) of hypotheses to a small number of axioms from which all the former are derivable. Not all the hypotheses indicated in Freud's writings will follow from ours. We believe, however, that a substantial part of them can be formulated as specializations of the basic models introduced here. Thus our reconstruction only provides the frame, the basis on which a full net of specializations (that is, in structuralist terminology, a theory-net[5]) can be worked out comprising the full range of Freudian ideas. Still some hypotheses will not be treatable in

[4]Compare Perrez (1979) for a review and critique of discussions before 1979, and later on Gruenbaum (1984).
[5]See Balzer, Moulines, & Sneed (1987), Chap.IV.

this way : they "get lost" in the process of reconstruction. We do not have to say new things about other Freudian topics, like his account of dreams or his later theories of the ego, id, and superego.

Freud's Basic Picture

Freud often uses physical metaphors which may serve as a guide through the abstract passages. For his early theories the "steam pot picture" seems particularly relevant: a closed pot filled with water is constantly heated up, and so from time to time the cover will be lifted and steam will escape. This picture by way of analogy models his view of the unconscious. Man in some respects is like the steam pot. It is constantly "heated up" by an ongoing flow of "drivings" ("Affekte"[6]). The steam is set analogous to "ideas" ("Vorstellungen"[7]), pressure to "suppressing" ("verdrängen"[8]), and escaping to "abreaction" ("Abreagieren", "assoziatives Verarbeiten"[9]). The term "abreaction" ("Abreagieren") is used in connection with drivings as well as with ideas[10], we restrict it to drivings here. Thus the drivings cause the production of ideas which usually give rise to abreactions, or actions. But what if the cover is locked, i.e. if those actions are not feasible? According to Freud the drivings then are blocked (his term is "eingeklemmt"[11]), pressure rises, and the ideas get suppressed, they become what he later calls unconscious. Here are some important passages.[12] "She [psychotherapy] takes back the effect of an idea originally not abreacted by allowing the blocked affect of it to run off through speech, and causes its associative correction by pulling it into ordinary consciousness..." (p. 97), "The pictures of "screening" an incompatible idea, of the origin of hysterical symptoms by conversion of psychical to bodily excitement, of the formation of a separate psychical group by means of the act of the will which leads to the screening, all this was seizably put before my eyes in this moment." (p. 222), "The screening reaches its aim of pressing the incompatible idea out of consciousness, if in the respective person, healthy up to then, sexual scenes are present as unconscious remembrances, and if the idea to be suppressed can be brought into logical or associative connection to such an infantile experience." (p. 447-8), "If in a person with disposition there is no ability for conversion while nonetheless for the sake of screening an unbearable idea this idea is cut off from its affect then this affect has to remain in the psychic field. The idea thus weakened remains in consciousness aside of all associations, its freed affect however joins other ideas, which by themselves are not incompatible but, by means of this 'false connection' become compulsive ideas." (p. 65-6). In later periods, the unconscious acquires its central position: "We learned from psychoanalysis that the essence of the process of suppression does not consist in the destruction of an idea representing the driving. Rather it consists in keeping the idea away from becoming conscious. We then say the idea is in a state of 'unconsciousness', and we can offer good proofs that, though unconscious, it can have effects; even effects that eventually reach 'consciousness'." [13]

---

[6]See, e.g. pp. 65, 66, 85, 97.

[7]E.g. pp. 63, 66, 75, 90, 97, 174.

[8]E.g. pp. 174, 181, 234, 386, 387, 388.

[9]E.g. pp. 87, 89, 90, 94, 97, 224.

[10]On pp. 87, 89, 94 it is used for drivings, on pp. 90, 97 for ideas.

[11]For instance on p. 97.

[12]Translations are ours.

[13]Freud (1963), p. 7. Translation ours.

In order to give a precise account of this, terminology needs to be fixed. We will use the term "event" in a broad sense including ideas, as well as all kinds of experiences a person may have, and actions. In particular, we will use the term such as to include possible events. It will be convenient to regard events as tokens rather than as types. The models to be considered will refer to a person's (possible) concrete experiences, ideas, and actions over some fixed period of time. These experiences, ideas and actions are represented by a set E of events. Besides event-tokens we also use event-types which we treat as classes of event-tokens similar in certain respects. The similarity-relation is left unspecified, and even implicit; it has to be chosen in each application appropriately. Event-types are denoted by k, k', and their collection by K, so that K is a subset of the power set of E. For reasons of simplicity we assume that event-types are disjoint. With a little extra effort at other places this assumption may be relaxed.

Some events are of special importance, for instance those which are conscious or those which are particularly horrible ("negative"). We introduce consciousness as a binary relation between instants and events: $C(t, e)$ means that the person at time t is conscious of event e.

Drivings are treated as ontologically different from events, they are entities of a new kind occurring in the psyche of humans. The set of drivings relevant for a person we denote by D. Drivings also are tokens rather than types. It is the particular driving, say, to eat at 3 a.m. under given circumstances rather than the type of driving we call "hunger" that occurs in the models.

Next, we use the notion of a driving being abreacted ("abreagiert"). We prefer to use the more neutral term "realization" instead. Realization is treated as a four-place relation between instants, drivings, events and event-types. $REAL(t, d, e, k)$ means that, at t, driving d is realized (abreacted) by event e of type k.

Since each model will refer only to one period in a single person's life there will be no need to represent that person in the model. All the concepts used in describing a model are always understood as referring just to one person's case.

A further primitive we use is that of a horrible event, horrible for the person under consideration. We will speak more neutrally of "negative" events, and represent them by a binary relation between instants and events: $N(t, e)$ means that, at t, the person experiences the negative event e. Roughly, negative events are those which cause drivings to be blocked from getting realized.

Our most important primitive is that of the unconscious which we introduce as a binary relation U between instants and events. $U(t, e)$ means that, at t, event ("idea") e is unconscious or suppressed. We need no special term for blocked drivings; these will be defined by means of the above terms.

Next, we use a function f to assign to each driving d the type of events by means of which d ordinarily, or naturally, is realized. We assume that each driving has exactly one such natural type of realizations. This assumption is more technical in nature, for different event-types may be joined to form one new, "bigger" type.

In order to round up the picture we use an ordering relation $\leq$ among instants, and a binary relation AS of association among events: $AS(e, e')$ means that events e and e' are associated for the person considered. Association plays an important role in psychoanalysis. However, from its role in Freud's theory as well as from the development of psychology later on we conclude that Freud's theory is not intended to give a special meaning to that term. We treat association as not explicitly depending on time. This indicates that the "mechanism" of association essentially works "across" time, depending only on the internal structure of the events involved.

It may be noted that our use of events to cover the actions, experiences, as well as ideas has no analogue in Freud's writing; it is an essential ingredient of our reconstruction. We chose events for their great unifying power. It also may be noted that consciousness and the corresponding actions might be omitted without essential loss. We include it, mainly in order to have a "complete" set of terms for the psychic structure: drivings-consciousness-unconsciousness, which motivates the label of unconsciousness so central in Freud.

Altogether we thus arrive at the following list of primitives: T, a set of instants; E, a set of events; D, a set of drivings; K, a set of event-types; $\leq$, an ordering-relation among instants; AS, an association-relation among events; C, consciousness; U, unconsciousness; N, negative events; $REAL$, relation of realization; f, assignment of event-types to drivings.

Potential Models and Models

By stating the precise "grammar" of these primitives, as well as some further, trivial requirements, we obtain the so called potential models of the theory.[14] These are possible systems in which all the primitives have some interpretation but which need not satisfy the theory's central axioms. Among such possible systems there may be real systems as well as purely abstract ones defined in terms of numbers or abstract sets. The class M_p of all potential models may be regarded as the set of "possible worlds" for Freud's theory. Any "world" (=potential model) which contains interpretations for all primitives is possible.

D1 x is a *potential model* of Freud's theory ($x \in M_p$) iff there exist $T, E, D, K, \leq, AS, C, N, U, REAL$ and f such that $x = \langle T, E, D, K, \leq, AS, C, N, U, REAL, f \rangle$ and

1) T, E, D are finite, non-empty sets, and pairwise disjoint;
2) K is a partition of E (i.e. $K \subseteq Po(E)$, all $k \in K$ are non-empty and pairwise disjoint, and $\bigcup\{k : k \in K\} = E$);
3) $\leq$ is a weak order on T (i.e. $\leq \subseteq T \times T$ is reflexive, transitive, and connected);
4) $AS \subseteq E \times E$;
5) $C \subseteq T \times E, N \subseteq T \times E$, and $U \subseteq T \times E$;
6) $REAL \subseteq T \times D \times E \times K$;
7) $f : D \Longrightarrow K$ is injective.

The set T of instants must not be confused with instants of physical time (which often are represented by real numbers). The elements of T simply serve as indices for ordering events and drivings as they occur one after another. Note that by D1-1, T is a finite set. It is best to imagine members of T as those (physical) instants at which something important

[14]See Balzer, Moulines, & Sneed (1987), Chap.I.

happens in the person's history: she experiences an event important from the point of view of psychology, or some sufficiently strong driving is present. The choice of T in an application is not much restricted theoretically but a wrong choice may lead to an uninteresting model. If T contains too many instants, the model will be overloaded with redundant data, if T is "too small" nothing interesting will happen in the model. It may be noted that T needs not cover the whole life of the person described.

In order to get used to this kind of representation, consider the following trivial, contrived example of a person B during an ordinary working day, say November 4, 1977. The instants will make up a list of the following kind: 7 a.m., 7.15, 7.35, 7.50, 8, 9, 11, 11.30, ... Of course, these instants are ordered in the natural way. The set E of events will comprise those events which in some sense are important, and to each event-token we may assign a corresponding event-type as given by the verbal description (which never can be as fine as a token). E may contain, among others, the event of being waked up (at 7 a.m.), of taking a shower (at 7.15), having breakfast (at 7.35), seeing an accident while sitting in the bus (7.50), entering office (at 8), getting an order (at 9) etc. The set of drivings contains those occurring during that day, like a little sexual excitement under the shower, a small feeling of hunger before breakfast, nervosity and anxiety while meeting the boss at 9, hunger at 11 etc. Some of the events experienced will get associated with other events in B's history: the event e1 of listening to some advertisement at breakfast will get associated with other, past, experiences $(e1)2, ..., (en)2$ of the same silly sentences, the event $e3$ of seeing a broken limb at the accident at 7.50 will get associated with the past event $e4$ of B himself breaking a leg. The association-relation AS will consist of a set of such pairs of associated events:
$AS = \{\langle e1, (e1)2\rangle, \langle e1, (e2)2\rangle, ..., \langle e1, (en)2\rangle, \langle e3, e4\rangle, ...\}$.

Consciousness is represented by those pairs $\langle t, e\rangle$ for which e is some event of importance which gets into the person's mind, and t is the instant at which it occurs. $\langle 7.50, e3\rangle$ and $\langle 9, e5\rangle$ are examples, if $e5$ is the event of B's getting a special order from his boss. So $C = \{\langle 7.50, e3\rangle, \langle 9, e5\rangle, ...\}$. Negative events in such an ordinary case will not occur, so N will be empty. The realization-relation will consist of events which abreact present drivings. One example here might be $\langle 11, d, e6, k\rangle$ where d is "hunger" and $e6$ the event of having lunch. Thus $REAL = \{\langle 11, d, e6, k\rangle, ...\}$. On the assumption that B is a psychically healthy person, there will be no important unconscious, suppressed events, i.e. $U = \emptyset$. If we put together all these sets in a 11-tuple we obtain a potential model which describes B during the particular day from Freud's psychological point of view.

Such a description is called a model of the theory if it satisfies the following axioms.

A1 If, at t, event e of type k realizes driving d then, at t, e is conscious, and of type k.

A2 Any negative event at t is conscious at t.

A3 Any event is associated with itself.

These are rather trivial, "analytic" statements concerning the use of the primitives. A1 rules out the case of e realizing d without e being conscious. Similarly, A2 rules out negative events from not being conscious at the time when they occur. A3 is simply a convention. In addition, there are four more substantial axioms. We say that e is a *natural realization* of driving d if $e \in f(d)$.

A4 An event e cannot be unconscious and a natural realization at the same time.

A5 If some driving d is realized by two events e and e' (possibly at different times) then these events are associated.

A6 For any two events which are associated and which both are natural realizations of the same driving: if one of the two is negative at t then the other will be unconscious at any later time.

A7 Any driving becomes realized at some time.

A4 imposes a restriction on the realization-relation. Only those events may occur as realizations of some driving which are not unconscious. In other words, unconscious, suppressed events cannot serve for natural realization. A5 says that associations of events are caused by their being linked to a common driving. In this form A5 certainly contains a strong element of idealization. We note, however, that realization of d by e implies that e is conscious (by A1), so e has to be rather strong and important. A6 represents the "mechanism" of suppression: if e at t is negative ("horrible") then any natural realization of the driving realized by e which is associated with e will get unconscious after t. A7 is the central axiom concerning the steam pot picture: any driving will lead to a corresponding realization.

By collecting these axioms and eliminating some ambiguities still present in the verbal formulation we obtain

D2 x is a *model* of Freud's theory ($x \in M$) iff there exist $T, E, D, K, \leq, AS, C, N, U, REAL, f$ such that $x = \langle T, E, D, K, \leq, AS, C, N, U, REAL, f \rangle$, $x \in M_p$ and
1) for all $t \in T$, $d \in D$, $e \in E$ and $k \in K$: if $REAL(t, d, e, k)$ then $C(t, e)$ and $e \in k$;
2) for all $t \in T$ and $e \in E$: if $N(t, e)$ then $C(t, e)$;
3) for all $e \in E : AS(e, e)$;
4) for all $t \in T, e \in E$ and $k \in K$ such that $e \in k$: not $[U(t, e)$ and (there exists $d \in D$ such that $REAL(t, d, e, k)$ and $k = f(d))]$;
5) for all $t, t' \in T, e, e' \in E, d \in D$ and $k, k' \in K$: if $REAL(t, d, e, k)$ and $REAL(t', d, e', k')$ then $AS(e, e')$;
6) for all $t, t' \in T, e, e' \in E$: if $N(t, e), t < t', AS(e, e')$, and if there exists $d \in D$ such that $e \in f(d)$ and $e' \in f(d)$ then $U(t', e')$;
7) for all $d \in D$ there exist $t \in T$, $e \in E$ and $k \in K$ such that $REAL(t, d, e, k)$.

The expression "$t < t'$" in A6 is of course defined in terms of $\leq$ in the usual way: $t < t'$ iff ($t \leq t'$ and not($t = t'$)). Obviously, $M \subseteq M_p$.

Neurosis

The formal models just introduced basically describe "normal" healthy persons but they also can be applied to psychically sick persons. One may wonder how this is possible because "sick" and "healthy" exclude each other, and a theory allowing for both would seem inconsistent. The first thing to note here is that the axioms are, in fact, consistent.

Theorem 1 M is not empty.

Proof : It is easy to check that $x = \langle\{t\},\{e,e'\},\{d\},\{\{e\},\{e'\}\},$
$\{\langle t,t\rangle\},\{\langle e,e\rangle,\langle e',e'\rangle\},\{\langle t,e\rangle,\langle t,e'\rangle\},\emptyset,\emptyset,\{\langle t,d,e,\{e\}\rangle\},$
$\{\langle d,\{e\}\rangle\}\rangle$ is a model.#

Secondly, it has to be noted that one single model cannot describe a sick and a healthy person at the same time. The distinction between sickness and health cannot be drawn within a single model; it has to be drawn in the class of models. We may regard M as being split up into two subsets, one subset, $HEALTH$, containing exactly the models describing healthy persons, and a second one, $SICK$, describing sick persons. Still the problem remains to characterize $SICK$, for how can a person be psychically sick (be described by an $x \in SICK$) and at the same time satisfy all the axioms for healthy, "normal" persons ($x \in M$)?

In order to see this let us reflect on how a person gets sick (neurotic) according to the scheme expressed in the axioms of D2. At some instant t the person realizes some driving d by means of event e of type k : $REAL(t,d,e,k)$. This causes sickness if e turns out as a horrible experience, $N(t,e)$, due to the reactions of other persons which our person could not anticipate. By D2-6, any event e' which would be a natural realization of d and which is associated with e at any later time t' will be unconscious: $U(t',e')$. In the light of D2-7 this is a source of inner stress for the person because, according to D2-7, the driving d "presses for" realization, but realization, by D2-4, is excluded by e being unconscious. More presicely, D2-7 yields some e' and t' such that $REAL(t',d,e',k')$. If k' is the natural type of realizations for d then $k' = k$ which, by D2-4, implies: not $U(t',e')$. But if $t < t'$ this contradicts to $U(t',e')$ above, so $t' \leq t$, and d can be realized by a natural event from $f(d)$ only at t, or later by events of a different type (neurotic symptoms). In other words, the negative event is conscious at the time t of its first being experienced, at which time it also is a realization of some corresponding driving. But this driving cannot get realized by natural realizations at any later time, it is blocked in this sense, and the person gets sick (neurotic) because of this suppression. The symptoms of neurosis on Freud's account occur because the driving gets dissociated from its natural realizations and, in order to find some abreaction at all, gets realized by those symptoms (this feature of the theory is not made explicit here). The cause of sickness thus is given by a pair $\langle d,e\rangle$ of a driving d and an event e such that $REAL(t,d,e,k)$ and $N(t,e)$. This derivation is central to Freud's theory, it shows how neurosis is caused, and therefore explains neurosis and psychical sickness. Because of its importance let us state the derivation as a formal proof.

Theorem 2 Let $x = \langle T,E,D,K,\leq,AS,C,N,U,REAL,f\rangle \in M$, and let $t \in T$, $d \in D, e \in E$ and $k \in K$ be such that
(1) $N(t,e), REAL(t,d,e,k)$ and $f(d) = k$.
Then

(2) there is no $t' \in T$ and no $e' \in E$ such that $t < t'$ and $REAL(t', d, e', k)$.

Proof : Suppose there exist $t' \in T$ and e' such that $t < t'$ and $REAL(t', d, e', k)$. By D2-4,
(3) not $U(t', e')$. By D2-5, (1), and the assumption,
(4) $AS(e, e')$. By (1), D2-1, and the assumption,
(5) $e \in k$ and $e' \in k$. From this and (1) we obtain $e, e' \in f(d)$ which by (1), (4) and D2-6 yields
(6) $U(t', e')$. From (5), (1) and the assumption we get
(7) $e' \in k$ and there exists $d \in D$ such that $REAL(t', d, e', k)$ and $k = f(d)$. But (7) and D2-4 yield: not $U(t', e')$, in contradiction to (6).#

The conclusion (2) of theorem 2 may be rephrased by saying that after t, driving d is blocked and the natural realizations for d are suppressed. Theorem 2 therefore may be restated as follows. If driving d gets realized at t by a negative event then any natural realization for d will be suppressed after t.

These considerations show how psychical sickness may occur in a model even if all axioms for a healthy person are satisfied. Sickness is caused by negative events. If there are no such events the person normally (not provably) will be healthy. If there are negative events they are realized at the moment of first being experienced (by which the axioms for normal development are satisfied), and afterwards the corresponding driving is blocked (the person gets sick). To put it differently: the axioms describing the "normal" case still provide room for sickness, they represent necessary, but not sufficient conditions for health.

We define a person to be psychically sick or neurotic precisely if some driving is blocked after a certain instant in the sense just introduced: d is *blocked after* t iff there is no $t' \in T$, no $e \in E$ and no $k \in K$ such that $t < t', REAL(t', d, e, k)$ and $k = f(d)$, and if there is some $t* \in T$ such that $t < t*$. The final clause here excludes the definition to be trivialized by taking t as the "last" point of time occurring in T. The models describing persons with blocked drivings form a subset $SICK$ of M.

D3 x is a *model of a psychically sick person* ($x \in SICK$) iff
1) $x = \langle T, E, D, K, \leq, AS, C, N, U, REAL, f \rangle \in M$;
2) there exist $t \in T$ and $d \in D$ such that d is blocked after t.

Clearly, $SICK \subseteq M$. This characterization of neurosis is theoretical, and does not refer to the real symptoms. In applications of the theory, one will start of course from the symptoms, infer "backwards" that the person is sick in the sense of D3, and then start to find the crucial items of the model: $D, U, REAL$, and f. Note that suppression takes place "immediately" after the negative event occurs (A6). This does not preclude, however, that neurotic symptoms may occur only much later, for we do not establish here the connections between the unconscious and neurotic symptoms in explicit terms. The unconscious remains in a rather theoretical status without explicit links to neurotic symptoms. Note also that negative events on this account are strongly theory-laden. The only indicator for the occurrence of such events is neurosis. If a person is not neurotic even the most dramatic events will not be counted as negative.

Constraints, Links, Measuring Models

According to structuralist meta-theory an empirical theory in general consists of a *formal core* K and a set I of *intended applications*. The core itself is made up of five items: classes M_p and M of potential models and models, constraints C and links L, some approximation apparatus U, and a distinction between theoretical and non-theoretical terms.

Constraints express assumptions of identity or stability "across" different models. In the present case such an assumption may be stated for association: if two events are associated in one potential model (i.e. for the person described by that model) then they also are associated in any other potential model describing any other person. Two features of this requirement should be noted. First, it is "across" different potential models. This is due to our representing different persons by different models. Second, the requirement applies only in cases where two persons "have" or experience identical events. This comes out clearly once we formulate the constraint in precise terms. We write E^x, AS^x, E^y etc. in order to denote the entitites E, AS etc. occurring in system $x = \langle T^x, E^x, ..., AS^x, ...\rangle$ and system $y = \langle T^y, ..., AS^y, ...\rangle$.

D4 X satisfies the *constraint* of Freud's theory ($X \in C$)
iff
1) $X \subseteq M_p$ and X is not empty;
2) for all $x, y \in X$ and all e, e' :
if $e \in E^x \cap E^y$ and $e' \in E^x \cap E^y$
then
$(AS^x(e, e')$ iff $AS^y(e, e'))$.

Any X satisfying the constraint may be called an admissible combination (of potential models). It is admissible inasfar as it represents a set of persons in which association is stable in the sense of D4. Of course, this constraint is very idealized, and will be satisfied only to some degree, but it nevertheless is crucial for applying the theory in psychoanalysis. For it allows to infer certain associations from other persons' associations or from earlier ones of the person under treatment. A second constraint which we do not formulate explicitly, requires stability of the function f which assigns types of natural events to drivings. The constraint says that "identical" drivings in different models (persons) get identical f-values (types of events).

The role of links in a theory is to "import" data, information and meaning from "outside", that is, from other, "surrounding" theories or from everyday experience. A first link for Freud's theory concerns the ordering of instants. This ordering is constituted mainly in physical terms. We may regard each potential model as being linked to a model of some theory of space-time such that the instants in the former correspond to instants in the latter, and the physical ordering in the latter determines the ordering of the corresponding instants in the psychological model. Note that this does not enforce an ontological identity of corresponding instants, so the existence of this link does not conflict with what was said about the interpretation of T above. Formally, the link may be represented by a class of pairs of potential models $\langle x, y\rangle$ ($x \in M_p$ and $y \in M_p(SP)$, the class of potential models of a theory of space-time) in which corrresponding instants are linked.

D5 If SP is a theory of space-time with class $M_p(SP)$ of

potential models such that the elements of $M_p(SP)$ contain an ordering relation $\leq'$ then
$\langle x, y \rangle$ ***satisfies the link to*** SP iff $x \in M_p$,
$y \in M_p(SP), x = \langle T, ..., \leq, ... \rangle, y = \langle T', ..., \leq', ... \rangle$ and there is a one-one mapping $g : T \Longrightarrow T'$ such that for all $t, t' \in T$:
$t \leq t'$ iff $g(t) \leq' g(t')$.

A second link can be established to theories of association. It imports information about the association-relation from association theory. A third link may be used which connects Freud's theory with theories dealing with consciousness. From these different links a ***global*** link L may be defined which consists of all systems x that are linked by each of the "individual" links to some system from another theory.

We skip the discussion about which terms of the theory are theoretical. Also, we cannot go into the details of describing a full-fledged approximation apparatus to be used in applying the above models. As the theory is completely qualitative the approximation apparatus has to be built up by exploiting the notion of qualitative similarity. Definitions like that proposed by Tversky[15] may be used to form neighbourhoods by means of which the idealized claims associated with the previous idealized items have to be blurred in order to yield realistic, non-trivial empirical claims.[16] We note that, in general, the need for approximation comes from idealizing features inherent in quantitative theories. If quantities (and therefore numbers) are involved, the theoretical pictures become much finer than reality, and therefore the theoretical picture can be claimed to represent reality ("to be true") at most approximatively. But Freud's theory is completely qualitative. Still, it contains some idealizing features. Instead of blurring these, it also seems possible to weaken some axioms. In order to obtain a more liberal version of D2-5, for instance, we could use an approximation of the following kind. The if-clause "if $REAL(t, d, e, k)$ and $REAL(t', d, e', k')$" might be strengthened to refer to repeated such experiences "if $REAL(t_i, d, e, k)$ and $REAL(t_i, d, e', k')$ at different times $t_i, i = 1, ..., n$". Approximation then could be "tacked on" at the number n of repetitions.

In addition to the items introduced so far it is of interest to investigate the means of measurement formally possible within the present theory. Such investigation, even if performed purely abstractly, may be helpful in evaluating the empirical performance or adequacy of the theory. Any model in which one of the primitives t is uniquely determined by the others we call a measuring model for t. This notion is helpful in two respects. First, if a term has no measuring model at all in the theory, this indicates that the term obtains its meaning from "outside", either from other theories or from everyday experience. Second, measuring models are an important tool to derive predictions or other singular statements to be used in confirming the theory.[17] We write $x\langle t/t' \rangle$ to denote the result of substituting t' in x for t.

D6 If $x = \langle T, E, D, K, \leq^x, AS^x, C^x, ..., f^x \rangle \in M_p$
and $t \in \{\leq^x, AS^x, C^x, ..., f^x\}$ we say that x is a
measuring model for t iff $x \in M$ and for all t' of the same

[15] Tversky (1977).
[16] A detailed account of such an approximative apparatus which works well for quantitative theories is found in Balzer, Moulines, & Sneed (1987), Chap.VII.
[17] Compare Balzer (1985) for a fuller account of measuring models.

type as t :
(*) if $x\langle t/t'\rangle \in M$ then $t = t'$.

(*) expresses that t in x is uniquely determined (by M): any possible other t' substituted for t in x by means of the axioms characterizing M is forced to be identical with t. So there is just one possibility for t in x.

We may ask what kinds of measuring models are possible in Freud's theory. A first answer - which some may find a bit astonishing - is that the theory provides measuring models for all its terms. Let us exemplifiy this for the unconscious, U.

Theorem 3 There exist measuring models for U in Freud's theory.

Proof: We define a potential model as follows. $T = \{t_0, t_1\}, E = \{e\}, D = \{d\}, K = \{\{e\}\}$, and for the relations exactly the following atomic statements are true: $t_0 \leq t_1, AS(e,e), C(t_0,e), N(t_0,e), REAL(t_0,d,e,\{e\}), f(d) = \{e\}$. We leave U undetermined. From these definitions it follows by D2-6 that $U(t_1,e)$, and by D2-4 that not$(U(to,e))$. That is, $U = \{\langle t_1, e\rangle\}$, and therefore is uniquely determined by the other components. It is easy to check that all axioms of D1 and D2 are satisfied. So $x = \langle T, ..., U, ..., f\rangle$ is a measuring model for U.#

The minimal example constructed in the proof exemplifies a general strategy for determining U. Find all relevant negative events, and use knowledge about association to determine all positive instances of unconsciousness by means of D2-6. Second, exclude as many events as possible from being unconscious by means of D2-4, using knowledge about the realization-relation. If this is to be carried out in a real case, the hypothetical steps will consist in making sure that the drivings occurring in D2-4 and 6 have the respective events as natural realizations. These hypotheses will refer to further theoretical knowledge about which drivings cause which natural realizations. It seems well possible that such knowledge be expressed by specializations of the present theory. The point of theorem 3 is only to show that if sufficient knowledge is available about the components different from U then U may be determined with the help of the axioms, and logics. Also, the knowledge about the other components used in the proof of theorem 3, and outlined in the previous discussion, seems to be of the sort realistically needed in applications.

Similar theorems can be proved for the other relations. This result is not too surprising. It shows that Freud's theory provides measuring models for all of its primitive relations, even for its time-ordering $\leq$. (With respect to $\leq$ this once again stresses that $\leq$ is not just the order of physical time.) This is to be expected from a theory which for the first time structures a new domain of phenomena, and which is not much concerned with operationalizing its primitives.

A final point to be discussed in connection with the formal concepts of the theory are the various forms of specializations by means of which a whole theory-net may be established on the basis of the present models. Each specialization corresponds to some special hypothesis which can be formulated in our vocabulary or in some extension of it. Such special hypotheses usually have a range of applications much more narrow than the basic axioms. We cannot go into the details of describing the specializations, we only can briefly indicate the forms they may take. The most important form of specialization concerns drivings. These may be analyzed and differentiated into various sorts. Together with this, different forms of natural realizations may be considered, and the special laws arising express which drivings have which natural realizations. In formal terms such specializations define special forms of the function f. A second way of specializing is to introduce "weaker" forms of the unconscious, the most famous being sublimation. In these cases, negative events are not suppressed, getting unconscious, but also they are not abreacted by natural types of events: they give rise to sublimation. A third form which is not clearly stated in Freud but may be important for psychology consists of weakening the notion of a negative event. Instead of one strong event we may consider a long sequence of "weakly" negative events (like little frustrations of the same type each day) which in the long run also may lead to some form of suppression (like depression). Finally, the realization-relation may be specialized by introducing a time-scale for drivings and connecting the occurrences of drivings to those of their realizations. In the present formulation, these connections are left very weak and general.

Intended Applications

A theory is empirical only if there exist real systems to which it is applied. These are called intended applications of the theory. In Freud's theory all the cases he reports himself will be intended applications. In addition, other cases, sufficiently similar to those mentioned by Freud usually also will be treated as intended applications. It is characteristic of empirical theories that the set I of all intended applications can not be described very sharply. The picture of how I is determined in first approximation may be drawn as follows. First, a very small subset I_0 of paradigm intended applications will be described ostensively (the cases mentioned by Freud himself), and second, intended applications in general are characterized as those real systems which are sufficiently similar to members of I_0. Often, the theory itself is used to decide which systems are "sufficiently similar". In Freud's case, as in medical theories in general, intended applications always are cases of sick persons. Only the subsumption of a case of sickness under the theory will count as success, the explanation of persons being healthy is not intended. This situation creates a difficulty when we want to formulate an empirical claim. Roughly, a theory's empirical claim is that its intended applications can be subsumed under the theoretical picture as represented by the models, that is, all intended applications "are" models. But now we have two classes that might serve as the relevant theoretical models: M and $SICK$. If we choose M as representing the theoretical image the claim would be that all intended cases fall under the general picture described in D1 and D2. This claim clearly is inadequate, it might be true even if all the persons considered were healthy. This claim has no implications for neurosis. We obtain an adequate claim only if we use $SICK$ as "theoretical picture". The resulting claim is that all intended cases are cases of psychically sick persons.

But now the problem occurs of what to do with M. If the empirical claim is formulated with $SICK$, could we not simply omit M altogether? Nothing will get lost - so it seems - because $SICK \subseteq M$.

This move seems tempting but there is a decisive objection. If we eliminate M we loose the "standard of health" which is an essential part of the theory's identity. For if we look at the models of psychically sick persons, how do we justifiy that they are models of "sick" persons? Of course, this is justified by pointing to the mechanism described by the axioms for "healthy" persons (D2) and the additional axiom for sickness (D3-2). But how can we separate these two groups of axioms from each other? Clearly, we have to refer to the content of the respective axioms. In general, therefore, it seems necessary to include some extra standard - axioms covering healthy cases - in order to draw the distinction between healthy and sick cases.

This distinction constitutes a clear formal difference between medical theories as contrasted to theories in the natural as well as in the social sciences. In medical or therapeutical theories a further component not present in other types of theories is necessary in order to identify the theory: a component characterizing health forming the standard or the background against which we may sensibly talk about sickness. We will therefore treat both classes M and SICK as basic constitutents of the theory. By summarizing all the items described by now we obtain the formal core $K(FREUD)$ of Freud's theory.

$$K(FREUD) = \langle M_p, M, SICK, C, L\rangle$$

The core comprises all those features of the theory that can be formulated in a precise way, it represents the "theoretical picture".

The empirical claim which may be formulated with the help of this picture in first approximation is that all intended applications "are" models of psychically sick persons and in addition satisfy the constraints and links. But if I is a set of real systems, what is the meaning of "are" in such a statement? How can a real system "be" a set theoretic structure? The answer is: it cannot. In order to make "real systems" on the one hand and "models" of $SICK$ on the other hand compatible there is only one way. We have to make further assumptions on the structure of the real systems (but of course assumptions which do not already imply that the systems are elements of $SICK$, for this would turn the empirical claim into a tautology).

Let's consider two "average" cases reported by Freud.[18] Katharina, a peasant girl in the alpes, suffers from depressions and anxiety. Her history turns out as follows. The girl lived with her uncle, and had to work in the house. Repeatedly, she was threatened by her uncle, but the character of the thread (sexual or punishing or otherwise) did not become clear to her. Twice she found him unexpectedly during intercourse with the maidservant. After some time she got depressed, and she suffers from anxiety on her long way to the village which she often has to go alone.

A second report is about a woman of 38 suffering from attacks of agoraphobia and mortal fear. Her history reveals a first such attack 21 years earlier, at her age of 17. Before that event she was out for preparations concerning a ball to which she was invited. Some days before, her girl-friend had died, and the event coincided with her critical days, the only ones she had in that year. When she passes by her friend's house she gets a first attack of giddiness, anxiety and swoon. She believes she will die. In the following she had similar attacks several times.

We may format both cases according to our terminology, thus specifying the instants and events important in both cases. Little information is given about association; we may assume that all important events were conscious when occurring for the first time. The negative events are clearly pointed out in both cases. By collecting these data we obtain two

[18]The peasant girl is found on pp. 184-95, the agoraphobia on p. 170f.

fragments of potential models, in which information, especially about $D, U, REAL, f$, but also about AS, is missing. Such fragments we call partial potential models.

D7 x is a *partial potential model* of Freud's theory ($x \in M_p$)
iff there exist $T, E, D, K, \leq, AS, C, N, U, REAL, f$ and
$T', E', D', K', \leq', AS', C', N', U', REAL', f'$, such that
1) $\langle T', ..., REAL', f' \rangle \in M_p$;
2) $x = \langle T, E, D, ..., REAL, f \rangle$;
3) $T \subseteq T', E \subseteq E', D \subseteq D', K \subseteq K', \leq \subseteq \leq', AS \subseteq AS', C \subseteq C'$,
$N \subseteq N', U \subseteq U', REAL \subseteq REAL'$, and $f = f'/K$
($= f'$, restricted to K).

In order to close the gap between "real systems" and "models" we now assume that all intended applications are partial potential models: $I \subseteq M_{pp}$. This assumption has two parts. First, it amounts to assuming that the real systems considered can be described in our vocabulary; all the primitives should be interpretable in such a system. Second, it means that other features of the system, which cannot be expressed in terms of the chosen primitives, are neglected as irrelevant. The assumption does *not* imply any theoretical connection, or structure, in the system. Roughly, we may regard intended applications as descriptions of all those data that can be obtained from the underlying real system.

By adding a set $I(FREUD)$ of intended applications, we complete our description. Freud's theory, which we call $FREUD$, then has the following form

$$FREUD = \langle K(FREUD), I(FREUD) \rangle.$$

Note that M_{pp} is explicitly defined in terms of M_p and therefore needs not to be mentioned in $K(FREUD)$.

Empirical Claim and Confirmation

Our assumption of representing intended applications as partial potential models leads to a relatively simple formulation of the theory's empirical claim. If the "given" systems are fragments of potential models the appropriate relation to proper models is that of extension, and the empirical claim will be that each intended application can be extended to a model of a psychically sick person (such that constraints and links are satisfied). The formal definition of extension is like in D7: y is an extension of x in case all components of x are subsets of the corresponding components of y.

D8 If $x = \langle u1, ..., u11 \rangle$ and $y = \langle v1, ..., v11 \rangle$ are partial potential
models of Freud's theory then y is *an extension of* x ($x \sqsubset y$)
iff, for all $i \leq 11 : ui \subseteq vi$. For $X \subseteq M_{pp}$ and $Y \subseteq M_p$ we write
"$Y \in e(X)$" as a shorthand for "for all $x \in X$ there is $y \in Y$
such that $x \sqsubset y$", and we then say that Y is *an extension of* X.

Note that $M_p \subseteq M_{pp}$, so an extension of $x \in I(FREUD)$ can be a full potential model. We now may state the empirical claim of $FREUD$ pertaining to sick persons in precise terms.

D9 The *empirical claim of* $FREUD$ is this:
There exists a set X such that

1) $X \in e(I(FREUD))$,
2) $X \subseteq SICK$,
3) $X \in C$,
4) $X \subseteq L$.

That is, the intended applications in $I(FREUD)$ can be extended such that the resulting set of extensions X ($X \in e(I(FREUD))$) is a set of models of psychically sick persons ($X \subseteq SICK$), satisfies the constraints ($X \in C$), and satisfies the links ($X \subseteq L$). This apparently simple statement in fact expresses very complex and holistic relations.

In the light of the two examples given in the previous section an intended application x typically contains data about times, events and negative events. Sometimes there may be some information about K, C, and AS, and, more rarely, about $U, REAL$, and f. If we assume such data to be collected for many different cases (persons) we get (part of) the set of intended applications. The empirical claim then is that further items like U, D, etc. can be "filled in" in order to obtain full models, and in a way which satisfies constraints and links. In other words, the data may be extended to full structures which satisfy all the axioms stated in D1, D2 and D4. In addition, the different association-relations and f-functions are constrained as described earlier, and all extensions have to be linked to appropriate structures (from space-time theories, and theories about association and consciousness).

The question now may be raised whether such a claim is an empirically non-trivial statement, a statement which can be tested, confirmed, and which might turn out false. This crucially depends on the particular systems making up the set $I(FREUD)$. If members of $I(FREUD)$ contain "large" parts of full potential models it may be difficult to extend them to proper models of $SICK$. In principle there even might occur full potential models in $I(FREUD)$ for which the question of extendability to models reduces to the question of whether the axioms of D2 are satisfied. Since we do not have at hand a complete list of all intended applications and the corresponding data which have been investigated by now, we have to resort to hypothetical reasoning: "What about the empirical claim if $I(FREUD)$ had this and that form?" Obviously, there exist "potential falsifiers" (i.e. sets $X \subseteq M_{pp}$ for which $SICK$ is not an extension): take an appropriate set of full potential models which do not satisfy the axioms of D2. As long as we do not worry about where the data in $I(FREUD)$ come from, such cases exist. However, reflection on real examples shows that, normally, only a small fragment of all the data making up a full potential model will be known. In such cases extension is a substantial procedure. If we go still one step further and assume that certain primitives, like U, will never be represented in $I(FREUD)$, and that extension consists in adding such missing relations, we obtain more interesting forms of possible falsifiers. In theorem 4 below we write

$$r(y) = \langle T, E, \emptyset, K, \leq, AS, C, N, \emptyset, \emptyset, \emptyset \rangle$$

if

$$y = \langle T, E, D, K, \leq, AS, C, N, U, REAL, f \rangle.$$

Theorem 4 There exists $X \subseteq M_{pp}$ such that
1) for all $x \in X$ there is $y \in M_p$ such that $x = r(y)$;
2) there is no $Y \subseteq SICK$ such that $\{r(y) : y \in Y\} = X$.

Proof: Let $X = \{x\}$ where $x = \langle T, E, \emptyset, K, \leq, AS, C, N, \emptyset, \emptyset, \emptyset \rangle \in M_{pp}$ such that

(1) $T = \{t_0, t_1\}$, $E = \{e_0, e_1\}$, $K = \{E\}$, and $t_0 < t_1$,
(2) not $(C(t_0, e_0))$, not $(C(t_0, e_1))$ and not $(C(t_1, e_0))$.
Suppose there exists some $y \in SICK$ such that $r(y) = x$. It follows that y has the form
$y = \langle T, E, D, K, \leq, AS, C, N, U, REAL, f \rangle$
and, by D3, satisfies
(3) there exist $t \in T$, $d \in D$ such that
(3.1) there is $t^* \in T$ such that $t < t^*$,
(3.2) for all t', e, k : not$(t < t'$ and $REAL(t', d, e, k)$ and $f(d) = k)$.
Let t and d be as in (3). From (3) and (1) it follows that
(4) $d \in D$ and $t = t_0$. As $y \in SICK$ we obtain from (4) and D1-7 that there is some k with $f(d) = k$, and by (1): $f(d) = E$. From this, (4) and (3.2) we obtain: for all t', e, if $t_0 < t'$ then not $REAL(t', d, e, E)$ and from this by (1):
(5) not: $REAL(t_1, d, e, E)$ for all $e \in E$. On the other hand, (4) and D2-7 yield
(6) there exist t_2, e_2, k_2 such that $REAL(t_2, d, e_2, k_2)$, and this, by D2-1 yields $C(t_2, e_2)$. From this by (1) and (2) we obtain $t_2 = t_1$ and $e_2 = e_1$, so, by (6) and (1):
(7) $REAL(t_1, d, e_1, E)$. But by (5): not $REAL(t_1, d, e_1, E)$ in contradiction to (7).#

Theorem 4 shows that there may be data which cannot be extended to proper models of $SICK$ by adding suitable $D, U, REAL$ and f. If such data occur in $I(FREUD)$ then the empirical claim will become false. Note that the data assumed to be present in the partial potential model x in the proof of theorem 4 are very "thin". They amount to knowing that just two instants and two events are present, that there is only one type of events and that both events are not conscious at the first point of time, and one of them also is not conscious at the second. Though the example itself is contrived, the *kind* of data used certainly is not. In the light of these considerations it seems difficult to maintain that $FREUD$ is not empirical.

Still, the objection may be held up that it cannot be seen how the empirical claim could be confirmed. For, it may be said, the crucial point is not whether there are potential falsifiers but rather how the data making up $I(FREUD)$ are collected. More precisely, if all the data in $I(FREUD)$ can be obtained only by assuming the theory to hold then the empirical claim of course will be true, and its truth will spring from the way the data are collected. Roughly, if we collect only those items that fit with the theory and call them data, we are sure that those data can be extended to models (i.e. satisfy the empirical claim). But then it seems impossible to test and to confirm the theory.

To this objection there are two replies. First, we do not think that the data are collected in a way that presupposes the theory in the sense of fully implying it. To be sure, the general picture drawn by the theory may be used but this only amounts to focussing on the "right" things, on those things to which the theory refers to. This does not mean that any determination of a datum is understood as being explicitly dependent on all the complex axioms of the theory being true in the situation of determination. We believe that a distinction has to be made between the act of determining a datum, and "presupposing" the theory in that act. "Presupposing the theory" here is of the same kind as "presupposing a concept" (say "table") in order to be able to "see" tables. In this trivial sense of course the theory is presupposed in any act of determination, and this holds for *all* empirical theories, in physics as well as, say, in economics. The interesting question is whether the theory is fully implied by the assumptions used in order to determine some datum. In some cases this is so but in others it is not.[19] In Freud's theory it seems natural to use the theory's axioms in order to determine the drivings, the unconscious, the realization-relation and the function f of the models (compare theorem 3 above). If this is done those parts should not occur in the descriptions of the intended applications, and in the light of the examples considered it is unlikely that they actually do occur.

Second, it has to be pointed out that the assumption underlying the previous discussion, namely that a theory can be tested or confirmed only on the basis of independent data, does not express the dominant view of confirmation to-day. The mainstream view concedes that also coherence may be used in order to confirm and justify a theory. A precise view of confirmation along these lines exists.[20] According to this view, confirmation consists in the coincidence of values (of the "same" function for the "same" argument) determined or computed along different lines, irrespective of whether the theory under consideration was used in the course of these computations. This view has some credit in the area of comprehensive theories in the natural sciences.[21] So, even if one is not convinced by our first reply, there still remains the possibility of changing one's view about confirmation.

By way of summary let us state that there is no proof that $FREUD$'s empirical claim is correct and well confirmed. Such proof is impossible for any empirical theory. But there are hypothetical falsifiers (even of a rather realistic kind, see theorem 4), and the difficulties in collecting independent data for $FREUD$ seem not very different from such difficulties in general. We therefore tend to conclude that the empirical claim of $FREUD$ is not very different from such claims in general.[22] Of course, there are other differences between $FREUD$ and theories from the natural sciences in connection with the reliability of measurement and repetition which we did not address. But these $FREUD$ shares with all theories in the social sciences.

References

Balzer, W. (1982). *Empirische Theorien: Modelle, Strukturen, Beispiele.* Braunschweig-Wiesbaden : Vieweg.

Balzer, W. (1985). *Theorie und Messung.* Berlin etc.: Springer.

Balzer, W. (1986). Theoretical Terms. A New Perspective. *The Journal of Philosophy*, **83**, 71-90.

Balzer, W., Moulines, C.U., & Sneed, J.D. (1987). *An Architectonic for Science.* Dordrecht: Reidel.

[19] An attempt to clarify the distinction discussed here is made in Balzer (1986).

[20] See Glymour (1980).

[21] Glymour even claims that the bootstrap method was applied by Freud, see Glymour (1980), pp. 263.

[22] A popular argument against $FREUD$ consists in pointing out the damage caused by psychotherapists in many cases. This argument, however, rests on grave misunderstanding. It does not show that $FREUD$ is badly performing empirically. It just shows that it is badly used or even misused, in the sense in which physics may be said to be misused for the construction of atomic missiles.

Freud, S. (1967). *Gesammelte Werke.* Volume 1, 5th ed. Frankfurt/Main: S.Fischer.

Freud, S. (1963). *Das Unbewußte.* Frankfurt/Main: S.Fischer.

Gruenbaum, A. (1984). *The Foundations of Psychoanalysis.* Berkeley: Univ. of California Press.

Glymour, C. (1980). *Theory and Evidence.* Princeton: University Press.

Perrez, M. (1979). *Ist die Psychoanalyse eine Wissenschaft?.* 2nd ed. Bern: Huber.

Stegmüller, W. (1986). *Theorie und Erfahrung. Dritter Teilband.* Berlin: Springer.

Tversky, A. (1977). Features of Similarity. *Psychological Review*, **84**, 327-352.

Chapter 3

Festinger's Theory of Cognitive Dissonance

A Revised Structural Reconstruction

Rainer Westermann

University of Göttingen

Abstract

In this chapter, the main results of a structuralist analysis of Festinger's theory of cognitive dissonance and of a typical dissonance experiment are presented and some methodological problems are discusssed from a structuralist point of view.

The informal set-theoretical axiomatizations of main theory-elements lead to a reduction of some difficulties and ambiguities with Festinger's terms and relationships. The basic theory-element of dissonance theory does not correspond to the general form of the theory presented by Festinger, but is a considerable simplification thereof.

For each area of application special theory-elements are generated by introducing new terms and special laws. For post-decisional and forced-compliance dissonance, uniqueness constraints and paradigmatic applications are exemplarily specified and it is demonstrated that modifications of the theory resulting from empirical failures lead to theory-elements with restricted sets of objects or less precise substantial laws.

For a precise assessment of the connections between the dissonance theory elements, new kinds of intra-theoretical relations (restriction, simplification, theoretical and non-theoretical enlargement) must be introduced. Like the common structuralist specialization and theoretization relations they are special cases of a general specialization relation. The theory net can be displayed graphically so that both general specializations and temporal developments are represented.

A reconstruction of the most specific theory-element representing the theoretical reference point of an exemplaric dissonance experiment shows that this element results from more general elements by simplifications and specializations, that it does not pertain to single subjects but to artificial systems of at least two experimental groups, that it contains ceteris paribus and probability clauses, and that there are indispensable inter-theoretical links representing ways of operationalization, statistical decision procedures, etc.

As the fundamental law does not contribute at all to the empirical content of the theory, empirical research can not be aimed at corroborating or falsifying the theory in general. Instead, it should lead to new delimitations of the sets of successful and unsuccessful applications, to modifications of special laws and to the introduction of new theory-elements.

Discussions in philosophy of science typically pertain to very simplified examples of substantial theories. Partly for that reason, many substantial researchers believe that philosophical problems and results are of no relevance for their daily work. It seems that the *structuralist view* of scientific theories (Balzer, 1982; Balzer & Sneed, 1977/1978; Diederich, 1981; Sneed, 1971, 1976; Stegmüller, 1976, 1979, 1986) may also run into this danger. To bridge the gap between philosophical and substantial disciplines it must be shown that the main characteristics of real psychological theories and theory-oriented research programs can be reconstructed clearly and comprehensively in terms of structuralist metatheory.

As an exemplaric first step, Festinger's (1957) *theory of cognitive dissonance* was analyzed and the methodological consequences of this analysis were discussed (Westermann, 1987,

1988). In this chapter a revised version of the structural reconstruction of dissonance theory is presented.

Cognitive dissonance is one of the most prominent theories in psychology and many important experiments pertaining to this theory have been published (Cooper & Fazio, 1984; Frey, 1978; Frey, Irle, Möntmann, Kumpf, Ochsmann & Sauer, 1982). Today, professional interest in dissonance theory has been considerably attenuated. Many researchers prefer to reinterpret dissonance phenomena from an attributional point of view. But even in the light of up-to-date theories of, say, action control, dissonance theory does not lose its attraction (Beckmann & Irle, 1985).

1 The Basic Element

Festinger's (1957) book can be devided into two distinct parts. Firstly, in Chapter 1 he presents the general principles which are assumed to hold in any application of the theory. Secondly, in Chapters 2 to 10 the applications of these principles in four different areas are described.

Section 1 of the present chapter is aimed at a structural reconstruction of the fundamental form of the theory. To be concrete, the actual models and the potential models of *general dissonance theory* are defined by an informal set-theoretical axiomatization (see Section 1.2). Section 1.1 is devoted to the formulation of these axioms.

1.1 Some Informal Set-Theoretical Formulations

The fundamental concept of dissonance theory is "cognition" or "cognitive element": *"By the term cognition ... I mean any knowledge, opinion, or belief about the environment, about oneself, or about one's behavior"* (Festinger, 1957, p. 3). Let K_ω be the set of all "elementary cognitions" that are considered. Then the power set $Po(K_\omega)$ encompasses all possible clusters of these elements which are called c_i,c_j, etc. In addition, T is a set of points of time and P is a set of persons or - more generally - observational objects.

A1 T is a non-empty set (of points of time),
P is a non-empty set (of observational objects),
K_ω is a non-empty set (of elementary cognitions).

With these three fundamental terms we can define the set K of objects that are of interest for further theoretical analyses, namely, those elementary cognititions or combinations thereof that are effectively held by a certain person p at a certain point of time t. This set K of present cognitions is defined as a subset of the cartesian product of the power set of K_ω, the set of persons, and the set of points of time. In addition, a temporal order relation O_T on the set T is introduced. For convenience, elements of O_T are called t and t_+, u and u_+, etc. with t being "not later than" t_+, etc.

A2 $K \subseteq Po(K_\omega) \times P \times T$ is a non-empty set (of present cognitions),
$O_T \subseteq T \times T$ is a reflexive, transitive, and antisymmetric relation
(partial temporal order).

There are three kinds of relations which may exist between pairs of cognitive elements, namely, irrelevance, dissonance, and consonance (Festinger, 1957, p. 11). Two elements "are in a dissonant relation if, considering these two alone, the obverse of one element would follow from the other" (p. 13). In the following Expression A3 these relationships are defined by introducing two relations D_p and C_p.

A3 $D_p \subseteq K \times K$ is a set (of dissonant pairs of cognitions) and
$C_p \subseteq K \times K$ is a set (of consonant pairs of cognitions)
with $D_p \cap C_p = \emptyset$.

Festinger (1957) does not only distinguish different kinds of relations between cognitions, but also considers different degrees of consonance and dissonance and states that they are functionally related to the importance of the elements. This is shown by the following two quotations.

> **P1** If two elements are dissonant with one another, the magnitude of the dissonance will be a function of the importance of the elements (p. 16).

> **P2** The magnitude of the dissonance (or consonance) increases as the importance or value of the elements increases (p.18).

Following Krause's (1972, S. 37) formalization, a real-valued importance function w and two functions D_m and C_m for the comparative concepts of dissonance and consonance are introduced in the following expression A4. In addition, some functions are already introduced in A4 that will be discussed below.

A4 Let $\mathbb{R}$ be the set of all real numbers. Then there are functions

$$
\begin{array}{llll}
w: & D_p \cup C_p & \Rightarrow \mathbb{R} & \text{(pairwise importance),} \\
D_m: & D_p & \Rightarrow \mathbb{R} & \text{(pairwise magnitude of dissonance),} \\
C_m: & C_p & \Rightarrow \mathbb{R} & \text{(pairwise magnitude of consonance),} \\
D_e: & K & \Rightarrow \mathbb{R} & \text{(elementwise magnitude of conflict),} \\
C_e: & K & \Rightarrow \mathbb{R} & \text{(elementwise magnitude of support),} \\
Q: & K & \Rightarrow \mathbb{R} & \text{(proportion of dissonant relations),} \\
D: & K & \Rightarrow \mathbb{R} & \text{(elementwise magnitude of dissonance),} \\
R: & K & \Rightarrow \mathbb{R} & \text{(strength of pressure to reduce dissonance),} \\
T_D: & P \times T & \Rightarrow \mathbb{R} & \text{(degree of tolerance for dissonance).}
\end{array}
$$

When we intend to transform P1 and P2 into a set-theoretical expression, we face the problem that Festinger (1957) does not specify the meaning of phrases of the form "x is a function of y" or "x increases as y increases". In my opinion, we get the best reconstruction of Festinger's intentions with set-theoretical expressions that are as general as possible. Therefore, in the following Expression A6 (Expression A5 is given below) relations are assumed to be strictly monotone increasing, differences and changes are expressed as numerical differences, and they are allowed to pertain to different persons, cognitions, and points of time.

A6 (a) For all $(c_{ipt}, c_{jpt}), (c_{iqu}, c_{jqu}), (c_{krv}, c_{lrv}), (c_{ksw}, c_{lsw}) \in D_p$,

$$
\begin{array}{lccccc}
\text{If} & w(i,p,t,j,p,t) & - & w(i,q,u,j,q,u) & < \\
 & w(k,r,v,l,r,v) & - & w(k,s,w,l,s,w), & \\
\text{then} & D_m(i,p,t,j,p,t) & - & D_m(i,q,u,j,q,u) & < \\
 & D_m(k,r,v,l,r,v) & - & D_m(k,s,w,l,s,w). &
\end{array}
$$

(b) For all $(c_{ipt}, c_{jpt}), (c_{iqu}, c_{jqu}), (c_{krv}, c_{lrv}), (c_{ksw}, c_{lsw}) \in C_p$,

$$\begin{array}{llcl} \text{If} & w(i,p,t,j,p,t) & - & w(i,q,u,j,q,u) \quad < \\ & w(k,r,v,l,r,v) & - & w(k,s,w,l,s,w), \\ \text{then} & C_m(i,p,t,j,p,t) & - & C_m(i,q,u,j,q,u) \quad < \\ & C_m(k,r,v,l,r,v) & - & C_m(k,s,w,l,s,w). \end{array}$$

Up to now we have only considered dissonance with respect to pairs of cognitions. In Festinger's theory there is another important concept of dissonance, namely, dissonance between a certain cognition c_{ipt} on the one, and and all the other present cognitions on the other hand. In A4 I have introduced the function D for the magnitude of this elementwise dissonance.

> **P3** assuming momentarily, for the sake of definition, that all the elements relevant to the one in question are equally important, the total amount of dissonance between this element and the remainder of the person's cognition will depend on the proportion of relevant elements that are dissonant with the one in question (Festinger, 1957, p. 17)

When the cognitive elements are not equally important,

> **P4** the total amount of dissonance ... is a function of the weighted proportion of all relevant relations ... that are dissonant. The term 'weighted proportion' is used because each relevant relation would be weighted according to the importance of the elements involved in the relation (p. 18).

Festinger also generalizes these definitions to deal with the magnitude of dissonance between one cluster of cognitions and all the rest of them. This case is automatically encompassed in our reconstruction, however, because, according to A2, the set K of cognitive elements refers to clusters of elementary cognitions.

In A5, loosely following Krause (1972), some further terms are defined which are needed for a precise set-theoretical formulation of P3 and P4.

A5 For all $c_{ipt} \in K$,

$$D_e(i,p,t) := \sum_j D_m(i,p,t,j,p,t),$$

with the summation over all $c_{jpt} \in K$ with $(c_{ipt}, c_{jpt}) \in D_p$,

$$C_e(i,p,t) := \sum_j C_m(i,p,t,j,p,t),$$

with the summation over all $c_{jpt} \in K$ with $(c_{ipt}, c_{jpt}) \in C_p$, and

$$Q(i,p,t) := \frac{D_e(i,p,t)}{D_e(i,p,t) + C_e(i,p,t)}.$$

According to A6, D_m and C_m are monotone functions of the importance function w. For that reason, $Q(i,p,t)$ is a precise representation of Festinger's notion of a "weighted proportion". As a result, we get A7 as a set-theoretical transformation of P3 and P4.

A7 For all $c_{ipt}, c_{jqu}, c_{krv}, c_{lsw} \in K$,

$$\begin{array}{lrcl} \text{If} & Q(i,p,t) - Q(j,q,u) & < & Q(k,r,v) - Q(l,s,w), \\ \text{then} & D(i,p,t) - D(j,q,u) & < & D(k,r,v) - D(l,s,w). \end{array}$$

Festinger (1957) himself stresses that the central point of his theory refers to the consequences of dissonance arousal and is summarized in the following quotation.

P5 The presence of dissonance gives rise to pressures to reduce that dissonance ... The strength of the pressure to reduce the dissonance is a function of the magnitude of the existing dissonance (p. 263).

The function R defined in A4 represents the magnitude of these pressures to reduce dissonance. As the following quotation P6 shows, R also depends on the person's momentary maximum tolerance for dissonance which is represented by the function T_D.

P6 There are, certainly, individual differences among people in the degree to which, and in the manner that, they react to the existence of dissonance ... Persons with low tolerance for dissonance should show more discomfort in the presence of dissonance and should manifest greater efforts to reduce dissonance than persons who have high tolerance (Festinger, 1957, pp. 266-267).

P5 and P6 can be summarized in the following manner.

A8 For all $c_{ipt}, c_{jqu} \in K$,

If $\quad 0 < D(i,p,t) - T_D(p,t) \; < \; D(j,q,u) - T_D(q,u),$

then $\quad R(i,p,t) \; < \; R(j,q,u).$

In general, existing dissonance between cognitive elements can be reduced or eliminated by changing one of these elements, by adding new elements, or by decreasing the importance of the elements involved (Festinger, 1957, pp. 18-19, 264). "Whether or not any of them change, and if so, which ones, will certainly be determined in part by the magnitude of resistance to change which they possess" (p. 24). This resistance primarily depends on the responsiveness to reality and the degree of consonance with other cognitions (pp. 24-28). Therefore, the magnitude of resistance to change can be represented by the function C_e as defined in A5 (Krause, 1972, S. 39).

It seems important to note "that the presence of pressures to reduce dissonance, or even activity directed toward such reduction, does not guarantee that the dissonance will be reduced ... In fact, it is quite conceivable that in the process of trying to reduce dissonance, it might even be increased" (p. 23). Dissonance theory does not predict that the magnitude of dissonances will be changed or reduced in the course of action. It only says *"that in the presence of a dissonance, one will be able to observe the attempts to reduce it"* (p. 24). It is the magnitude of these attempts that are represented by the function R.

1.2 Models and Potential Models

The fundamental form of Festinger's theory shall be reconstructed as a theory-element that is called *general dissonance theory* and that is abbreviated as *DissA*. As a result of the foregoing subsection we have the expressions A6 to A8 corresponding to the main theoretical principles presented by Festinger (1957) in Chapter 1 of his book, and we have the expressions A1 to A5 by which the necessary terms are introduced. In D1 below the set of *potential models* of *DissA* is defined by using A1 to A5 as defining conditions or "axioms". In the terminology of Balzer, Moulines and Sneed (1987, pp. 5-20) T, P, and K_ω are *principal base sets*, $\mathbb{R}$ is an *auxiliary base set* which is assumed to be antecedently available, and the remaining terms are sets that are defined on this basis. Although the terms D_e, C_e, and Q are completely defined by A5, they are included for clarity's sake, for the corresponding concepts in Festinger's (1957) exposition are of some importance.

D1 x is a *potential model* of general dissonance theory,
i.e. $x \in M_p(DissA)$,
if and only if there are
$T, P, K_\omega, \mathbb{R}, K, O_T, D_p, C_p, w, D_m, C_m, D_e, C_e, Q, D, R, T_D$ such that
(a) $x = \langle T, P, K_\omega, \mathbb{R}, K, O_T, D_p, C_p, w, D_m, C_m, D_e, C_e, Q, D, R, T_D \rangle$
and
(b) A1 to A5 from Section 1.1 are satisfied.

The axioms A1 to A5 are descriptions, typifications, and characterizations of the base and non-base sets. Put into other words, they determine the "conceptual framework" to which all potential models of the theory-element must belong. Loosely speaking, they are purely "terminological" axioms.

The *actual models* of a theory-element must also satisfy those axioms that represent substantial, lawlike connections between these terms. So the actual models of *DissA* are defined as those potential models for which the axioms A6 to A8 are also satisfied.

D2 x is an *actual model* of general dissonance theory,
i.e. $x \in M(DissA)$,
if and only if there are
$T, P, K_\omega, \mathbb{R}, K, O_T, D_p, C_p, w, D_m, C_m, D_e, C_e, Q, D, R, T_D$ such that
(a) $x \in M_p(DissA)$ according to D1 and
(b) A6 to A8 from Section 1.1 are satisfied.

The "partial potential models" or - in short - the *partial models* of a theory-element T can be derived from the potential models by eliminating all those terms that are *T-theoretical*, i.e. that are *theoretical with respect to the theory* T (Sneed, 1971, p. 41; Balzer, Moulines & Sneed, 1987, pp. 57, 83). The set of potential models that can be reduced to a certain partial model y by eliminating the theoretical terms is called the set of *theoretical enlargements* of y. This elimination can be described by a cutting-off function r_τ. For any theory-element *DissT* we get the following definition.

D3 $M_{pp}(DissT)$ is the set of *partial models* of theory-element *DissT*
if and only if
there are $B_1, ..., B_b, t_1, ..., t_n, n_1, ..., n_m$ such that
(a) $x = \langle B_1, ..., B_b, t_1, ..., t_n, n_1, ..., n_m \rangle \in M_p(DissT)$,
(b) $B_1, ..., B_b$ are base sets,
(c) $t_1, ..., t_n$ are *Diss*-theoretical terms,
(d) $n_1, ..., n_m$ are *Diss*-non-theoretical terms,
(e) r_τ: $M_p(DissT) \Longrightarrow M_{pp}(DissT)$ is a function
with $r_\tau(\langle B_1, ..., B_b, t_1, ..., t_n, n_1, ..., n_m \rangle) = \langle B_1, ..., B_b, n_1, ..., n_m \rangle$,
(f) $M_{pp}(DissT) := \{y : y = r_\tau(x) \text{ and } x \in M_p(DissT)\}$.

To give a well-founded distinction between *Diss-theoretical* and *Diss-non-theoretical* terms, we must first investigate how the theory is used in empirical research (see Sections 2.2 and 2.3). Then it will also become possible to circumscribe the sets I of *intended applications* for some dissonance theory-elements. When $M_{pp}(T)$ is the set of partial models of a theory-element T, then the set I of intended applications of T can be defined as a subset of the power set of M_{pp}. In contrast to the set M_{pp} of all *possible applications*, the set I of all *intended applications* is not defined in a formal manner but by determining a subset of *paradigmatic applications* and by other informal semantic and pragmatic means (Balzer, Moulines & Sneed, 1987, pp. 20-23, 86-89).

For clarity's sake and following Balzer's (1982) first structuralist treatment of a psychological theory, I have attached verbal labels to all terms introduced in A1 to A4. These labels in these axioms and the quotations and explanations given in the text of the preceding subsection can be considered as a partial characterization of the *basic intended interpretations* of the terms of general dissonance theory. Thus, strictly speaking, my definitions of actual models, potential models, and partial models are not purely formal. Nevertheless, there is a clear-cut distinction between the primarily formal *core* K of a theory-element with M_p, M, and M_{pp} on the one hand and the irreducibly pragmatic set I on the other.

It will become evident below (Sections 2.2 and 2.3) that the general dissonance theory $DissA$ does not adequately represent the theoretical basis of all empirical studies pertaining to dissonance theory. Firstly, empirical research refers to additional terms and relationships. Secondly, empirical dissonance research does not make use of all terms and relations of our element $DissA$. Therefore, another theory-element $DissB$ is introduced which is a simplification of $DissA$. $DissB$ seems to represent the common theoretical reference point of all dissonance research and is hypothesized to be the basic element of all theory-nets by means of which various parts and versions of dissonance theory can be reconstructed.

As empirical research seems to refer neither to A6 and A7 nor to the concept of dissonance tolerance, the set of actual models of $DissB$ can be defined by means of the three "terminological" axioms A1 to A3, one simplified "terminological" axiom A4', and one simplified substantial axiom A8'.

A4' Let $\mathbb{R}$be the set of all real numbers. Then there are functions
$D: \quad K \Rightarrow \mathbb{R}$ (elementwise magnitude of dissonance)
$R: \quad K \Rightarrow \mathbb{R}$ (strength of pressure to reduce dissonance)

A8' For all $c_{ipt}, c_{jqu} \in K$,
If $\quad D(i,p,t) \quad < \quad D(j,q,u)$,
then $\quad R(i,p,t) \quad < \quad R(j,q,u)$

D4 (a) $x \in M_p(DissB)$ if and only if there are
$T, P, K_\omega, \mathbb{R}, K, O_T, D_p, C_p, D, R$ such that
(aa) $x = \langle T, P, K_\omega, \mathbb{R}, K, O_T, D_p, C_p, D, R\rangle$ and
(ab) A1, A2 and A3 from Section 1.1 as well as A4' are satisfied.
(b) $x \in M(DissB)$, if and only if
(ba) $x \in M_p(DissB)$, and
(bb) A8' is satisfied.

By definition D4, the set of actual models of $DissB$ consists of those potential models of this element that satisfy the substantial axiom A8'. Therefore, the common notion of a theoretical assertion or a scientific law can be reconstructed structurally by the transition from the set of potential models to the set of actual models. In this sense, we can say that the *fundamental law* of dissonance theory is reconstructed by the actual models of the *basic element DissB*, whereas *special laws* of the theory are reconstructed by means of theory-elements that are specializations of $DissB$ (see Section 2 below).

1.3 Uniqueness Constraints

Structural reconstructions of empirical theories reveal the important role of *constraints* between different possible applications of the theory (Sneed, 1971, pp. 65-95; Balzer, Moulines & Sneed, 1987, pp. 40-47).

For psychological theories the most important kind of constraints are *uniqueness constraints*. Let both $x^m = \langle T^m, P^m, K^m_\omega, \mathbb{R}, K^m, O^m_T, D^m_r, C^m_r, D^m, R^m \rangle$ and $x^n = \langle T^n, P^n, K^n_\omega, \mathbb{R}, K^n, O^n_T, D^n_r, C^n_r, D^n, R^n \rangle$ be elements of $M_p(DissB)$. Now suppose that there are two elementary cognitions c_i and c_j that are both in $Po(K^m_\omega)$ and $Po(K^n_\omega)$, that there are corresponding present cognitions c_{ipt} and c_{jqu} for persons p and q and times t and u in K^m, and that there are two present cognitions c_{irv} and c_{jsw} for persons r and s and times v and w in K^n.

Further suppose that we have applied the theory with respect to, say, the potential model x^m and that the fundamental axiom A8' is satisfied, i.e. that both $D^m(i,p,t) < D^m(j,q,u)$ and $R^m(i,p,t) < R^m(j,q,u)$. If we now want to predict the results of a study with x^n, this is only possible if we assume that the values of the functions D and R in x^n are a strictly monotone function of corresponding values in x^m. Put into other words, D and R must be unique up to strictly monotone transformations.

Uniqueness constraints are not methodological requirements which are added *a posteriori*. They are part of the theory, because they are directly implied by the substantial connections specified in the theory. The monotone relationship between D and R in A8', for example, implies that both variables must be measured at least at ordinal-scale level. If this is not the case, the set of actual models of $DissB$ does not remain constant under admissible transformations of these variables. In the terminology of Suppes and Zinnes (1963), A8' is not *empirically meaningful* if D and R do not have at least ordinal-scale level. More specific theoretical relationships imply uniqueness constraints that correspond to higher levels of measurement. A7, for example, is meaningful at interval-scale level, but not at ordinal-scale level.

Though constraints play an essential role, for example, in any theory-based prediction, they usually remain implicit. Any constraint for a theory-element T corresponds to a subset of the power set of $M_p(T)$ (Balzer, Moulines & Sneed, 1987, p. 47). As an example, a set U is defined in D5 for the uniqueness constraints of $DissB$.

D5 Let $x^m = \langle T^m, P^m, K^m_\omega, \mathbb{R}, K^m, D^m_r, C^m_r, D^m, R^m \rangle \in M_p(DissB)$,
$x^n = \langle T^n, P^n, K^n_\omega, \mathbb{R}, K^n, D^n_r, C^n_r, D^n, R^n \rangle \in M_p(DissB)$,
$c_i, c_j \in Po(K^m_\omega) \cap Po(K^n_\omega)$; $p, q \in P^m$; $r, s \in P^n$; $t, u \in T^m$ and $v, w \in T^n$.
Then y is an element of the set of uniqueness constraints of basic dissonance theory, i.e. $y \in U(DissB)$, if and only if
(a) $y \in Po(M_p(DissB))$
(b) for all $(x^m, x^n) \in y \times y$,
for all $c_{ipt}, c_{jqu} \in K^m$, and
for all $c_{irv}, c_{jsw} \in K^n$

$$\begin{array}{llcl} \text{if} & D^m(i,p,t) & < & D^m(j,q,u), \\ \text{then} & D^n(i,r,v) & < & D^n(j,s,w), \\ \text{and} & & & \\ \text{if} & R^m(i,p,t) & < & R^m(j,q,u), \\ \text{then} & R^n(i,r,v) & < & R^n(j,s,w). \end{array}$$

According to D5 the functions D and R should be unique up to strictly monotone transformations over different observational objects and times. Such general uniqueness constraints imply a high predictive power of the theory, but they are often not tenable empirically. For that reason, much weaker uniqueness constraints are used in practice. These constraints can be formulated as special cases of D5. For example, when we additionally demand $p = r = q = s$, the resulting special uniqueness constraint $U_p \subset U$ only encompasses potential models that refer to the same observational object.

Because of the general importance of uniqueness constraints they must also be taken into account when the *empirical content* of any theory-element T is discussed. Following Balzer, Moulines and Sneed (1987, pp. 82-85), in D6 a subset $G(T)$ of the power set of the set $M_{pp}(T)$ of partial models of T is introduced. This subset results from applying the elimination function r_τ (see D3) to those sets of potential models that are actual models and satisfy the uniqueness constraints $U(T)$.

D6 $G(T) := \{y : y \in Po(M_{pp}(T))$ and for all $y_i \in y$:
$y_i = r_\tau(x_i)$ with $x_i \in x$ and $x \in Po(M(T)) \cap U(T)\}$.

In the structuralist terminology, $G(T)$ is usually called the empirical content of T. In order to avoid any confusion with the well-known concept of the empirical content of a theory in the sense of Popper (1975), I prefer calling $G(T)$ the *empirical extent* of theory-element T. Put simply, the expirical extent consists of those empirical systems for which both the substantial axioms and the constraints of the theory are satisfied.

2 A Theory-Net

In this section the main parts of Festinger's dissonance theory are reconstructed as a net of theory-elements. Each theory-element T is a tupel $\langle K, I\rangle$ where $K = \langle M_p, M, M_{pp}, U\rangle$ is the theory-core and I is a domain of intended applications of K (Balzer & Sneed, 1977-78). In general, connections between theory-elements can be described by so-called links and inter-theoretical relations (Balzer, Moulines & Sneed, 1987, pp. 57-62, 247-322). For clarity's sake, I use the term *intra-theoretical relations* for connections between elements of the same theory-net. Some of them are defined in the following subsection.

2.1 Intra-Theoretical Relations

Balzer and Sneed (1977/1978) argue that there are three basic kinds of intra-theoretical relations: theoretization, reduction, and specialization. They call a theory-element $T' = \langle M_p', M', M_{pp}', U', I'\rangle$ a *specialization* of another theory-element $T = \langle M_p, M, M_{pp}, U, I\rangle$, if $M' \subseteq M$, $U' \subseteq U$, $I' \subseteq I$, $M_p' = M_p$, and $M_{pp}' = M_{pp}$. If this is the case, I write $T'\sigma T$.

According to this definition, a specialization of T means that the sets of actual models, uniqueness constraints and intended applications of T can be restricted to subsets, whereas the sets of potential and partial models remain invariant. This can be the result of "new" substantial axioms or uniqueness constraints that refer to the "old" terminology.

As is shown in this section, an adequate reconstruction of a psychological theory like the dissonance theory requires the use of other intra-theoretical relations. These can be defined as special cases of a *general* specialization relation which is symbolized by Σ. The most important of them are the *enlargement* and the *restriction* relations. The specialization relation σ of Balzer and Sneed (1977-78), too, is such a special case. Therefore, I shall call σ a "specialization in the strict sense" or a *strict specialization.*

The definition of the general specialization relation Σ and the special cases thereof is based on a cutting-off function r_ε which connects the potential models of certain pairs of theory-elements.

D7 If

(a) S_T is a set of theory-elements,
(b) $\Sigma \subseteq S_T \times S_T$ is a binary relation on S_T,
(c) $T = \langle M_p, M, M_{pp}, U, I\rangle$ and
$T' = \langle M'_p, M', M'_{pp}, U', I'\rangle$ are two elements of S_T,
(d) $x = \langle B_1, ..., B_b, f_1, ..., f_k\rangle \in M_p$ and
$x' = \langle B_1, ..., B_b, f_1, ..., f_k, ..., f_{k+l}\rangle \in M'_p$.
with k and l beeing two natural numbers.
(e) $r_\varepsilon : M'_p \Longrightarrow M_p$ is a function with
$r_\varepsilon(\langle B_1, ..., B_b, f_1, ..., f_k, ..., f_{k+l}\rangle) = \langle B_1, ..., B_b, f_1, ..., f_k\rangle$,
(f) $R_\varepsilon(M') = \{x : x \in M_p \text{ and } x = r_\varepsilon(x') \text{ with } x' \in M'\}$ and
$R_\varepsilon(U') = \{x : x \in Po(M_p) \text{ and for all } x_i \in x:$
$x_i = r_\varepsilon(x'_i) \text{ with } x'_i \in x' \text{ and } x' \in U'\}$

then
$T' \sum T$ (T' is a *(general) specialization* of T),
if and only if
(g) $R_\varepsilon(M') \subseteq M$ or
(h) $R_\varepsilon(U') \subseteq U$.

According to this definition the function r_ε "eliminates" some terms of the potential models of T' so that we get potential models of T. If this function is applied only to those potential models that are also actual models of T', the result is a subset of M_p which is called $R_\varepsilon(M')$. If this subset is also a subset of the set M of actual models of T, then T' is defined to be a specialization of T. Various special cases of this general specialization relation Σ are first defined in D8 and then verbally explained.

D8 Let T and T' be two theory-elements with $T' \Sigma T$ according to D7. Then

(a) $T' \Sigma^e T$ (T' is a *true specialization* of T),
if and only if
$R_\varepsilon(M') \subset M$ or $R_\varepsilon(E') \subset E$.
(b) $T' \sigma T$ (T' is a *strict specialization* of T),
if and only if $l = 0$.
(c) $T' \tau T$ (T' is a *theoretization* of T),
if and only if $l > 0$ and $M_p = M'_{pp}$.
(d) $T' \varepsilon_\tau T$ (T' is a *theoretical enlargement* of T),

if and only if $l > 0$ and $M_{pp} = M'_{pp}$.

(e) $T' \varepsilon_\nu T$ (T' is a *non-theoretical enlargement* of T), if and only if $l > 0$ and neither $T' \tau T$ nor $T' \varepsilon_\tau T$.

(f) $T' \eta T$ (T' is a *restriction* of T), if and only if

(fa) $T' \varepsilon_\nu T$,

(fb) $f_{k+j} \subseteq f_i$ for at least one term $f_i (1 \leq i \leq k)$ and one term $f_{k+j} (1 \leq j \leq l)$.

(g) $T \upsilon T'$ (T is a *simplification* of T'), if and only if T is introduced later than T'.

According to part (a) of D8, T' is called a *true specialization* of T ($T' \Sigma^e T$), if $R_\epsilon(M')$ is a proper subset of M. This is the case when additional substantial axioms are used to define the actual models of T' that are not satisfied by all actual models of T. True specialization can also result when there are additional uniqueness constraints for T'. In both cases, $G(T')$, the empirical extent of T', is smaller than $G(T)$. As a consequence, true specializations have a greater empirical content in the Popperian sense.

In D7 potential models of T' were symbolized by $x' = \langle f_1, ..., f_k, ..., f_{k+l} \rangle$. If $l = 0$, i.e. if there are no additional terms in T', we get $M'_p = M_p$, $M'_{pp} = M_{pp}$, and $I' \subseteq I$. In this case T' is a specialization of T, if and only if M' is a subset of M or if U' is a subset of U. This shows that Balzer and Sneed's *strict specialization* relation σ is also a special case of the (general) specialization relation Σ (D8b, cf. Stephan (this volume), who defines a similiar differentiation relation δ). As a consequence of D8 (a) and (b), T' can be called a *true strict specialization* of T, if T' is a strict specialization of T (D8b) and if M' is a true subset of M or if U' is a true subset of U (D8a).

In D8c, d, e and f special relations are defined for the case that T' is a specialization of T, but not in the strict sense. In this case the parameter l in D7 is larger than zero, i.e. there are more terms in T' than in T.

If all additional terms are theoretical with respect to T', whereas the terms that are T-theoretical are T'-non-theoretical, the set of partial models of T' is equivalent to the set of potential models of T: $M'_{pp} = M_p$. This means that the "theoretical level" of T has become the "non-theoretical level" of T'. As a consequence, T can be "explained" by the theoretical terms and relationships of T'. According to D8c, T' is called a *theoretization* of T: $T' \tau T$ (Diederich, 1981; Balzer & Sneed, 1977/1978; see Balzer, Moulines & Sneed, 1987, p. 251, for more general definitions of theoretizations in the weak and the strong sense.)

If all T'-theoretical terms are either additional terms or terms that are also theoretical with respect to T, l is greater than 0 and M'_{pp} equals M_{pp}. In this case T' is called a *theoretical enlargement* of T: $T' \varepsilon_\tau T$ (D8d). This relation corresponds to the "enlargement" relation ε of Diederich (1981, pp. 78-81). Theoretical enlargement and theoretization are equivalent, of course, if there are no T-theoretical terms, i.e. if $M_p = M_{pp}$.

If at least one additional term in T' is not T'-theoretical, T' is a *non-theoretical enlargement* of T: $T' \varepsilon_\nu T$ (D8e). In this case, the partial models of T' are structures that are terminologically richer than the partial models of T.

As is shown by the reconstruction of dissonance theory, a new non-theoretical term is often introduced because a set of non-base objects (e.g. present cognitions) must be restricted to a certain subset. Therefore, the *restriction relation* η is defined in D8f as a special case of the non-theoretical enlargement relation.

The specialization relations discussed so far do not include any temporal notion. Nevertheless, somebody reading that a theory-element T' is reconstructed as a specialization, theoretization, or enlargement of T, probably has a strong tendency to believe that T' has been introduced later than T. Often, however, the more specific element T' is the first one, and T is introduced afterwards, for example, in order to keep matters simple in experimental applications of the theory. Therefore, a *simplification* relation υ is defined in D8g.

Take, as an illustration, the theory-elements $DissA$ and $DissB$ discussed in Section 1.2. From a formal point of view, $DissA$ is an enlargement of $DissB$, because the actual models of $DissA$ are structures with additonal terms (w, D_m, C_m, etc.) which fulfil additional substantial axioms (A6 and A7). As these terms will turn out to be $Diss$-theoretical (see Section 2.4), $DissA$ is a theoretical enlargement of $DissB$. From a pragmatic point of view, however, $DissB$ is a simplification of $DissA$.

In a more sophisticated fashion, theory-development can be reconstructed by considering a sequence of theory-nets and by introducing diachronic and pragmatic concepts such as historical periods and scientific communities (Balzer, Moulines & Sneed, 1987, pp. 216-223). But this is beyond the scope of this chapter.

In a very general way, we can define a *theory net*, N, as a structure consisting of a set S_T of theory-elements and one or more relations $R_1, R_2, \ldots$ each of which is a subset of $S_T \times S_T$. More specifically, N is a *specialization net* if $R_1, R_2, \ldots$ are the general specialization relation Σ and some of its special cases defined in D8.

It follows from Definition D7 that the general specialization relation Σ is transitive, reflexive and antisymmetric. The relation is not complete, however, because there may be pairs of theory-elements for which neither $T \ \Sigma \ T'$ nor $T' \ \Sigma \ T$ hold. Therefore, any theory-net $N = \langle S_T, \Sigma \rangle$ is a *partial order*.

Balzer, Moulines and Sneed (1987, p. 172 - 177) define theory-nets as structures consisting of a set of theory-elements and the relation σ which I call the strict specialization relation. This seems to be too narrow a conceptualization for the reconstruction of psychological theories, however. In the theory-nets by which parts of dissonance theory will be reconstructed, for example, most relations between theory-elements are not strict specializations, but other special cases (enlargements, restrictions, simplifications, etc.) of the general specialization Σ. Thus, our dissonance theory-nets will usually be of the form $N = \langle S_T, \Sigma, \sigma, \varepsilon_\tau, \varepsilon_\nu, \eta, \upsilon \rangle$.

Usually, a theory-net will be accepted as a reconstruction of one distinct empirical theory only if it is connected, i.e. if any two theory-elements either are general specializations of a third element or if they have a common specialization. Moreover, many, if not all substantial theories seem to be reconstructable as "theory-trees", i.e. as theory-nets that are connected and have a single basic element with all other elements being (general) specializations thereof (Balzer, Moulines & Sneed, 1987, p. 172-177).

All dissonance theory-nets turn out to consist exclusively of elements that are specializations of $DissB$. Put into other words, the substantial axioms of $DissB$ are hypothesized to be satisfied in all applications of the theory. Therefore, *DissB* represents the *fundamental law* of the theory and is called the *basic element* of dissonance theory. Each specialization, on the other hand, corresponds to a *special law* of the theory.

Festinger (1957) describes four areas of application for his theory: consequences of decisions, effects of forced compliance, voluntary and involuntary exposure to information, and the role of social support. In the following Sections 2.2 and 2.3 the most important theoretical and empirical aspects of the first two areas are reconstructed as parts E and F of the dissonance theory-net.

2.2 Part E of the Theory-Net: Consequences of Decisions

According to Festinger (1957) "dissonance is an almost inevitable consequence of a decision" between two (or more) alternatives, because "all those elements that, considered alone, would lead to action other than the one taken are dissonant with the cognitive elements corresponding to the action taken" (p. 36).

P7 When a decision has been made,
(a) the more important the decision,
(b) the greater the relative attractiveness of the unchosen alternatives to the chosen alternative, and
(c) the smaller the cognitive overlap between the two alternatives, i.e. the greater the qualitative distinction between them, the greater the magnitude of dissonance (Festinger, 1957, pp. 37-47).

P8 The presssure to reduce postdecisional dissonance will manifest itself mainly in attempts to add or change cognitions in order
(a) to increase the attractiveness of the chosen alternative or to decrease the attractiveness of the unchosen alternative, and
(b) to enlarge the cognitive overlap between chosen and unchosen alternatives (Festinger, 1957, p. 52-56).

In contrast to P1 to P6, P7 and P8 refer only to a certain subset of present cognitions which I call K_E. Each $c_{ipt} \in K_E$ is a subject's cognition that, in a certain decision situation, he or she has preferred a certain alternative A to an other alternative (or set of alternatives) B. In A9, five new functions are defined on this subset of cognitions to reconstruct Festinger's (1957) special theoretical account of postdecisional dissonance. To keep matters as simple as possible, Festinger's (1957, p. 37) notion of the relative attractiveness of chosen and unchosen alternatives is formalized by differences, not by proportions.

A9 $K_E \subseteq K$ is a non-empty set (of cognitions concerning a decision that has been) made with the functions

$w_c:$	$K_E \Rightarrow \mathbb{R}$	(subjective importance)
$s:$	$K_E \Rightarrow \mathbb{R}$	(subjective similarity between chosen and unchosen alternatives)
$a_g:$	$K_E \Rightarrow \mathbb{R}$	(attractivity of the chosen alternative)
$a_n:$	$K_E \Rightarrow \mathbb{R}$	(attractivity of the unchosen alternative)
$a_r:$	$K_E \Rightarrow \mathbb{R}$	with $a_r(i,p,t_+) = a_g(i,p,t_+) - a_n(i,p,t_+)$ (relative attractivity of chosen versus unchosen alternative).

P7 and P8 give rise to two special substantial axioms A10 and A11 which are given below.

Two aspects of these and the following axioms need a prior explanation. A statement like P7 on the antecedent conditions of dissonance can be formulated by means of several "If ..., then ..." - phrases. But the theory does not say that always if, for example, there is a larger subjective importance, then dissonance becomes larger (cf. A7a). For example, when there is also a smaller relative attractiveness of the nonchosen alternative, the theory does not allow clear predictions. Thus, it is implicitly assumed that any other factor F_x that has an influence on the magnitude of dissonance (whether known or unknown) remains constant when the factor F_i of interest varies. Alternatively, the weaker assumption can be made that F_i is stochastically independent of any F_x, i.e. that they do not covary in any systematic way. Assumptions of this kind can be summarized as *ceteris paribus clauses.* They are an essential, albeit implicit part of all causal hypotheses and theories in science (see Johansson, 1980; Secord, 1986; Steyer, 1985; for further details). For that reason they are made explicit in the formulations of our special substantial axioms. Instead of repeatedly using lengthy phrases like "If ... and if all other factors are constant or do not vary systematically, then ..." we write in short "If$_{cp}$ ..., then ..."

Though most of Festinger's theoretical statements are worded in a deterministic manner, he would certainly not claim to have a theory of inevitable consequences of certain antecedent conditions. Phrases like "The implications of the theory ... would lead one to expect that at least occasionally we should be able to observe ..." (Festinger, 1957, p. 98) clearly show that his theory deals only with cognitive or behavioral tendencies. In addition, Festinger does not pretend to know all possible manifestations of pressures to reduce dissonance. For each area of application, he discusses only the main ways in which dissonance can be reduced.

For these reasons, a probabilistic formulation of the special axioms in our reconstruction seems necessary, although it reduces falsifiability and empirical content in Popper's (1975) sense. Dissonance theory does not allow us, however, to give further specifications of probability spaces and exact values of p. We can only assume that *ceteris paribus* each probability p for a consequence B given a condition A is larger than the corresponding probability p_0 of B in the case that A is not given. As an abbreviation, I use "*then*$_p$..." instead of "then with probability $p > p_0$ ..."

A10 For all $c_{ipt}, c_{jqu} \in K_E$,

$$\begin{array}{llrcl} \text{if}_{cp} & \text{(a)} & w_c(i,p,t) & < & w_c(j,q,u), \\ \text{or} & \text{(b)} & a_r(i,p,t) & > & a_r(j,q,u), \\ \text{or} & \text{(c)} & s(i,p,t) & > & s(j,q,u), \\ \text{then}_p & & D(i,p,t) & < & D(j,q,u). \end{array}$$

A11 For all $c_{ipt}, c_{ipt+}, c_{jqu}, c_{jqu+} \in K_E$,

$$\begin{array}{llrcl} \text{if}_{cp} & \text{(a)} & R(i,p,t) & < & R(j,q,u), \\ \text{then}_p & \text{(b)} & 0 \leq \; a_r(i,p,t_+) - a_r(i,p,t) & < & a_r(j,q,u_+) - a_r(j,q,u) \\ \text{or} & \text{(c)} & 0 \leq \; s(i,p,t_+) - s(i,p,t) & < & s(j,q,u_+) - s(j,q,u). \end{array}$$

A11 presupposes that there are at least two present cognitions concerning decisions at times t and u and that these cognitions are still present at the subsequent points of time t_+ and u_+. The premise (a) states that there are smaller pressures to reduce dissonance connected with c_{ipt} than with c_{jqu}. The conclusion refers to changes with respect to cognition c_i (between

t and t_+) and c_j (between u and u_+). Point (b) deals with changes in the relative attractivity of chosen and unchosen alternatives, and (c) with changes in the similarity of the alternatives. If the premise is satisfied, then, according to P8, changes in both "relative attractivity" and "similarity" should be smaller for c_{ipt} than for c_{jqu}. In addition, the inequalities in (b) and (c) contain the information that both relative attractivity and similarity become larger.

The sets of actual models and potential models of a new theory-element $DissE1$ are now defined with the special axioms A9, A10, and A11.

D9 $x \in M_p(DissE1)$ if and only if
there are $T, P, K_\omega, \mathbb{R}, K, O_T, D_p, C_p, D, R, K_E, w_c, s, a_g, a_n, a_r$ such that
(a) $x = \langle T, P, K_\omega, \mathbb{R}, K, O_T, D_p, C_p, D, R, K_E, w_c, s, a_g, a_n, a_r\rangle$,
(b) $\langle T, P, K_\omega, \mathbb{R}, K, O_T, D_p, C_p, D, R\rangle \in M_p(DissB)$ according to D4, and
(c) A9 is satisfied.

D10 $x \in M(DissE1)$ if and only if
(a) $x \in M_p(DissE1)$ according to D9, and
(b) A8', A10 and A11 are satisfied.

In comparison to actual models of $DissB$, actual models of $DissE1$ have to satisfy two more substantial axioms which pertain to terms that are newly introduced in A9. As these terms will turn out to be non-theoretical with respect to dissonance theory (cf. Sec. 2.4), $DissE1$ is a non-theoretical enlargement of $DissB$ as defined in D8: $DissE1 \; \varepsilon_\nu \; DissB$. In addition, $DissE1$ comprises *special uniqueness constraints*. Because of the use of differences in the special substantial axiom A11, the terms a_r and s must be at least unique up to positive-linear transformations.

If A8', A10, and A11 are satisfied for a potential model x of $DissE1$, i.e. if x is an actual model of $DissE1$, the following T1 is satisfied, too. In this sense, T1 is a "theorem" implied by the three "axioms". It consists of the premises of A10 and the conclusions of A11. As it pertains exclusively to terms that are *Diss*-non-theoretical, it is called an "empirical theorem."

T1 If $x \in M(DissE1)$, then for all $c_{ipt}, c_{ipt+}, c_{jqu}, c_{jqu+} \in K_E$,

$$\begin{array}{llrcl} \text{if}_{cp} & \text{(a)} & w_c(i,p,t) & < & w_c(j,q,u) \\ \text{or} & \text{(b)} & a_r(i,p,t) & > & a_r(j,q,u) \\ \text{or} & \text{(c)} & s(i,p,t) & > & s(j,q,u), \\ \text{then}_p & \text{(d)} & 0 \leq a_r(i,p,t_+) - a_r(i,p,t) & < & a_r(j,q,u_+) - a_r(j,q,u) \\ \text{or} & \text{(e)} & 0 \leq s(i,p,t_+) - s(i,p,t) & < & s(j,q,u_+) - s(j,q,u). \end{array}$$

In precedent versions of my reconstruction of dissonance theory I preferred to define the set of actual models of theory-elements with one special substantial axiom like T1 instead of two special axioms like A10 and A11. Using this approach, it was possible to work with two distinct and exhaustive classes of substantial axioms, namely, basic axioms like A8' which refer to theoretical terms and special axioms like T1 without theoretical terms. Then, a "theoretical axiom" like A8' stands for the transition from the set of potential models of the basic element to the set of its actual models, i.e. it stands for the fundamental law of the theory. A "non-theoretical" axiom like T1, on the other hand, would directly represent a *special law* of the theory, for it would stand for the transition from potential models to actual models of a theory-element that is a specialization of the basic element. These interpretative

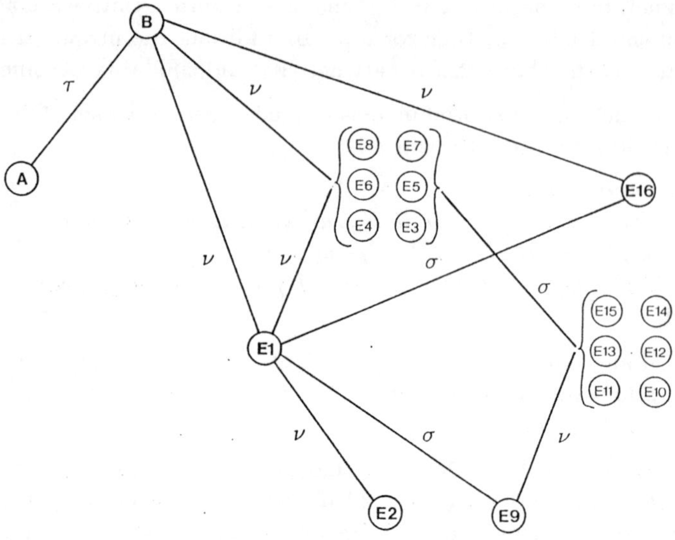

Figure 1: *Relations between some theory-elements for post-decisional dissonance*

Note.
If theory-elements Ti and Tj are connected by one line
and if Ti is above Tj,
then Tj is a specialization of Ti ($Tj \Sigma Ti$, according to D7).
If, in addition, Ti is to the right of Tj,
Ti is a simplification of Tj ($Ti v Tj$, according to D8 g).
Special cases of the general specialization relation Σ are labeled by
τ: theoretical enlargement
ν: non-theoretical enlargement
σ: strict specialization
η: restriction.

advantages notwithstanding, the present manner of axiomatization has been chosen because it is more general and corresponds more closely to Festinger's original exposition of his theory.

Different (groups of) scientists are considered as holding the same theory as long as they accept the same basic element with the same fundamental law. Special axioms and laws, however, are more or less modified, for example, as a result of empirical research or new theoretical reflection. For post-decisional dissonance, this will be illustrated by some examples (cf. Figure 1).

Firstly, besides the most prominent ways to reduce dissonance (see above P8), Festinger (1957, pp. 55-61, 83) discusses another manifestation of the pressure to reduce dissonance, namely, a higher subjective confidence that the decision was the right one. Such a supplement to the theory can be reconstructed by adding a definition of a function sh to the "terminological" axiom A9 and a strictly monotonic relationship of sh and R to the substantial axiom A11. By the resulting modified axioms, the actual models of a new theory-element can be defined which is called *DissE*2. It is a non-theoretical enlargement of both *DissE*1 and *DissB*.

Secondly, new theory-elements can be introduced to reconstruct the fact that usually only one part of A10 and one part of A11 are used in empirical applications of the theory. Elimination of part (b) and (c) of A10 and part (c) of A11, for example, leads to two new special substantial axioms which the actual models of a theory-element called *DissE*3 must fulfil and which imply the following empirical theorem.

T2 If $x \in M(DissE3)$ then for all $c_{ipt}, c_{ipt+}, c_{jqu}, c_{jqu+} \in K$,

$$\begin{array}{llcl} \text{if}_{cp} & w_c(i,p,t) & < & w_c(j,q,u), \\ \text{then}_p & 0 \leq a_r(i,p,t_+) - a_r(i,p,t) & < & a_r(j,q,u_+) - a_r(j,q,u). \end{array}$$

In the same manner, the other five possible combinations of parts of A10 and A11 lead to new theory-elements *DissE*4 to *DissE*8. Combination of part (b) of A10 and part (b) of A11 leads to *DissE*4, A10c and A11b to *DissE*5, etc. According to definition D8 *DissE*1 is a non-theoretical enlargement of each of *DissE*3 to *DissE*8, whereas from a pragmatic point of view *DissE*3 to *DissE*8 are simplifications of *DissE*1, i.e., for example, both $DissE3 v DissE1$ and $DissE1 \varepsilon_\nu DissE3$ hold. Thirdly, the most important modifications of special axioms result as consequences of empirical results. In the case of post-decisional dissonance, there were some early studies showing not divergent but convergent changes in the attractiveness of chosen and unchosen alternatives as immediate consequences of decisions. This so-called *regret effect* is not in accordance with the special substantial axioms introduced so far. Following Festinger (1957, p. 270; 1964, pp. 97-110), regret effects do not contradict *general dissonance theory*, however. So it is possible to introduce new specializations of the basic element *DissB* that encompasses this effect by means of cut-off points t_g and u_g between t and t_+, and u and u_+, respectively. The theory-elements *DissE*9 to *DissE*16 (see Figure 1) are examples of such specializations.

When we assume that there *must* be a regret effect for subjective importance, attractivity, and similarity, a corresponding modification of A11 leads to theory-element *DissE*9 that is a specialization in the strict sense of *DissE*1. By combining the parts of its substantial axioms we get the theory-elements *DissE*10 to *DissE*15 which are simplifications of *DissE*9 and strict specializations of *DissE*3 to *DissE*8.

When we only assume that a regret effect *may* occur, modifying A11 leads to a theory-element that is called *DissE*16. Both *DissE*1 and *DissE*9 are strict specializations of *DissE*16.

In Figure 1, the formal relations between theory-elements are represented by their vertical position. If *Tj* is a general specialization of *Ti* according to definition D7, *Tj* stands below *Ti*. The horizontal positions respresent some pragmatic relations. If *Tj* is introduced later than or as a simplification of *Ti*, it is depicted more to the right side.

To be sure, we have analyzed only some typical specializations of the basic element for post-decisional dissonance and Figure 1 is only a small portion of part *E* of the theory-net by which post-decisional dissonance theory can be reconstructed.

Up to now, I have discussed only cores of theory-elements, not their intended applications. Festinger (1957, pp. 48-83) describes four empirical studies as applications of his theory to post-decisional phenomena. Only Brehm's (1956) experiment, however, pertains to one of the prominent ways to reduce dissonance, namely, changes in the relative attractivity of chosen and unchosen objects. As the relation of these changes to pre-decisional attractivity is studied, Brehm's experiment can be taken as a paradigmatic application for theory-element *DissE*4.

Brehm's experiment is indeed a paradigmatic application of dissonance theory on post-decisional phenomena, because it has given rise to a large number of similar experiments (see, for a review, Irle & Möntmann, 1978, pp. 304-315). Brehm and Cohen (1959), for example, study the relative attractiveness of toys after choices between toys of different similarity. So they refer to part (c) of A10, part (b) of A11, and, as a consequence, to element *DissE*5. Other experiments (see Irle & Möntmann, 1978, pp. 309-315) correspond to intended applications of theory-elements in the right side of Figure 1 (*DissE*9 to *DissE*16), because they study the "regret effect".

2.3 Part F of the Theory-Net: Forced Compliance Dissonance

Forced compliance is a "public compliance without private acceptance" (Festinger, 1957, p. 87). "There are circumstances in which persons will behave in a manner counter to their convictions or will publicly make statements which they do not really believe ... such a state of affairs is acompanied by dissonance and by various manifestations of pressure to reduce the dissonance" (p. 84).

P9 Following a forced compliance,
(a) the more important the opinions or behavior involved, and
(b) the smaller the promised reward or threatened punishment,
the greater is the magnitude of dissonance that is created (pp. 90-94).

P10 Pressures to reduce forced compliance dissonance may be manifested in
(a) a reduction of the importance of the opinion involved,
(b) an enhancement of the subjective importance or magnitude of the promised reward or threatened punishment,
(c) a change of private opinion in accordance with public behavior
(pp. 94-97).

Festinger's special theoretical statements refer to cognitions or behaviors that contradict personal opinions. This subset is called K_M. Opinions are usually treated in a quantitative manner by assessing the strength of a belief or the degree of an evaluation. Hence, in A12 below a function m_e for the real personal opinion and another function m_v for the opinion as expressed in open behavior are introduced. In addition, we need a function w_c for the importance of the cognitions (cf. A9) and a function b for the subjective magnitude of the promised reward or threatened punishment.

A12 $K_M \subseteq K$ is a non-empty set
(of cognitions on behaviors contrary to personal opinions)
with the functions
b: $K_M \Rightarrow \mathbb{R}$ (subjective magnitude of reward or punishment),
w_c: $K_M \Rightarrow \mathbb{R}$ (subjective importance),
m_e: $K_M \Rightarrow \mathbb{R}$ (real opinion),
m_v: $K_M \Rightarrow \mathbb{R}$ (opinion expressed in behavior).

By means of these special terms we can state the following special substantial axioms corresponding to P9 and P10.

A13 For all $c_{ipt}, c_{jqu} \in K_M$,

$$\begin{array}{llrcl} \text{if}_{cp} & \text{(a)} & w_c(i,p,t) & < & w_c(j,q,u) \\ \text{or} & \text{(b)} & b(i,p,t) & > & b(j,q,u), \\ \text{then}_p & \text{(c)} & D(i,p,t) & < & D(j,q,u). \end{array}$$

A14 For all $c_{ipt}, c_{ipt+}, c_{jqu}, c_{jqu+} \in K_M$,

$$\begin{array}{lllcl} \text{if}_{cp} & \text{(a)} & 0 < \quad R(i,p,t) & < & R(j,q,u), \\ \text{then}_p & \text{(b)} & 0 \geq \quad w_c(i,p,t_+) - w_c(i,p,t) & > & w_c(j,q,u_+) - w_c(j,q,u) \\ \text{or} & \text{(c)} & 0 \leq \quad b(i,p,t_+) - b(i,p,t) & < & b(j,q,u_+) - b(j,q,u) \\ \text{or} & \text{(d)} & |m_e(i,p,t_+) - m_v(i,p,t)| & < & |m_e(i,p,t) - m_v(i,p,t)| \\ & \text{and} & |m_e(j,q,u_+) - m_v(j,q,u)| & < & |m_e(j,q,u) - m_v(j,q,u)| \\ & \text{and} & |m_e(i,p,t_+) - m_e(i,p,t)| & < & |m_e(j,q,u_+) - m_e(j,q,u)|. \end{array}$$

Part (d) of A14 may need some further explanation. According to the first two lines personal opinions are changed so that there is a smaller difference with the opinions expressed in open behavior. The last line says that the amount of change is smaller for c_{ipt} than for c_{jqu}.

The complete form of Festinger's theory for forced compliance situations is reconstructed by the theory-element $DissF1$. Like $DissE1$, it is a non-theoretical enlargement of $DissB$. There is no need to give the definitions of its actual models and potential models, because they are very similar to D9 and D10 in Section 2.2. Again, the two special substantial axioms imply an "empirical theorem" like T1. Furthermore, we get six different specializations of $DissF1$ by ignoring parts of the special axioms (see Figure 2). For example, by combining part (a) of A13 and part (b) of A14, we get the theory-element $DissF2$, and the special substantial axioms of $DissF7$ comprise part (b) of A13 and part (d) of A14 (cf. Figure 2).

Festinger (1957, pp. 98-122) illustrates his theory for forced compliance situations by means of five empirical studies. Two of them, however, are not published in detail. The remaining three studies (King & Janis, 1956; Janis & King, 1954; Kelman, 1953) can be considered as paradigmatic applications of elements in part F of the dissonance theory-net. There can be little doubt that another paradigmatic application is given by the experiment of Festinger and Carlsmith (1959) which has had a great influence on subsequent research. As predicted by dissonance theory, subjects who had to present a dull task as very interesting, gave a more positive evaluation of the task when rewarded with 1 dollar than when rewarded with 20 dollar. Hence, Festinger and Carlsmith (1959) refer to $DissF7$ as defined above and their experiment gives rise to a partial model of $DissF7$ which is an element of its set of paradigmatic applications. The same is true for Kelman's (1953) study. Many other forced compliance experiments (see, for a review, Irle & Möntmann, 1978, pp. 323-334) are highly similar to these two paradigmatic applications. As is demonstrated in Section 3, the theoretical reference point of each of these experiments can be much more closely reconstructed by a strict specialization of $DissF7$. This is symbolized by the theory-element $DissF8$ in Figure 2.

The results of forced compliance experiments are not generally in accordance with dissonance theory, however. It seems that there are dissonance reduction effects as predicted by

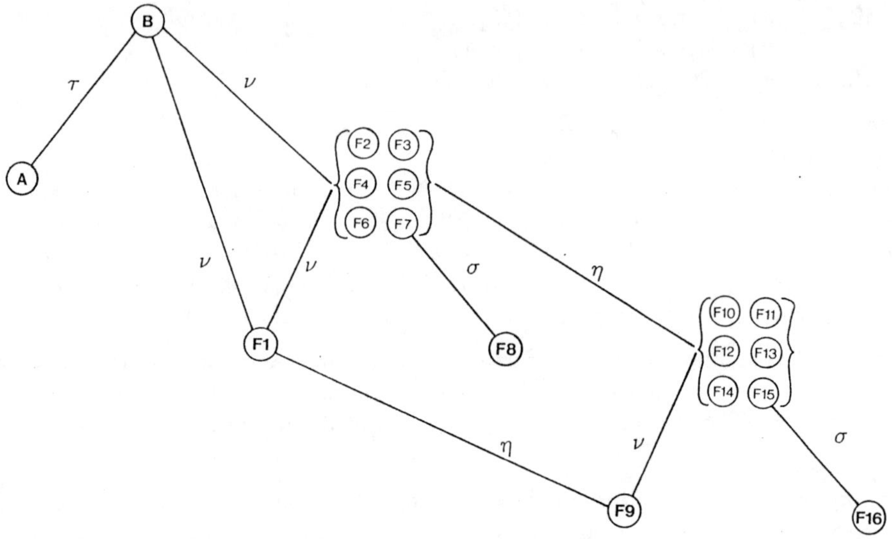

Figure 2: *Relations between some theory-elements for forced-compliance dissonance*

Note.
If theory-elements Ti and Tj are connected by one line
and if Ti is above Tj,
then Tj is a specialization of Ti ($Tj \Sigma Ti$, according to D7).
If, in addition, Ti is to the right of Tj,
Ti is a simplification of Tj ($Ti v Tj$, according to D8 g).
Special cases of the general specialization relation Σ are labeled by
τ: theoretical enlargement
ν: non-theoretical enlargement
σ: strict specialization
η: restriction.

the theory only if subjects can decide freely whether or not to engage in behavior which is contrary to their opinion and if their engagement is made public (Irle & Möntmann, 1978, p. 332). Otherwise, the magnitude of opinion change is often positively related to the magnitude of reward or punishment. Such a *reinforcement effect* is also observed when the magnitude of reward is relatively high (Frey et al., 1982, p. 285).

As a reaction to these empirical results, several modifications of dissonance theory were put forth. Brehm and Cohen (1962) stress that a personal "commitment" is necessary for cognitive dissonance. Aronson (1968) suggests that there is cognitive dissonance only if the individual's open behavior is not only inconsistent with personal opinions but also with his or her self-concept. For an exemplaric reconstruction of Aronson's modification, a subset $K_{MS} \subseteq K_M$ of cognitions on such behaviors is introduced and the special axioms A12, A13 and A14 are restricted to this subset.

A15 (a)$K_M \subseteq K$ is a non-empty set
(of cognitions on behaviors contrary to personal opinions), and
$K_{MS} \subseteq K_M$ is a non-empty set
(of cognitions on behaviors contrary
to personal opinions and the personal self-concept).
(b) As A12 with K_{MS} instead of K_M.

A16 As A13 with K_{MS} instead of K_M.

A17 As A14 with K_{MS} instead of K_M.

Let *DissF*9 be the theory-element to reconstruct the general Aronson modification. The sets of its actual models and potential models are defined as follows.

D11 $x \in M_p(DissF9)$ if and only if there are
$T, P, K_\omega, \mathbb{R}, K, O_T, D_p, C_p, D, R, K_M, K_{MS}, b, w_c, m_e, m_v$
such that
(a) $x = \langle T, P, K_\omega, \mathbb{R}, K, O_T, D_p, C_p, D, R, K_M, K_{MS}, b, w_c, m_e, m_v \rangle$,
(b) $\langle T, P, K_\omega, \mathbb{R}, K, O_T, D_p, C_p, D, R \rangle \in M_p(DissB)$
according to D4 in Section 1.2 and
(c) A15 is satisfied.

D12 $x \in M(DissF9)$ if and only if
(a) $x \in M_p(DissF9)$ according to D11 and
(b) A8', A16, and A17 are satisfied.

*DissF*9 is a *restriction* η of *DissF*1 in the sense of *D*8 in Section 2.1. A paradigmatic application of *DissF*9 is given by the experiment of Nel, Helmreich and Aronson (1969). Again, by ignoring parts of the special axioms we get simplifications of *DissF*9. Each of these theory-elements *DissF*10 to *DissF*15 is a restriction of the corresponding element in the set running from *DissF*2 to *DissF*7. These relationships are sketched in Figure 2. (The theory-element *DissF*16 in this figure will be discussed in Section 3.)

2.4 Theoretical and Non-Theoretical Terms

Sneed (1971) has initiated the development of new answers to the outstanding problem of distinguishing between theoretical and non-theoretical terms. According to the informal structualist criterion of theoreticity a concept f is called theoretical relative to theory T (or simply *T-theoretical*), if and only if every determination of f that is adequate according to existing expositions of the theory presupposes the existence of at least one actual model of T (Balzer, Moulines & Sneed, 1987, pp. 55, 67-68).

Of course, there may be a measuring procedure for a term f that is independent of the theory T but that is not yet discovered or that is not accepted as valid by the most influential proponents of the theory. As in these cases, too, the term f is classified as T-theoretical, the informal criterion is basically pragmatic. For a more precise identification of T-theoretical terms, a formal criterion has been developed (Balzer, 1983; Balzer, Moulines & Sneed, 1987, pp. 73-76). Formal and informal criteria are not equivalent, however. Many terms are classified as T-theoretical by the formal, but as T-non-theoretical by the informal criterion. The reason for this result lies in the fact that the formal criterion takes into account only those methods of determination that can be represented in the conceptual frame of T, whereas the informal criterion covers "all kinds of methods ... including those available in other theories ..." (Balzer, Moulines & Sneed, 1987, p. 77). For this reason I suggest that the informal and pragmatic criterion is more appropriate for the structural reconstruction of dissonance theory.

As indicated in Sections 2.2 and 2.3, experimental dissonance research typically studies dependent and independent variables such as similarity between alternatives, strength of opinions, degree of attractivity, magnitude of reward, etc. The corresponding terms do not belong to the basic element, but are first introduced in axioms like A9 and A12, i.e. for specializations of the basic element like $DissE1$ and $DissF1$. The various assessment methods for these terms depend on the validity of measurement theories, auxiliary hypotheses, and other kinds of assumptions. But they do not at all depend on the validity of dissonance theory. Thus, these terms are $Diss$-non-theoretical.

The same is true for terms designating special subsets of cognitions (K_E, K_M, etc.) which must be introduced for every area of application. Take, as an example, the set K_{MS} defined in A15. The question if a cognition on counter-attitudinal behavior is inconsistent with the individual's self-concept or not is not answered by dissonance theory, but by recourse to paradigmatic applications (Aronson, 1968; Bramel, 1968; Nel, Helmreich & Aronson, 1969) or well-known approaches to the psychology of the self (Rosenberg & Kaplan, 1982; Kihlstrom & Cantor, 1984; Gergen, 1984).

When, as in our example, the meaning of a term occuring in partial models of a theory-element T is (partly) determined through another theory T', this can be reconstructed by an *intertheoretical link.* I do not introduce links in the present reconstruction of dissonance theory, for this would require the specification and reconstruction of at least one of the preceding theories of the self.

I now turn to the terms introduced in A1 to A4 for general dissonance theory $DissA$ and the basic element $DissB$. The terms P for persons or observational objects, T for points of time, and O_T for temporal order are clearly $Diss$-non-theoretical because they are used in their common-sense meaning. The terms K, K_ω, D_p and C_p are also classified as $Diss$-non-theoretical, for they can be further specified by many other psychological conceptions. For example, the distinction between dissonant, consonant, and irrelevant pairs of cognitions can be traced back to a personal "follows from"-relation the assessment of which is independent of dissonance theory (Festinger, 1957, pp. 278-279).

Note that all base sets of dissonance theory have been classified as $Diss$-non-theoretical by applying the informal criterion. Balzer, Moulines and Sneed (1987) assert that "it would be a characteristic of all empirical theories ... that their base sets ... are determined either pre-theoretically in ordinary language or by means of underlying theories" (p. 49).

The terms in A4, however, are classified as $Diss$-theoretical. Although Krause (1972) argues for a direct assessment of such terms as dissonance strength and pressure to reduce it, dissonance researchers unanimously do not try to assess these terms directly and idependently of dissonance theory. Instead, they study empirical relationships between variables corresponding to $Diss$-non-theoretical terms which are decribed in what I have called "empirical theorems".

When the results of a study are in accordance with such a theorem, these empirical associations can be given a *theoretical explanation* by assigning different values of theoretical variables to the different values of the corresponding non-theoretical variables and by referring to the fundamental law of the theory. Let there be, for example, a study on changes in relative attractivity for decisions differing in importance. Under certain conditions this study leads to a partial model a of $DissE3$. When empirical results show a strict monotone relationship between importance and change in attractivity, the empirical theorem T2 of $DissE3$ from Section 2.2 can be considered as satisfied and the partial model a can be called a *non-theoretical model* of $DissE3$. This empirical relationship can be explained theoretically when we choose values for the theoretical functions D and R so that, according to A10, the more important the decision (w_c) the greater the strength of dissonance (D), and that, according to A11, the larger the change in relative attractivity (a_r) the larger the pressure to reduce dissonance (R).

As there is no problem to specify situations not in accordance with T2, the empirical extent $G(T)$ is smaller than the power set of the set of partial models. Thus, $DissE3$ has empirical content in the Popperian sense. The same is true for all special theory-elements like $DissE1$ to $DissE16$ and $DissF1$ to $DissF16$. The basic element $DissB$, however, has no empirical content. This is illustrated by the fact that its substantial axiom A8' must be satisfied if, for example, T2, A10, and A11 are satisfied. Therefore, any partial model of $DissE3$ can be enlarged to an actual model if it is a non-theoretical model, i.e. if the empirical theorem and the special substantial axioms are satisfied. The general theory-element $DissA$, too, has no empirical content. Its theoretical terms and axioms can be used, however, for a further theoretical explanation of the different magnitudes of dissonance strength D and the fundamental law relationship between D and R.

When an empirical application of the theory turns out to be unsuccesful, i.e. when the results are not in accordance with the empirical theorem, researchers usually conclude that cognitive dissonance has not been aroused by the experimental conditions or that it had too low a strength. Explanations of that kind have led to the modifications of the theory like that of Aronson or Brehm and Cohen.

As hinted earlier, the *partial models* of a theory-element can be derived from its potential models when $Diss$-theoretical and $Diss$-non-theoretical terms have been differentiated. A comparison of Definitions D2 and D4 in Section 1.2 shows that, according to our classification, the terms that are in $DissA$ but not in $DissB$ are exclusively $Diss$-theoretical terms. Thus, the sets of partial models of both theory-elements are equal. We can define these sets on the basis of Definition D1 of potential models of $DissA$.

D13 x is a *partial model* of general dissonance theory
and of the basic element of dissonance theory,
i.e. $x \in M_{pp}(DissA)$ and $x \in M_{pp}(DissB)$
if and only if there are $T, P, K_\omega, \mathbb{R}, K, O_T, D_p, C_p$ such that
(a) $x = \langle T, P, K_\omega, \mathbb{R}, K, O_T, D_p, C_p \rangle$ and
(b) A1, A2, and A3 from Section 1.1 are satisfied

The sets of partial models of the other theory-elements can be defined in the same manner. As an illustration, D14 defines the partial models of $DissE1$.

D14 $x \in M_{pp}(DissE1)$ if and only if there are
$T, P, K_\omega, \mathbb{R}, K, O_T, D_p, C_p, K_E, w_c, s, a_g, a_n, a_r$ such that
(a) $x = \langle T, P, K_\omega, \mathbb{R}, K, O_T, D_p, C_p, K_E, w_c, s, a_g, a_n, a_r \rangle$,
(b) $\langle T, P, K_\omega, \mathbb{R}, K, O_T, D_p, C_p \rangle \in M_{pp}(DissB)$ according to D13, and
(c) A9 from Section 2.2 is satisfied.

3 Theory and Experiment

Up to now, published applications of the structuralist view have primarily dealt with some rudimentary forms of scientific theories. Relationships between theories and empirical data in real scientific research programs, however, have been neglected. For dissonance theory, I have made some first steps toward a detailed reconstruction of this central aspect of any empirical science (Westermann, 1987). To be concrete the experiment of Frey and Irle (1972) and its connections to the theory have been analyzed in structuralist terms and problems of experimental validity were discussed from a structural point of view. In this section, some basic aspects of this reconstruction are resumed. To be sure, certain aspects of this experiment can be criticized and there may be better exemplars of dissonance research. Nevertheless, it is a typical and often-cited experiment, and the main features and problems of a structuralist account of actual empirical research can be illustrated quite well by considering this study.

The experiment pertains to "the relation of reward and attitude change after a person has performed some counter-attitudinal behavior" (Frey & Irle, 1972, p. 45). In many respects, the experiment is similar to the paradigmatic forced-compliance applications of Kelman (1953), Janis and King (1954), King and Janis (1956), and Festinger and Carlsmith (1959). But the authors' theoretical reasoning also includes Aronson's (1968) modification of dissonance theory. Thus, their experiment pertains to $DissF9$ the actual models of which have been defined in D12 and to the simplification of this theory-element which has been called $DissF15$ (cf. Fig. 2). The axioms for defining the actual models of $DissF15$ are stated below as A18, A19, and A20. They follow directly from axioms A15, A16, and A17 for $DissF9$, which, in turn, are modifications of A12, A13, and A14, respectively, by which the actual models of $DissF1$ have been defined.

A18 $K_M \subseteq K$ is a non-empty set
(of cognitions of behaviors contrary to personal opinions) and
$K_{MS} \subseteq K_M$ is a non-empty set
(of cognitions of behaviors contrary to personal opinions
and the personal self-concept)
with the functions
$b: \quad K_{MS} \Rightarrow \mathbb{R}$ (subjective magnitude of reward or punishment),
$m_e: \quad K_{MS} \Rightarrow \mathbb{R}$ (real opinion),
$m_v: \quad K_{MS} \Rightarrow \mathbb{R}$ (opinion expressed in behavior).

A19 For all $c_{ipt}, c_{jqu} \in K_{MS}$,
if_{cp} (a) $b(i,p,t) > b(j,q,u)$,
then_p (b) $D(i,p,t) < D(j,q,u)$.

A20 For all $c_{ipt}, c_{ipt+}, c_{jqu}, c_{jqu+} \in K_{MS}$,

if$_{cp}$	(a)	$R(i,p,t)$	$<$	$R(j,q,u)$,
then$_p$	(b)	$\lvert m_e(i,p,t_+) - m_v(i,p,t)\rvert$	$<$	$\lvert m_e(i,p,t) - m_v(i,p,t)\rvert$
and	(c)	$\lvert m_e(j,q,u_+) - m_v(j,q,u)\rvert$	$<$	$\lvert m_e(j,q,u) - m_v(j,q,u)\rvert$
and	(d)	$\lvert m_e(i,p,t_+) - m_e(i,p,t)\rvert$	$<$	$\lvert m_e(j,q,u_+) - m_e(j,q,u)\rvert$.

With these axioms, the sets of actual models and partial models of $DissF15$ can be defined in the usual manner.

D15 $x \in M(DissF15)$, if and only if there are
$T, P, K_\omega, \mathbb{R}, K, O_T, D_p, C_p, D, R, K_M, K_{MS}, b, m_e, m_v$ such that
(a) $x = \langle T, P, K_\omega, \mathbb{R}, K, O_T, D_p, C_p, D, R, K_M, K_{MS}, b, m_e, m_v\rangle$
(b) $\langle T, P, K_\omega, \mathbb{R}, K, O_T, D_p, C_p, D, R\rangle \in M(DissB)$ according to D4, and
(c) A18, A19 and A20 are satisfied.

D16 $x \in M_{pp}(DissF15)$ if and only if there are
$T, P, K_\omega, \mathbb{R}, K, O_T, D_p, C_p, K_M, K_{MS}, b, m_e, m_v$ such that
(a) $x = \langle T, P, K_\omega, \mathbb{R}, K, O_T, D_p, C_p, K_M, K_{MS}, b, m_e, m_v\rangle$,
(b) $\langle T, P, K_\omega, \mathbb{R}, K, O_T, D_p, C_p\rangle \in M_{pp}(DissB)$ according to D13 and
(c) A18 is satisfied.

According to D16 an empirical system can be considered as a partial model of $DissF15$ when

(a) there are at least two pairs of succeeding points of time ($(t, t_+), (u, u_+) \in O_T$, where t may equal u) and two observational objects ($p, q \in P$),

(b) there is, for each object, at least one present cognition of counter-attitudinal and self-inconsistent behavior ($c_{ipt}, c_{jqu} \in K_{MS}$, where i may be equal to j),

(c) there are, for each cognition, numerical values for the associated magnitude of promised reward and expressed opinion at the first point of time ($b(i,p,t), b(j,q,u), m_v(i,p,t), m_v(j,q,u)$),

(d) there are, for each cognition and point of time, numerical values for personal opinions ($m_e(i,p,t)$, $m_e(i,p,t_+)$, $m_e(j,q,u)$, $m_e(j,q,u_+)$).

I start with the supposition that Frey and Irle's experimental setting, i.e. their situational and procedural conditions and requirements, can be reconstructed as aiming at the creation of a partial model of this theory-element $DissF15$. To begin with, the time before and after writing the essay correspond to one pair (t, t_+) of points of time mentioned in point (a) above. As the observational objects p and q are better discussed later, we turn to a closer examination of point (b).

Frey and Irle's subjects (high school seniors) had to write an essay against a planned reduction of voting age, although they clearly preferred it. Because all subjects in the experimental groups had the same theme for their essays, we can set $i = j$. As a consequence, according to the definitions given in Section 1.1 both present cognitions c_{ipt} and c_{iqt} refer to the same "cluster" c_i of elementary cognitions which can be considered as consisting of two dissonant elementary cognitions of a personal opinion and of an open behavior, respectively.

The authors reason that the self-concept is not threatened when the counter-attitudinal behavior is entirely anonymous and when the subject has no choice to refuse compliance.

Under these circumstances, an incentive effect is hypothesised, i.e. a positive relationship between magnitude of reward and magnitude of attitude change. A dissonance effect, however, is expected when public commitment and free choice are given.

To test these hypotheses, eight experimental conditions were created by combining three independent variables.

(i) low (1 DM) vs. high (8 DM) reward (abbreviated here as B_1 and B_2),
(ii) explicit choice vs. no explicit choice (E^+ and E^-), and
(iii) publicity vs. anonymity of the essays (P^+ and P^-).

As the counter-attitudinal behavior is considered as threatening the self-concept only for the subjects in the E^+/P^+-condition, only this condition leads to an intended application of *DissF*15. The other conditions can give rise, however, to intended applications of more general theory-elements like *DissF*7.

After writing the essays, each subject was asked to indicate his or her opinion on the issue on an eleven-point rating scale. The results correspond to the functional values $m_e(i,p,t_+)$ and $m_e(i,q,t_+)$ (cf. point (d) above). As indicated above, for the E^+/P^+-condition more positive attitudes are expected in condition B_1 than in B_2 (dissonance effect), whereas the reverse (incentive) effect is expected in the E^-/P^--condition. As is usual in experimental psychology, these expectations are not tested with respect to individuals, but by statistical comparisons of group means. Frey and Irle (1972, p. 51) see their hypotheses corroborated by the attitude-scale means and significance tests. Thus, the theory is not applied to individual subjects but to randomized experimental groups B_1 and B_2. The elements p and q of the set P of observational objects (point (a) above) refer to these two groups. In general, theory-oriented psychological experiments give rise to partial models of theory-elements that are artificial empirical systems consisting of at least two differently treated groups of persons.

The two experimental conditions B_1 and B_2 differ only in the promised reward. Thus, they correspond to the two present cognitions c_{ipt} and c_{iqt} with two different numerical values for associated magnitude of promised reward. When objective and subjective monetary reward are assumed to be equal, we get $b(i,p,t) = 1$ and $b(i,q,t) = 8$ (cf. point (c) above).

As Frey and Irle's experimental groups are created by randomization, no systematic differences are expected for pre-experimental and expressed attitudes. According to the results of a control group, the real attitudes for the first point of time ($m_e(i,p,t) = m_e(i,q,t)$) are assumed to be positive, whereas attitudes as expressed in behavior ($m_v(i,p,t) = m_v(i,q,t)$) are assumed to be negative. When we include these simplifying conditions in the premise of A20, we get a modified substantial axiom A20' by means of which a further theory-element *DissF*16 is defined. Its actual models must satisfy the following empirical theorem T3.

T3 For all $c_{ipt}, c_{iqt} \in K_{MS}$,

$$\begin{array}{llllllll}
\text{if}_{cp} & \text{(a)} & b(i,p,t) & < & b(i,q,t), & & \\
\text{and} & \text{(b)} & m_e(i,*,t) & := & m_e(i,p,t) & = & m_e(i,q,t) > 0, \\
\text{and} & \text{(c)} & m_v(i,*,t) & := & m_v(i,p,t) & = & m_v(i,q,t) < 0, \\
\text{then}_p & \text{(d)} & m_e(i,p,t_+) & < & m_e(i,q,t_+) & < & m_e(i,*,t).
\end{array}$$

*DissF*16 is a strict specialization of *DissF*15, because T3 includes additional conditions which usually can be considered as satisfied only if the partial model refers to experimental groups for which the probability for a systematic difference in any other than the manipulated variable b has been minimized by randomization. Therefore, the sets of possible and intended applications of this theory-element consist of experimental situations with an adequate degree of "internal validity".

In the present reconstruction, $DissF16$ is the most specific theoretical reference point of Frey and Irle's (1972) experiment. To be sure, it is possible to introduce further specializations by taking into account special characteristics of this study such as essay writing as a specific form of attitude-contrary behavior or self-rating as one possibility to operationalize personal opinions. As a consequence, studies using, say, different attitude scaling methods would pertain to different theory elements. This does not seem to be an adequate reconstruction of the role of theory in experimental research, however. Sets of (hypothetical) studies differing only in some aspects of method are usually better understood as leading to different classes of partial models of the same theory-element. Nevertheless, it may be advisable to incorporate such an aspect into the reconstructed theory when it turns out to be a moderator variable which helps to distinguish the areas of successful and unsuccessful applications of the theory or of different theory-elements.

For each theory-element $T = \langle K, I \rangle$ there is the *empirical claim* that all elements of the set I are also elements of the empirical extent $G(T)$ as defined by D6 in Section 1.3, i.e. that they can be enlarged to actual models satisfying the constraints (Balzer, Moulines & Sneed, 1987, pp. 89-92). Put into simpler words, it is claimed that all intended applications are also successful applications.

Any theory-oriented empirical study usually corresponds to at most one of the infinite number of possible partial models. Each study thus can be considered as testing the *empirical hypothesis* that a concrete partial model is an element of the empirical extent of a certain theory-element.

For example, we can conlude from the foregoing discussion that the entire situational and procedural conditions of Frey and Irle's (1972) experiment for the E^+/P^+-condition lead to a partial model of theory-element $DissF16$. Let a be the name of this partial model. When we identify $m_e(i, *, t)$ with the mean attitude of the control group, the last line of T3 corresponds to the main theoretical prediction for this experiment. The test of this prediction can be reconstructed as a test of the empirical hypothesis that the partial model a is an element of the empirical extent of $DissF16$, i.e. that it can be enlarged to an actual model of $DissF16$ and that the uniqueness constraints are satisfied. This can be only the case if the empirical theorem T3 is satisfied for this empirical system.

Any theory-oriented experiment does not only refer to a single specific theory-element, but, at least implicitly, also to all more general elements. $DissF16$, for example, is the most specific element in a distinct series of theory-elements which begins with the general dissonance theory $DissA$ and the basic element $DissB$ and which includes Festinger's (1957) full enlargement of his theory for forced-compliance situations ($DissF1$), Aronson's theory modification by restriction to self-threatening cognitions ($DissF9$), and a simplification thereof ($DissF15$) (cf. Fig. 2). When we use the specialization concept in the general sense (relation Σ, according to D7 in Section 2.1), we can say that any "experimental" theory-element like $DissF16$ results from simplifications and *successive specializations* from the general form of the theory.

No empirical theory can be expected to be exactly consistent with data. Instead, some degree of inaccuracy must be admitted. Balzer, Moulines and Sneed (1987, pp. 325-364) deal with this basic feature of science by introducing uniformities on the class M_p. Any uniformity or *blurr* is a set of potential models that are considered as "approximately equal." But I doubt that this conception leads to an adequate reconstruction of actual practice in behavioral and social sciences. As exemplified by Frey and Irle's experiment, in theory-oriented psychology the special axioms of the most specific theory-elements are considerably less precise than in physics. Empirical hypotheses typically do not pertain to exact functional values but only to rank orders.

When hypotheses of these kind are tested, the problem of approximation is not of primary importance. Especially when only two means are considered, the order of empirical means usually corresponds to the rank order in the substantial axiom. In this case, the theory is considered as successfully applied if, in addition, some standard statistical test turns out to be significant. The problem of approximation only arises when the empirical means are not in full accordance with the predicted rank order. But even in this case, the problem is not dealt with by blurring theoretical structures. Instead, significance testing procedures are applied to decide whether matches and divergences between experimental data and theoretical predictions are systematic or random. Often the theory is considered as valid if some over-all trend test is significant.

For our exemplaric experiment, we can reconstruct this way of hypothesis testing by means of a further specialization of $DissF16$ which includes the main features of Frey and Irles's statistical analysis (analysis of variance F-tests with 1 and 30 *degrees of freedom*, and 0.05 as significance level). It is clear that the corresponding additional terms are "imported" into dissonance theory from an "auxiliary" theory. We can describe this by inter-theoretical links between the new theory-element and certain elements of a theory-net that represent statistical test theories and actual practice of significance testing. The new element can also be considered as a specialization of these statistical theory-elements. Details of such a reconstruction are beyond the scope of this paper. As the main characteristics of the common statistical decision procedures usually do not depend on the substantial theory or hypothesis that is studied, they need not be incorporated in a structural reconstruction of a psychological theory. Nevertheless, their advantages and shortcomings can be analyzed from a structuralist point of view (Westermann, 1987, 1988).

4 References

Aronson, E. (1968). Dissonance theory: Progress and problems. In R.P. Abelson, E. Aronson, W.J. McGuire, T.M. Newcomb, M.J. Rosenberg & P.H. Tannenbaum (Eds.), *Theories of cognitive consistency: A sourcebook* (pp. 5-27). Chicago: Rand-McNally.

Balzer, W. (1982). *Empirische Theorien: Modelle - Strukturen - Beispiele.* Braunschweig: Vieweg.

Balzer, W. (1983). Theory and measurement. *Erkenntnis*, **19**, 3-25.

Balzer, W., & Moulines, C.U. (1980). On theoreticity. *Synthese*, **44**, 467-494.

Balzer, W., Moulines, C.U., & Sneed, J.D. (1987). *An architectonic for science.* Dordrecht: Reidel.

Balzer, W., & Sneed, J.D. (1977, 1978). Generalized net-structures of empirical theories. *Studia Logica*, **36**, 195-211, **37**, 167-194.

Beckmann, J., & Irle, M. (1985). Dissonance and action control. In J. Kuhl & J. Beckmann (Eds.), *Action control: From cognition to behavior*. Berlin: Springer-Verlag.

Bramel, D. (1968). Dissonance, expectation, and the self. In R.P. Abelson, E. Aronson, W.J. McGuire, T.M. Newcomb, M.J. Rosenberg & P.H. Tannenbaum (Eds.), *Theories of cognitive consistency: A sourcebook* (pp. 355-365). Chicago: Rand-McNally.

Brehm, J.W. (1956). Post decision changes in the desirability of alternatives. *Journal of Abnormal and Social Psychology*, **52**, 384-389.

Brehm, J.W., & Cohen, A.R. (1959). Re-evaluation of choice alternatives as a function of their number and qualitative similarity. *Journal of Abnormal and Social Psychology*, **58**, 373-378.

Brehm, J.W., & Cohen, A.R. (1962). *Explorations in cognitive dissonance*. New York: Wiley.

Cooper, J., & Fazio, R.H. (1984). A new look at dissonance theory. In L. Berkowitz (Ed.), *Advances in experimental social psychology: Vol. 17* (pp. 229-266). New York: Academic Press.

Diederich, W. (1981). *Strukturalistische Rekonstruktionen*. Braunschweig: Vieweg.

Festinger, L. (1957). *A theory of cognitive dissonance*. Stanford, CA: Stanford University Press.

Festinger, L. (Ed.) (1964). *Conflict, decision, and dissonance*. Stanford, CA: Stanford University Press.

Festinger, L., & Carlsmith, J.M. (1959). Cognitive consequences of forced compliance. *Journal of Abnormal and Social Psychology*, **58**, 203-210.

Frey, D. (1978). Die Theorie der kognitiven Dissonanz. In D. Frey (Ed.), *Kognitive Theorien der Sozialpsychologie* (pp. 243-292). Bern: Huber.

Frey, D., & Irle, M. (1972). Some conditions to produce a dissonance and an incentive effect in a "forced-compliance" situation. *European Journal of Social Psychology*, **2**, 45-54.

Frey, D., Irle, M., Möntmann, V., Kumpf, M., Ochsmann, R., & Sauer, C. (1982). Cognitive dissonance: Experiments and theory. In M. Irle (Ed.), *Studies in decision making* (pp. 281-310). Berlin: de Gruyter.

Gergen, K.J. (1984). Theory of the self: Impasse and evolution. In L. Berkowitz (Ed.), *Advances in experimental social psychology: Vol. 17* (pp. 49-115). New York: Academic Press.

Irle, M., & Möntmann, V. (1978). Die Theorie der kognitiven Dissonanz: Ein Resümee ihrer theoretischen Entwicklung und empirischen Ergebnisse 1957 - 1976. In L. Festinger, *Theorie der kognitiven Dissonanz* (pp. 274-413). Bern: Huber.

Janis, I.L., & King, B.T. (1954). The influence of role playing on opinion change. *Journal of Abnormal and Social Psychology*, **49**, 211-218.

Johansson, I. (1980). Ceteris paribus clauses, closure clauses and falsifiability. *Zeitschrift für allgemeine Wissenschaftstheorie*, **11**, 16-22.

Kelman, H.C. (1953). Attitude change as a function of response restriction. *Human Relations*, **6**, 185-214.

Kihlstrom, J.F., & Cantor, N. (1984). Mental representation of the self. In L. Berkowitz (Ed.), *Advances in experimental social psychology: Vol. 17* (pp. 1-47). New York: Academic Press.

King, B.T., & Janis, I.L. (1956). Comparison of the effectiveness of improvised versus non-improvised role-playing in producing opinion changes. *Human Relations*, **9**, 177-186.

Krause, M.S. (1972). An analysis of Festinger's cognitive dissonance theory. *Philosophy of Science*, **39**, 32-50.

Nel, E., Helmreich, R., & Aronson, E. (1969). Opinion change in the advocate as a function of the persuasibility of his audience: A clarification of the meaning of dissonance. *Journal of Personality and Social Psychology*, **12**, 117-124.

Popper, K.R. (1975). *The logic of scientific discovery* (8th ed.). London: Hutchinson.

Rosenberg, M., & Kaplan, H.B. (Eds.) (1982). *Social psychology of the self-concept.* Arlington Heights, IL: Harlan Davidson.

Secord, P.E. (1986). Explanation in the social sciences and in life situations. In D.W. Fiske & R.A. Shweder (Eds.), *Metatheory in social science* (pp. 197-221). Chicago: University of Chicago Press.

Sneed, J.D. (1971). *The logical structure of mathematical physics* (1st ed.). Dordrecht: Reidel. (2nd ed. published 1979)

Sneed, J.D. (1976). Philosophical problems in the empirical science of science: A formal approach. *Erkenntnis*, **10**, 115-146.

Stegmüller, W. (1976). *The structure and dynamics of theories.* Berlin: Springer-Verlag (Original work published 1973).

Stegmüller, W. (1979). *The structuralist view of theories.* Berlin: Springer-Verlag.

Stegmüller, W. (1986). *Theorie und Erfahrung: Dritter Teilband. Die Entwicklung des neuen Strukturalismus seit 1973.* Berlin: Springer-Verlag.

Steyer, R. (1985). *The theory of causal regressive dependencies: An overview.* Trierer Psychologische Berichte, 12.

Suppes, P., & Zinnes, J.L. (1963). Basic measurement theory. In R.D. Luce, R.R. Bush & E. Galanter (Eds.), *Handbook of mathematical psychology: Vol. 1* (pp. 1-76). New York: Wiley.

Westermann, R. (1987). *Strukturalistische Theorienkonzeption und empirische Forschung in der Psychologie.* Berlin: Springer-Verlag.

Westermann, R. (1988). Structuralist reconstruction of psychological research: cognitive dissonance. *German Journal of Psychology*, **12**, 218-231.

Chapter 4

A Net of Psychological Utility Theories

Ekkehard Stephan
University of Cologne

Abstract

A net of ten psychological utility theories is described in the frame of the structuralist metatheory. The basic and simplest theory element is a "general theory of utility maximizing" which seems to be the core of a whole cluster of psychological theories dealing with learning, attitudes, and achievement motivation. One of the results of the reconstruction is the insight that — contrary to a widespread intuition — theories of achievement motivation cannot be conceived of as specializations of the theory of subjective expected utility. Other results concern the divergence between the theories to be tested and the theories actually being tested, the testability of achievement motivation theories, the "holism" of psychological utility theories, and the nature of the intertheoretical relationships in the social sciences in contrast to those in the natural sciences.

1 Introduction

The present chapter has several intentions. First of all, it will demonstrate in detail that and how psychological theories can be reconstructed in the structuralist framework. The fact that structuralism - like almost all theories of science - has chosen physics as its preferred object science does not mean that it is not applicable to theories from other disciplines. In my opinion, the corresponding pessimism of some writers (e.g. Herrmann, 1976, p. 42) is based on the misunderstanding that the logical structure of a theory is tied to a certain stage of development of the discipline. Thus, a structuralist view of psychological theories is compatible with the judgement that psychology, as a whole, is still on a "pre-paradigmatic" level.

But why *should* psychological theories be reconstructed structuralisticly? First, there is the demand for a systematization of the arsenal (or better: lumber-room) of psychological theories (Wiswede, 1988). Not only the student in introductary social psychology courses is haunted by questions like: Which theory in which way derives from another one? Can two theories be regarded as equal branches of a common trunk? How are the intended applications of two theories related to each other? Which theories compete with each other, and which complement each other? Which of two theories is the "deeper" one? In what sense can a subsequent theory be regarded as scientific progress with respect to its predecessors? If such considerations want to go beyond the level of mere plausibility, the basic theoretical assumptions and their intended applications must be described precisely and the relations between the theoretical assumptions and between the intended applications must be explicated. So far, structuralism has proved itself to be qualified for that purpose in the field of physical and economic theories.

A more inner-philosophical advantage of the structuralist concept of a theory is its ability to "reunite" the historical and the systematic perspective within the theory of science. How can different kinds of scientific progress be distinguished? How can the difference between ordinary and revolutionary scientific change be defined? How can a progressive research program in the sense of Lakatos be explicated? The "rationality" of scientific development can only be discussed when we have a common terminology. Thus, structuralism can prove itself to be useful for future discussions of the development of psychological theories, e.g. Herrmann's (1976) notion of type-b-research programs.

Furthermore, the structuralist approach may correspond more closely to the scientists' intuitions and actual behavior in the field of testing, rejecting, and maintaining theories. A good deal of what - for an orthodox falsificationist - seems to be methodologicly questionable or seems to spring from a "dogmatic spirit" (Popper, 1974), finds rather natural explanations when looked at from the structuralist point of view. In structuralism, a strict distinction is made between the theory itself, which consists of a formal core and a variable set of intended applications, and the empirical claims related to the theory. An unsuccessful attempt to extend the range of intended applications does not force the rejection of the theory.

Another point is that several theories have proved to be immune against "falsification" in more than one respect. The structuralist point of view sets the discussion about "immunization of theories" into a new light. In addition, the idea of allowing the range of applications of a theory to be determined by the theory itself, no longer appears absurd.

The above mentioned arguments suggest a structuralist approach to psychological theories, they are not, however, compelling yet. The strongest argument in favor of such an approach is, in my view, a certain parallel between the logical structures of physical and psychological theories. Some psychological theories face the same problem in establishing substantial empirical claims (without running into logical problems) which Sneed has found in physical theories, and this problem can be solved in the same manner as Sneed has demonstrated for physical theories. The solution of the problem finally led to the structuralist view of theories. The problem is known as the *problem of theoretical terms*[1]. These terms appear in psychological theories as well as in physical, economic and biological theories.

However, it is interesting to note that this problem has been discussed in psychology - although under a different label and in a different context - since the middle of fifties: in the framework of axiomatic measurement theory. The present chapter tries to demonstrate that the testable axioms of representation theorems reflect the empirical content of (primitive) Ramsey-Sneed-sentences.

2 The Theory-Net

Theories of utility serve to analyse decision making of individuals or collectives. Decision making can be considered from a descriptive and from a normative point of view. The normative perspective is presented - with different intentions - in applied economics and ethics, the descriptive perspective in psychology. The methodological problems which arise

[1] It is sometimes disputed that there exists a problem of theoretical terms at all, e.g. by Hucklenbroich (1982) and Gadenne (1984, 1985). For a detailed discussion of this critique see Stegmüller (1986a).

by the use of the term "utility" in descriptive theories, become evident when analyzing the content resp. the testability of these theories. On the one hand, the statement that an actor always chooses that alternative which offers the greatest (expected) utility to him, can actually explain every decision (but can it also predict decisions?), on the other hand, it can be considered as a mere definition of utility, thus having no empirical content.

Because of the ambiguous character of the principle of utility maximizing (which is fundamental for all theories considered here), the question concerning the content of these theories is of special interest in our investigations. Closely linked to this question is the problem of the measurability of utility. It is important to know under which conditions utility can be measured at all, and what levels these measurements have. Both problems lead directly to the theory of fundamental measurement and their axiomatizations of (utility) theories. Occasionally, the customary theory and practice of testing utility theories is criticized on the basis of measurement-theoretical results.

Aside from the structuralist reconstruction of individual theories, the present chapter tries to elucidate the relations between them. It is explicated what it means that Atkinson's risk-taking theory is a special case of Lewin's resultant valence theory, whereby the latter is a special case of a (hithero undiscussed) general theory of achievement motivation. However, the explication of intertheoretical relations can lead to the revision of current ideas about such relations. For example, we will point out that theories of achievement motivation cannot be conceived of as specializations of subjective expected utility theory.

Finally, it is demonstrated that we need more complex conceptual tools to describe the relations between psychological theories than those tools which serve to describe the relations between theories of the natural sciences. Conceptual "differentiation" seems to be an important and characteristic means of theoretical advancement in the social sciences.

2.1 Overview

A short overview of the net of utility theories (see Fig.1) should provide a better orientation.

The basic element "General Theory of Utility Maximizing" (GUM) essentially comprises nothing more than the above cited statement, which apparently varies between analytical truth and universal explanation of action. An ordinal utility function u is constructed on the set of action alternatives H which must be put into a preference order.

This basic element can be differentiated into three other theory elements: to the "Additive General Theory of Utility Maximizing" ($AGUM$), to the "Maximin Theory" (MT), and to the "General Theory of Achievement Motivation" (GAM). $AGUM$ and MT represent the alternatives as complex risky consequences. The alternative h, for example, may stand for the complex event that event e_1 occurs with probability w_1 (as the risky consequence k_1), and event e_2 occurs with probability w_2 (as the risky consequence k_2).

A second utility function u' is defined on these risky consequences, which is additive in $AGUM$ (the utility u of a complex risky consequence equals the sum of the utilities u' of their components), and which is non-additive in MT (the action is preferred, which, "at the worst", offers the greatest utility).

GAM deals with choices between tasks with different degrees of difficulty, as a very special class of actions.

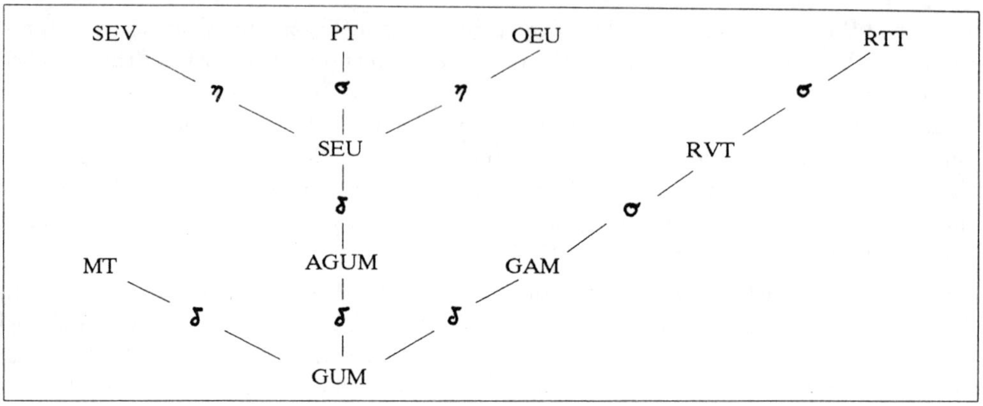

Figure 1: *The net of utility theories*

GAM and *AGUM* form the basis of further theory elements. *GAM* is specialized to Lewin's "Resultant Valence Theory" (*RVT*), which, in turn, is specialized to Atkinson's "Risk-Taking Theory" (*RTT*). *AGUM* is differentiated to the "Subjective Expected Utility Theory" (*SEU*), according to which the utility of a risky consequence equals the product of the subjectively evaluated probability w and the subjective value of the event e. Both, multiplicativity of subjective probability and value, and additivity of the utilities are usually regarded as the two main characteristics of *SEU*. In the course of the present reconstruction these principles occupy different positions in the theory net. Additivity (and, as a consequence, independence) of the utilities seems to be the more fundamental psychological principle, because it does not presume an extensive decomposition of the alternatives as presupposed in *SEU*. The different degrees of "cognitive analysis" of the alternatives are reflected by the separate and hierarchically ordered reconstructions of the principles of additivity and multiplicativity.

Finally, *SEU* is specialized, on the one hand, to Kahneman & Tversky's "Prospect Theory" (*PT*), and, on the other hand, it is de-theorized in two different ways. In the "Subjective Expected Value Theory" (*SEV*) the de-theoretization refers to the subjective value function, in the "Objective Expected Utility Theory" (*OEU*) it refers to the subjective probability function. In *SEV* the subjective values are set equal to objective (money) values, in *OEU* the subjective probabilities are set equal to objective probabilities.

It should be noted that this reconstruction, by no means, takes into account all hithero developed utility theories. Therefore, the theory net is an open one. Extensions are possible in all directions: "downwards" to more general theories, "upwards" to further specializations and differentiations, and "sidewards" to different arithmetic combinations between probabilities and values and between utilities. Not only do the theory cores have a rather exemplary character, but so do their ranges of intended applications. In this respect, the net could be extended considerably, too.

The theories may appear to be unnecessarily restrictive, as well. It is possible to formulate weaker probabilistic, and, consequently, more realistic versions of all theory cores. But this would complicate the reconstructions considerably, and would thus distract attention from the philosophical essentials.

2.2 General Theory of Utility Maximizing (GUM)

D1 $GUM(x)$ iff there exist $S, H, \succ, u$ such that
(1) $x = \langle S, H, \succ, u \rangle$;
(2) S is a finite, non-empty set (of actors);
(3) H is a finite, non-empty set (of action alternatives);
(4) $\succ$ is a relation with $D_I(\succ) = S \times H \times H$ and $D_{II}(\succ) = H$ such that
(a) $\succ (s, h_i, h_j) = h_i$ iff s prefers h_i to h_j
(b) $\succ (s, h_i, h_j) = h_i \longleftrightarrow \succ_s (h_i, h_j) = h_i \longleftrightarrow h_i \succ_s h_j$;
(5) u is a function with $D_I(u) = S \times H$ and $D_{II}(u) \subseteq \mathbb{R}$ and $u(s, h) = u_s(h)$;
(6) $\forall s \in S, (h_i, h_j) \in H \times H \ : \ h_i \succ_s h_j \longleftrightarrow u_s(h_i) > u_s(h_j)$.

$M(GUM) = \{x \ : \ GUM(x)\}$

The predicate GUM (General Theory of Utility Maximizing) attaches to each actor (individual, group, organization) a real valued function u which is defined on the action alternatives H. The experimental paradigma for the choice between the action alternatives is the paired comparison. In the case of n alternatives $(n^2 - n)/2$ paired comparisons are required. The resulting empirical preference relation, specific for the actor s, is $\succ_s$. The principle of utility maximizing is expressed by D1 - (6): From two alternatives, the one is always chosen which offers the greater utility to the actor. "Obviously [it] is not a 'pure conventional matter' or a 'mere convention' or another 'tautological statement'. On the other hand, the proposition revealed by this law is so indeterminate [...] and consequently open enough to resist any possible refutation." Stegmüller's (1980, p. 186) remark, made in the course of his discussion of the status of Newton's Second Law, applies to the principle of utility maximizing, too. That the definition of utilities by means of choices is inappropiate, can be seen by considering choices under pressure or altered states of consciousness or unseriousness of the actor. On the other hand, the principle of utility maximizing is so vague that it is hard to imagine what empirical evidence could falsify it. Every choice can be "explained" by this principle. Obviously altruistic decisions can be reconceiled with it in such a way that the utility - in form of increased self-esteem, e.g. - which the individual gains by adhering to his or her value system is greater than the utility which would have emerged from any other decision.

In what way is it possible to confirm a claim like "$y \in M(GUM)$"? In a logically incontestable way only by determining the preferences and utilities *separately* and by verifying D1 - (6) for every person and every paired comparison. However, it is impossible to measure utilities independently from preferences. The methodological situation is similar to that which Sneed (1979, p. 15 ff) and Stegmüller (1986, p. 33 ff) described by means of the equal arms balance example. If, for example, one intends to test whether an actor has decided between h_i and h_k in favor of h_i in accordance with D1 - (6), one might - in avoiding the petitio principii - proceed in the following indirect way: One application of the theory might result in $u_s(h_i) > u_s(h_j)$ (from $h_i \succ_s h_j$), whereas a second application in $u_s(h_j) > u_s(h_k)$ (from $h_j \succ_s h_k$). It follows $u_s(h_i) > u_s(h_k)$, from which the empirical hypothesis $h_i \succ_s h_k$, by virtue of D1 - (6), can be derived. This derivation, however, presupposes that two other applications are models of the theory, i.e the validity of two other claims "$y' \in M(GUM)$" and "$y'' \in M(GUM)$".[2] The confirmation of claims like "$y \in M(GUM)$" leads to an infinite regress (in the case that the number of the alternatives is infinite) or to a circle (in the case that it is finite).

These logical problems can be avoided by the Ramsey-substitute of this claim:

$$\exists y(r(y) \in M_{pp}(GUM) \wedge y \in M(GUM)) \qquad (A1)$$

Thus, it is stated that there *exists* a function u which expands a partial potential model to a model of the theory. Potential and partial potential models are defined in D2 and D3, respectively.

D2 $PGUM(x)$ iff there exist $S, H, \succ, u$ such that
(1) - (5) like D1 - (1) to (5)

$M_p(GUM) = \{x : PGUM(x)\}$

$r(GUM)(\langle S, H, \succ, u\rangle) = \langle S, H, \succ\rangle$

D3 $PPGUM(x)$ iff there exist $S, H, \succ$ such that
(1) $x = \langle S, H, \succ\rangle$
(2) - (4) like D1 - (2) to (4)

$M_{pp}(GUM) = \{x : PPGUM(x)\}$

What are the conditions which guarantee the existence of the function u so that D1, especially D1 - (6) is valid? This question is nothing else than the representation problem for ordinal measurement. Necessary and sufficient for the existence of u are the following regularities[3] :

$(GUM1)$ $\forall(h_i, h_j) \in H^2, s \in S :$
$h_i \succ_s h_j \rightarrow \neg(h_j \succ_s h_i)$

$(GUM2)$ $\forall(h_i, h_j, h_k) \in H^3, s \in S :$
$\neg(h_i \succ_s h_j) \wedge \neg(h_j \succ_s h_k) \rightarrow \neg(h_i \succ_s h_k)$

The preferences must be asymmetric and negative transitive. Thus, the confirmation of $(A1)$ is merely an empirical problem which does not presuppose the validity of the theory at any point. At the same time, $(GUM1)$ and $(GUM2)$ describe the empirical content of $(A1)$.

Next, we introduce the following constraint: The utility order of two alternatives remains unchanged in different applications. This means that if these alternatives occur in different

[2]Implicitly, it was also made use of an identity constraint (which will be defined below).
[3]For a proof see Roberts (1979, p.104 ff).

contexts (of other alternatives), their utility order remains constant ("context independency of utilities"). Let

$$x_i = \langle S_i, H_i, \succ_i, u_i \rangle$$

and

$$x_j = \langle S_j, H_j, \succ_j, u_j \rangle$$

be two elements of a set X of potential models of GUM. Then the constraint of context independency of utilities, formulated in terms of set theory, reads as follows:

$X \in C(GUM) \longleftrightarrow \forall (x_i, x_j) \in X^2$:
$[s \in (S_i \cap S_j) \land (h, h') \in (H_i^2 \cap H_j^2) \land u_i(s,h) > u_i(s,h')] \rightarrow [u_j(s,h) > u_j(s,h')]$

With the help of this constraint predictions can be made which go beyond one application of the theory.

The range of intended applications shall only be restricted by the conditions that the alternatives are judged according to the same criterion (one-dimensionality of the alternatives to be judged) and that they differ clearly in respect to their utilities (summation of subliminal utility-differences does not occur - see Orth, 1974, p. 44 f). Further assumptions are attentiveness and seriousness on behalf of the actors.

With the previous discussion, all components of the the theory element are defined.

$TE(GUM) = \langle \langle M_p(GUM), M(GUM), M_{pp}(GUM), r(GUM), C(GUM) \rangle, I(GUM) \rangle$

2.3 Additive General Theory of Utility Maximizing (AGUM)

D4 $AGUM(x)$ iff there exist $S, H, K, \succ, \succ', \circ, u, u'$ such that

(1) $x = \langle S, H, K, \succ, \succ', \circ, u, u' \rangle$
(2) - (6) like D1 - (2) to (6)
(7) K is a finite, non-empty set (of risky consequences)
(8) $\succ'$ is a relation with $D_I(\succ') \subseteq S \times K \times K$ and $D_{II}(\succ') = K$ such that
  a) $\succ' (s, k_i, k_j) = k_i$ iff s prefers k_i to k_j
  b) $\succ' (s, k_i, k_j) = k_i \longleftrightarrow \succ'_s (k_i, k_j) = k_i \longleftrightarrow k_i \succ'_s k_j$
(9) $\circ$ is a binary operation with $D_I(\circ) \subseteq K \times K$ and $D_{II}(\circ) = K \cup H$ such that
  a) $\circ(k_i, k_j, k_l)$ iff k_i and k_j are concatenated to a complex risky consequence k_l
  b) $\circ(k_i, k_j, k_l) \longleftrightarrow k_i \circ k_j = k_l$
(10) u' is a function with $D_I(u') \subseteq S \times K$ and $D_{II}(u') \subseteq \mathbb{R}$ such that
  $u'(s,k) = u'_s(k)$
(11) $\forall s \in S, (k_i, k_j) \in K^2$:
  a) $k_i \succ'_s k_j \longleftrightarrow u'_s(k_i) > u'_s(k_j)$
  b) $u'_s(k_i \circ k_j) = u'_s(k_i) + u'_s(k_j)$
(12) $\forall (k_i, k_j, h_l) \in \circ, s \in S$:
  $\tau[u'_s(k_i \circ k_j), u_s(h_l)] = 1$

$M(AGUM) = \{x : AGUM(x)\}$

D5 $PAGUM(x)$ iff there exist $S, H, K, \succ, \succ', \circ, u, u'$ such that
(1) - (10) like D4 - (1) to (10)

$M_p(AGUM) = \{x : PAGUM(x)\}$

D6 $PPAGUM(x)$ iff there exist $S, H, K, \succ, \succ', \circ, u$ such that
(1) $x = \langle S, H, K, \succ, \succ', \circ, u \rangle$
(2) - (9) like D4 - (2) to (9)

$M_{pp}(AGUM) = \{x : PPAGUM(x)\}$

D4 to D6 define the models, potential models, and partial potential models of $AGUM$-theory. Compared to GUM, the following components have been added: The set of the risky consequences K, the preference relation $\succ'$ defined on K, and the concatenation-operation $\circ$ as non-theoretical components and the $AGUM$-theoretical utility function u'. K can comprise uncertain events ("e will occur with probability w") as well as certain events. If k_1 is "e_1 will occur with probability w_1" and k_2 "e_2 will occur with probability w_2", then $k_3 = k_1 \circ k_2$ is the complex uncertain event "e_1 will occur with probability w_1 and e_2 will occur with probability w_2".

(9) implies that $\circ$ is not closed in respect to the union of $H \cup K = A$; it is closed only in respect to the subset $K \subseteq A$. This, however, does not restrict the measurability and scalability of the $k \in K$ (compare Orth, 1974, p. 47). H was integrated in the range of $\circ$ because it comprises the (global) action alternatives h from GUM which are to be decomposed in $AGUM$ into their particular components $k \in K$ (see the figure below). This decomposition, however, does not go beyond the risky consequences. (A further decomposition, namely of the risky consequences, will be subject of the SEU-theory.) $AGUM$ deals only with the utilities of the consequences as such and of their concatenations.

(11a) demands ordinal scalability of the preferences between the risky consequences, (11b) demands additivity of the utilities u'. (12) relates the $u-$ and $u'-$values to each other. If the alternatives $h_l, l = 1, 2, ...,$ consist of complex uncertain events $k_i \circ k_j$,

$$\begin{array}{lcl} h_1 \nearrow k_1 & = & (w_1, e_1) \\ h_1 \searrow k_2 & = & (w_2, e_2) \\ h_2 \nearrow k_3 & = & (w_3, e_3) \\ h_2 \searrow k_4 & = & (w_4, e_4) \\ \cdot & \cdot & \cdot \\ \cdot & \cdot & \cdot \\ \cdot & \cdot & \cdot \ , \end{array}$$

then the rank orders of the $u(h_l)$- and the corresponding $u'(k_i \circ kj)$-values are the same. Thus, if the preference order among the alternatives $h \in H$ is predicted on the basis of the $u'(k_i \circ k_j)$-values, it has to coincide with the empirically determined choices in H. (Because the u-values are unique only up to monotonely increasing transformations, it cannot be demanded that $u'(k_i \circ k_j) = u(h_l)$.) This restriction for the u-values is expressed by the condition that Kendall's rank-order correlation coefficient τ (Tau) between the u- and u'-values equals one.[4]

The test of the claim "$y \in M(AGUM)$" runs into the same difficulties as the test of "$y \in M(GUM)$". The crucial point again is that the u'-values have to be known in order to check whether D4 - (11) and (12) are valid for a certain potential model. Nevertheless, the claim that there *exists* a function u', which expands a partial potential model of $AGUM$ to a model, can be tested in a straightforward way. The existence of u' requires the following empirical regularities to be fulfilled:

(AGUM1) $\succ'$ is a strict order for all $s \in S$
($\succ'$ is asymmetric and negatively transitive)

(AGUM2) $\forall k_1, k_2, k_3 \in K, s \in S$:
$k_1 \circ (k_2 \circ k_3) \approx_s (k_1 \circ k_2) \circ k_3$[5]

(AGUM3) $\forall k_1, k_2, k_3 \in K, s \in S$:
$$k_1 \succ'_s k_2 \longleftrightarrow (k_1 \circ k_3) \succ'_s (k_2 \circ k_3) \longleftrightarrow (k_3 \circ k_1) \succ'_s (k_3 \circ k_2)$$

(AGUM1) - (AGUM3) are necessary axioms of an extensive measurement structure (strict order, associativity, monotony). If one assumes, in addition, that the Archimedian axiom

(AGUM4) $\forall k_1, k_2, k_3, k_4 \in K, s \in S$:
$$k_1 \succ'_s k_2 \rightarrow \exists n \in \mathbb{N}^+ : (nk_1 \circ k_3) \succ'_s (nk_2 \circ k_4)$$[6]

holds, D4 - (11) can be proved.[7] The u'-values are unique up to multiplication with a constant, thus, u' is a ratio scale.

For $AGUM$, a special constraint shall be introduced.[8] Let x_i and x_j be two potential models of $AGUM$:

$$x_i = \langle S_i, H_i, K_i, \succ_i, \succ'_i, \circ_i, u_i, u'_i \rangle$$
$$x_j = \langle S_j, H_j, K_j, \succ_j, \succ'_j, \circ_j, u_j, u'_j \rangle.$$

They shall belong to a set $X \subseteq M_p(AGUM)$. Then, the constraint can be stated as follows:

$$X \in C(AGUM) \longleftrightarrow \forall (x_i, x_j) \in X^2: [s \in (S_i \cap S_j) \wedge (k, k') \in (K_i^2 \cap K_j^2)] [(u'_i(s,k)/(u'_i(s,k') = u'_j(s,k)/(u'_j(s,k')]$$

The fractions of the actor-specific utilities of two risky consequences k and k' must be identical in all applications in which k and k' appear. (The multiplicative constants, up to which the scales are unique, can cancelled be from the fractions.)

The intended applications of $AGUM$ are situations in which the actors have to arrange a series of simple or complex (risky) consequences according to their preferences. The consequences must be independent of each other (necessary for monotony and associativity), and

[4]For the definition of Kendall's rank-order correlation coefficient and a comparison between Kendell's and Spearman's coefficients, see Hays (1973, p.792 ff).

[5]$x \approx_s y \longleftrightarrow \neg(x \succ'_s y) \wedge \neg(y \succ'_s x)$

[6]$1k = k, 2k = k \circ k, 3k = 2k \circ k, ..., nk = (n-1)k \circ k$

[7]See, for example, Roberts (1979, p.128 ff).

[8]Here and in the subsequent sections, the general constraints (in the present case: $C(GUM)$) are not mentioned again. Of course, they must be fulfilled, too.

may not have an "infinite" utility for the actor (violation of the Archimedean axiom). Thus, the range of intended applications of $AGUM$ is more restricted than that of GUM.

In what relation does the theory element

$$TE(AGUM) = \langle\langle M_p(AGUM), M(AGUM), M_{pp}(AGUM), r(AGUM), C(AGUM)\rangle, I(AGUM)\rangle$$

stand to $TE(GUM)$?

According to the previous discussion

$r(GUM)(\langle S, H, \succ, u\rangle) = \langle S, H, \succ\rangle$
$r(AGUM)(\langle S, H, K, \succ, \succ', \circ, u, u'\rangle) = \langle S, H, K, \succ, \succ', \circ, u\rangle$
$re(AGUM)(\langle S, H, K, \succ, \succ', \circ, u\langle) = \rangle S, H, \succ, u\rangle$
$r\delta(AGUM) = re(AGUM)r(AGUM)$
$(r\delta(AGUM))^1(M(AGUM)) \subset M(GUM)$ (via D4 - (12))
$(r\delta(AGUM))^2(C(AGUM)) \subset C(GUM)$ (the combinations of potential models of $AGUM$ are a subset of $C(GUM)$ - compare the previous footnote)

$r\Delta(AGUM) = r(GUM)re(AGUM)$
$(r\Delta(AGUM))^2(I(AGUM)) \subset I(GUM)$

From this it follows that

$$(r\Delta(AGUM))^2[(r(AGUM))^2(Pot(M(AGUM)) \cap C(AGUM))] \subset (r(GUM))^2(Po(M(GUM)) \cap C(GUM))$$

which can be simplified to

$$(r\Delta(AGUM))^2(Ge(K(AGUM))) \subset Ge(K(GUM)).$$

Thus, $TE(AGUM)$ is a *differentiation* of $TE(GUM)$:

$$TE(AGUM)\ \delta\ TE(GUM)$$

2.4 Maximin Theory (MT)

Apart from the differentiation of the basic theory element $TE(GUM)$ to $TE(AGUM)$, which is characterized by a simple additive utility algebra, a great number of theory cores with non-additve utility functions is conceivable. The utilities of the consequences may depend on each other, the combination rule may be multiplicative, the utility values may be weighted prior to the combination, etc.[9] Furthermore, it is possible to think of complex combinations of

[9]For example, D4 - (11b) can be modified to:

$$u_s'(k_i \circ k_j) = \frac{w_i(u_s'(k_i)) + w_j(u_s'(k_j))}{w_i + w_j}$$

whereby $w = a + b(u_s'(k)) + c(u_s'(k))^2$ and $a, b,$ and c are empirically determinable constants.

According to Lynch & Cohen (1978), this model describes a very special class of decisions: whether an individual does or does not render help to another individual in a certain situation. The special implication of this model lies in the fact that the utility of a complex consequence is particularly influenced by the extreme (negative or positive) utilities of the simple consequences. Lynch & Cohen offer the following explanation for additive and non-additive principles. As an example for non-additive models, the "Maximin Theory" (MT) shall be reconstructed here. In most cases, this strategy is understood as a rational criterion for "decisions under ignorance" (of the event-probabilities), but it is also applicable to "decisions under risk" (compare Stegmüller, 1969, p. 389-391, and Werbik, 1978, p. 67-70).

In a first step, the most unfavorable consequences of all action alternatives are considered, i.e. those consequences with the lowest utility per alternative (minimizing). In a second step, the most unfavorable consequences of the alternatives are ordered in respect of their utilities. The relatively "most favorable" of these (unfavorable) consequences determines the choice of the actor (maximizing). That is, the actor chooses that action which "at worst" leads to the relatively best outcome. By virtue of this "pessimistic" strategy the sure profit is maximized resp. the possible loss is minimized.

The determinants to use this strategy in decision making may be, on the one hand, certain personality factors, and, on the other hand, certain characteristics of the consequences, for example, consequences which jeopardize the financial or physical existence of the decision maker. In D7, this strategy is axiomatized.

D7 $MT(x)$ iff there exist $S, H, K, \succ, \succ', \circ, u, u'$ such that
(1) - (10) like D4 - (1) to (10)
(11) $\forall k_i, k_j, k_l \in K, s \in S:$
$a) k_i \succ'_s k_j \longleftrightarrow u'_s(k_i) > u'_s(k_j)$
$b) u'_s(k_i \circ k_j) = min[u'_s(k_i), u'_s(k_j)]$
(12) like D4 - (12)

$M(MT) = \{x \ : \ MT(x)\}$

D8 $PMT(x)$ iff there exist $S, H, K, \succ, \succ', \circ, u, u'$ such that
(1) - (10) like D7 - (1) to (10)

$M_p(MT) = \{x \ : \ PMT(x)\}$

D9 $PPMT(x)$ iff there exist $S, H, K, \succ, \succ', \circ, u$ such that
(1) $x = \langle S, H, K, \succ, \succ', \circ, u \rangle$
(2) - (9) like D7 - (2) to (9)

$M_{pp}(MT) = \{x \ : \ PPMT(x)\}$

The predicate MT is probably realistic only for those decision making situations, in which all consequences have sufficiently different utilities, i.e. it must holds for all $s \in S$ and $k_i, k_j \in K : k_i \succ'_s k_j$ or (in the exclusive sense) $k_j \succ'_s k_i$. If two complex consequences $(k_1 \circ k_2)$ and $(k_2 \circ k_3)$ have the same minimum, the decision usually will be made in favor of the greater maximum. In the case of more complex consequences $(k_i \circ k_j \circ k_l ...)$ an endless number of mixed strategies is conceivable - however, this will not be discussed here. The predicate MT

their model: "... humans have limited information-processing capacities. The decison maker may consider only a sample of the possible consequences of a behavioral alternative, but this sample gives heaviest weight to consequences with extreme (important) implications" (1978, p. 1148). The utility of a consequence is conceptualized as the product of the subjective probability and the subjective value of the anticipated event. This "product-rule" is presented in the next paragraph in the context of the SEU-theory, which, however, combines the utilities of the consequences additively.

describes a strict maximin strategy which considers two complex consequences with the same minimum as indifferent.

A special constraint shall not be introduced for MT.

The restriction function $r(MT)$ is identical to $r(AGUM)$.

It seems adequate to conceptualize the intended applications of $AGUM$ and MT as disjunct: $I(AGUM) \cap I(MT) = \emptyset$

Then the two theory elements do not compete with each other but complement each other.

The relation to $TE(GUM)$ is that of a differentiation, because MT relates to GUM in the same way as $AGUM$ does, with the exeption that

$$(r\delta(AGUM))^2(C(MT)) = C(GUM),$$

as there are no special constraints for MT. Thus, the hithero developed theory net has the form

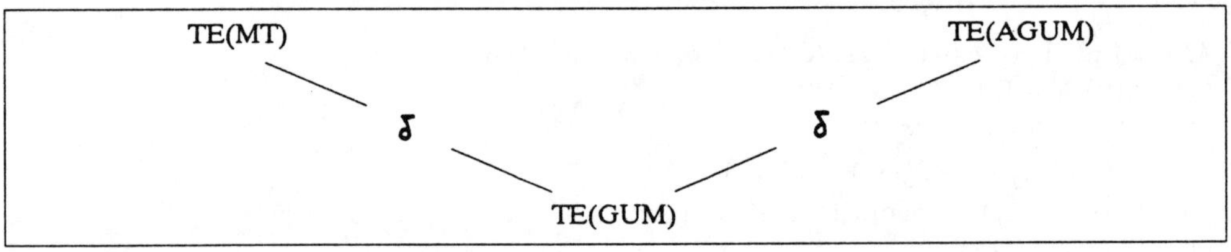

2.5 Theory of Subjective Expected Utility (SEU)

In this section, $AGUM$ is differentiated to the theory of Subjective Expected Utility (SEU). The fundamental law of this theory can be outlined as follows: The utility of an action is equal to the sum of the products deriving from the subjective values of the outcomes and the subjective probabilities of the outcomes of the action. What has been called "consequence" in $AGUM$ and MT, is in SEU decomposed into an outcome e which occurs with probability w. In referring to the graphical representation of the components of $AGUM$ (compare p. 70), this can be illustrated as follows.

$$\begin{array}{lccc}
 & (w_1, e_1) & = & k_1 \\
h_1 & & & \\
 & (w_2, e_2) & = & k_2 \\
 & (w_3, e_3) & = & k_3 \\
h_2 & & & \\
 & (w_4, e_4) & = & k_4 \\
\vdots & \vdots & & \vdots \\
\downarrow & \downarrow\downarrow & & \downarrow \\
(\text{function } u & p\ v & & u')
\end{array}$$

The probability specifications may (but need not) meet Kolmogoroff's axioms for a probability measure, qualitative specifications like "most probable", "less probable" etc. are allowed, too. The outcome e may be the receipt of a certain amount of money, or e may be a certain quantity or quality of material or immaterial commodities.

Compared to $AGUM$, the extension of the non-theoretical components will consist of the introduction of the sets W and E, that is, of probability specifications $w \in W$ and of the outcomes $e \in E$, together with the relation $\otimes \subseteq W \times E \times K$. If k consists of the outcome e which occurs with probability w, it holds: $(w, e, k) \in \otimes$.

The two SEU-theoretical functions p and v are defined on W and E, respectively. p assigns subjective probabilities to the probability specifications in W, and v assigns subjective values to the outcomes in E. u'' represents another SEU-theoretical function. u'' is a utility function and is used to formulate the above mentioned fundamental law of this theory element: The utility of a consequence $k, u''(k)$, consisting of the outcome e which occurs with probability w, is equal to the product of the subjective probability of the outcome, $p(w)$, and its value $v(e)$ (compare D10 - (19)).

The following definitions introduce the models, the potential models, and the partial potential models of the theory element SEU.

D10 $SEU(x)$ iff there exist $S, H, K, \succ, \succ', \circ, W, E, \otimes, u, u', u'', p, v$ such that

(1) $x = \langle S, H, K, \succ, \succ', \circ, W, E, \otimes, u, u', u'', p, v \rangle$

(2) - (12) like D4 - (2) to (12)

(13) W is a finite, non-empty set (of probability specifications)

(14) E is a finite, non-empty set (of outcomes)

(15) $\otimes$ is a relation with $\otimes \subseteq W \times E \times K$ such that
$\otimes(w, e, k)$ iff the risky consequence k consists of the outcome e which occurs with probability w
$\otimes(w, e, k) \longleftrightarrow (w \otimes e) = k$

(16) u'' is a function with $D_I(u'') = S \times K$ and $D_{II}(u'') \subseteq \mathbb{R}$ such that
$u''(s, k) = a \longleftrightarrow u''_s(k) = a$

(17) p is a function with $D_I(p) = S \times W$ and $D_{II}(p) \subseteq \mathbb{R}^+$ such that
$p(s, w) = a \longleftrightarrow p_s(w) = a$

(18) v is a function with $D_I(v) = S \times E$ and $D_{II}(v) \subseteq \mathbb{R}$ such that
$v(s, e) = a \longleftrightarrow v_s(e) = a$

(19) $\forall s \in S, (w, e, k) \in \otimes$:
$(w, e, k) \in \otimes \rightarrow u''_s(k) = p_s(w) \cdot v_s(e)$

(20) $u'_s = a \cdot (u''_s)^b$, with $a \in \mathbb{R}$ and $b \in \mathbb{R}^+$

$M(SEU) = \{x \ : \ SEU(x)\}$

D11 $PSEU(x)$ iff there exist $S, H, K, \succ, \succ', \circ, W, E, \otimes, u, u', u'', p, v$, such that

(1) - (18) like D10 - (1) to (18)

$M_p(SEU) = \{x \ : \ PSEU(x)\}$

D12 $PPSEU(x)$ iff there exist $S, H, K, \succ, \succ', \circ, W, E, \otimes, u, u'$ such that
(1) $x = \langle S, H, K, \succ, \succ', \circ, W, E, \otimes, u, u' \rangle$
(2) - (15) like D10 - (2) to (15)

$M_{pp}(SEU) = \{x : PPSEU(x)\}$

The identity of p and v in different applications shall be a special constraint for the present theory element.[10]

Let $x_i = \langle S_i, H_i, K_i, \succ_i, \succ'_i, \circ_i, W_i, E_i, \otimes_i, u_i, u'_i, u''_i, p_i, v_i \rangle$
and $x_j = \langle S_j, H_j, K_j, \succ_j, \succ'_j, \circ_j, W_j, E_j, \otimes_j, u_j, u'_j, u''_j, p_j, v_j \rangle$

be two elements of a set X of potential models of SEU. Then the constraint $C(SEU)$ can be defined as follows:

$$X \in C(SEU) \longleftrightarrow \forall (x_i, x_j) \in X^2 :$$
$$[(k, k') \in (K_i^2 \cap K_j^2) \wedge (w, e, k) \in \otimes_i \wedge (w', e', k') \in \otimes_j] \rightarrow$$
$$[(p_i(s, w)/p_i(s, w') = p_j(s, w)/p_j(s, w')) \ \wedge \ (v_i(s, e)/v_i(s, e') = v_j(s, e)/v_j(s, e'))].$$

Since p and v are ratio scales[11], the multiplicative constants up to which the scales are unique, can be cancelled.

The empirical content of a claim

$$\exists y (r(SEU)(y) \in M_{pp}(SEU) \wedge y \in M(SEU))$$

is given by the testable axioms of a two-dimensional multiplicative conjoint measurement structure.[12]

These axioms are

(SEU1) $\succ'$ is a strict order

---

[10]The psychological assumption implied by this constraint seems to be too restrictive for natural decision sequences: it excludes learning processes. For learning - as behavior modification due to experience - can be interpreted in the framework of SEU theory as the change of probability evaluations. Conditioning by means of negative reinforcement means that the reaction R, which is to be learned, is always followed by the interruption of an unpleasant stimulus S^-. Provided that the (negative) valuation of the stimulus S^- remains unchanged, the expected utility of the reaction R increases, because the subjective probability of the interuption of S^- after R increases the longer the conditioning persists. - This dynamic aspect of decision making is not considered in the present reconstruction (but could be included without any problems). Nevertheless, within a limited period of time, it is not unrealistic to assume constant subjective probabilities and values of the outcomes.

[11]D10 - (19) is the representation for multiplicative conjoint measurement structures (see Krantz & Tversky, 1971; Krantz et al., 1971, p. 316 ff), which has in the case of two independent components generally the form $\phi = \phi_1 \cdot \phi_2$. The uniqueness theorem for such structures says that ϕ, ϕ_1 and ϕ_2 are log-interval scales. That means, with ϕ' as another admissible scale, it holds: $\phi' = a[\phi(x)]^b$. The admissible transformations of ϕ, ϕ_1 and ϕ_2, however, are characterized by the same exponent b. Thus, multiplication and division of numerical measurements, which is meaningful for ratio scales, is meaningful for these special log-interval scales, too. This justifies the characterization of p and v (and of u'', consequently) as ratio scales.

[12]Tversky (1967a) tested the fundamental law of SEU theory by checking the axioms of an additive conjoint measurement structure. According to our notation, he tested - instead of $u'' = p \cdot v$ - the additive representation $\mathrm{u}'' = \mathrm{p} + \mathrm{v}$, with $\mathrm{u}'' = \ln u'', \mathrm{p} = \ln p$, and $\mathrm{v} = \ln v$. As long as the ranges of u'', p and v are only positive numbers, this "reduction" of multiplicative structures to additive structures is possible. However, we want to treat the more general case in which the scale-values can be positive, negative and zero.

(SEU2) E can be separated into the subsets E^+, E^- and E^0 such that for all $e^+ \in E^+, e^- \in E^-$ and $e^0 \in E^0$ and all $w, w' \in W$:
$w \otimes e^+ \succ' w' \otimes e^+ \longleftrightarrow w \otimes e^- \prec' w' \otimes e^-$
$w \otimes e^0 \approx' w' \otimes e^0$
(Sign-dependence)

(SEU3) $\forall w, w', w'' \in W,\ e, e', e'' \in E$:
$(e' \in E^0 \wedge w \otimes e' \approx' w' \otimes e'' \wedge w' \otimes e \approx' w'' \otimes e') \rightarrow$
$(w \otimes e \approx' w'' \otimes e'')$
(Thomsen-condition)

(SEU4a) $\forall w, w', w'' \in W,\ e, e', e'' \in E^+$:
$(w \otimes e' \succ' w' \otimes e'' \wedge w' \otimes e \succ' w'' \otimes e') \rightarrow$
$(w \otimes e \succ' w'' \otimes e'')$

(SEU4b) $\forall w, w', w'' \in W,\ e, e', e'' \in E^-$:
$(w \otimes e' \prec' w' \otimes e'' \wedge w' \otimes e \prec' w'' \otimes e') \rightarrow$
$(w \otimes e \prec' w'' \otimes e'')$
(Double cancellation)

(SEU5a) $\forall w, w', w'', w''' \in W,\ e, e', e'', e''' \in E^+$:
$(w \otimes e' \succ' w'' \otimes e''' \wedge w''' \otimes e''' \succ' w' \otimes e' \wedge w' \otimes e \succ' w''' \otimes e'') \rightarrow$
$(w \otimes e \succ' w'' \otimes e'')$

(SEU5b) $\forall w, w', w'', w''' \in W, e, e', e'', e''' \in E^-$:
$(w \otimes e' \prec' w'' \otimes e''' \wedge w''' \otimes e''' \prec' w' \otimes e' \wedge w' \otimes e \prec' w''' \otimes e'') \rightarrow$
$(w \otimes e \prec' w'' \otimes e'')$
(Triple cancellation)

It should be noted that $(SEU3)$ to $(SEU5)$ can be derived from $(SEU1)$ and $(SEU2)$, if, additionally, the non-testable axioms of unrestricted solvability and an Archimedean axiom are supposed as valid.[13] These four axioms (strict order, sign-dependence, unrestricted solvability, Archimedean axiom) are, at the same time, sufficient for the representation of D10 - (19).[14] But $(SEU3)$ to $(SEU5)$ are - as we will see in the following - necessary and, what is more, testable axioms, thus characterizing the empirical content of the theory.

E^+, E^- and E^0 are the positively, negatively, and resp. indifferently evaluated outcomes. $(SEU2)$ implies the independence of probabilities and values. If probability w is greater than probability w', every combination of w and a positively evaluated outcome $e^+, w \otimes e^+$, will be preferred to $w' \otimes e^+$; every combination $w' \otimes e^-$ will be preferred to $w \otimes e^-$. Thus, the preferences do not depend on the particular $e^+ \in E^+$ resp. $e^- \in E^-$, with which the probabilities are combined. They depend only on the *sign* of the evaluation of the outcomes. Outcomes with opposite signs invert the preferences. Different probabilities of a "neutral" outcome (e.g., to win 10 Dollars and to lose 10 Dollars) do not produce preferences.
The Thomsen-condition can be illustrated by the means of indifference-curves (cf. Figure 2).

[13]See Krantz et al. (1971, p. 340-348).
[14]For a proof see Krantz et al. (1971, p. 357-361).

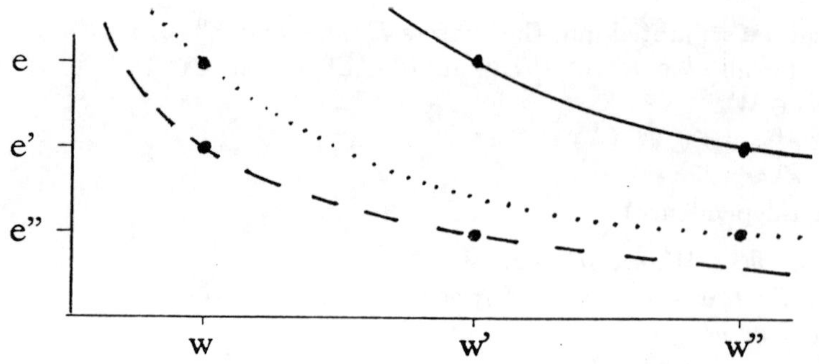

Figure 2: *Illustration of the Thomsen-Condition (after Krantz et al., 1971, p.251)*

The premise of $(SEU3)$ postulates that $w \otimes e'$ and $w' \otimes e''$ lie on one indifference-curve (dotted line in Fig. 2), $w' \otimes e$ and $w'' \otimes e'$ lie on another (full line). As a consequence, $w \otimes e$ and $w'' \otimes e''$ must lie on one indifference-curve (pointed line). The necessity of the Thomsen-condition can be seen from its numerical implications:

$$\begin{aligned}&[p(w)\cdot v(e') = p(w')\cdot v(e'') \ \wedge \ p(w')\cdot v(e) = p(w'')\cdot v(e')] \rightarrow\\ &\qquad [p(w)/v(e'') = p(w')/v(e') = p(w'')/v(e)] \rightarrow\\ &\qquad [p(w)\cdot v(e) = p(w'')\cdot v(e'')].\end{aligned}$$

Double cancellation $(SEU4)$ refers to 3×3-submatrices of the completely crossed factorial design:

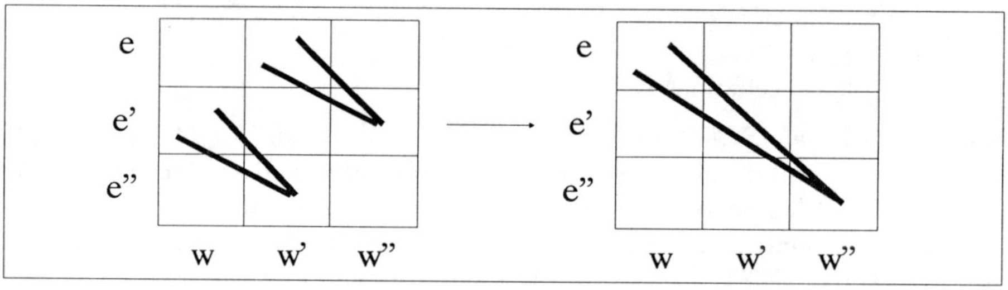

Figure 3: *Illustration of the double cancellation*

In Figure 3, the $>$ symbolize the preferences. The implication must be fulfilled for all 3×3-submatrices. The necessity of double cancellation becomes obvious when one replaces the equality relation in the above derivation of the necessity of the Thomsen- condition by the "greater than" relation. (In the axiom of double cancellation, simply the $\approx'$ relation in the Thomsen-condition is replaced by the $\succ'$ relation. For negatively evaluated outcomes the relations are inverted, see $(SEU4b)$.)

The triple cancellation demands from all 4×4-submatrices what is illustrated in Figure 4.

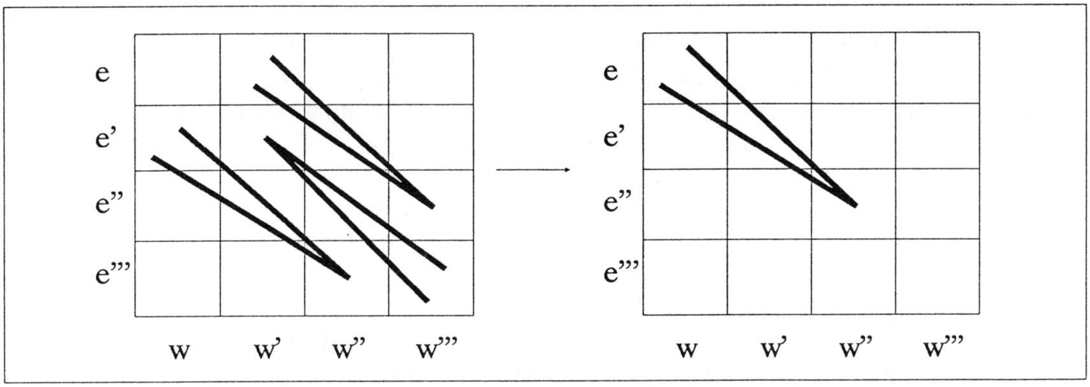

Figure 4: *Illustration of the triple cancellation*

The premises of $(SEU5a)$ imply:

(1) $p(w) \cdot v(e') > p(w'') \cdot v(e''')$
(2) $p(w''') \cdot v(e''') > p(w') \cdot v(e')$
(3) $p(w') \cdot v(e) > p(w''') \cdot v(e'')$

From (1) and (3) it can be derived

(4) $p(w) \cdot v(e) > (p(w'') \cdot v(e''') \cdot p(w''') \cdot v(e''))/(p(w') \cdot v(e'))$.

(4) and (2) imply

(5) $p(w) \cdot v(e) > p(w'') \cdot v(e'')$.

With this, the necessity of triple cancellation has been demonstrated. For negatively evaluated outcomes the relations are inverted, compare $(SEU5b)$.

The identity constraint excludes all combinations of potential models which may fulfill the conditions $(SEU1)$ to $(SEU5)$ separately, but whose overlappings do not have the same $u''-, p-$ and $v-$ values.

The range of intended applications $I(SEU)$ is more restricted than $I(AGUM)$, because the consequences to be compared by the subjects must consist of the complete combination of a set of probability specifications and a set of outcomes: $K = W \times E$. (In $AGUM$, no restrictions were made in this respect.)

For $I(SEU)$ Tversky's experiment (1967a) can be considered as paradigmatic. He offered to male prisoners (with a minimum intelligence quotient of 100) risky consequences which the subjects could "sell" in a hypothetical situation. The subject's utility of a consequence was found by his minimum selling price. Various quantities of packs of cigarettes and sugar (which is the usual currency in prison) could be won with (objective) probabilities of 0.20, 0.40, 0.60 and 0.80. By means of additive conjoint measurement (the axioms of which were fulfilled to a satisfactory degree) the subjective values of the packs of cigarettes and sugar as well as the subjective probabilities were calculated, in a first step. In a second step, these subjective probabilities and values were used to predict the selling prices of complex risky consequences (to win x packs of sugar with probability p and y packs of cigarettes with probability q). The predicted selling prices corresponded quite well to the empirically determined selling prices.

(To my knowledge, research is lacking which tried to extend the range of applications of the *SEU* theory systematically, i.e. in respect to the subjects, situations and commodities.)

In social psychology the core of *SEU* theory is used to explain *attitudes* (Rosenberg, 1965; Fishbein, 1963; Fishbein & Ajzen, 1975; Vroom, 1964). According to Fishbein & Ajzen an attitude "is a predisposition to respond in a consistently favorable or unfavorable manner with respect to a given object" (1975, p. 6). The evaluation of the attitude object comprises cognitive ("beliefs") and affective components ("evaluative responses") which are related to each other in the following way:

> (1) An individual holds many beliefs about an object; i.e., the object may be seen as related to various attributes, such as other objects, characteristics, goals, etc. (2) Associated with each of the attributes is an implicit evaluative response, i.e., an attitude. (3) Through conditioning, the evaluative responses are associated with the attitude object. (4) The conditioned evaluated responses summate, and thus (5) on future occasions the attitude object will elicit this summated evaluative response, i.e., the overall attitude.
>
> According to the theory, a person's attitude toward any object is a function of his beliefs about the object and the implicit evaluative responses associated with those beliefs. The central equation of the theory can be expressed as follows:
>
> $$A_O = \sum_{i=1}^{n} b_i e_i,$$
>
> where A_O is the attitude toward some object, O; b_i is the belief i about O, i.e., the subjective probability that O is related to attribute i; e_i is the evaluation of attribute i; and n is the number of beliefs. (Fishbein & Ajzen 1975, p. 29)

Whereas *SEU* theory (and all other presently reconstructed utility theories) deals with the evaluation of and choice between behavioral alternatives, attitude theory deals with the evaluation of attitude objects. However, there is a close relation between actions and attitudes. Attitudes (e.g. towards interaction partners, political parties, merchandise) result most frequently in acts of selection (selection of interaction partners, voting decision, purchase).[15] Attitude theorists frequently have pointed out the close relationship of attitude theory and *SEU* theory.[16] Expressed in structuralist terminology: They correctly identified their theory cores as the core of *SEU* theory.

The numerous variants and further developments of attitude theories should not be considered here in detail. Instead of that, we want to discuss exemplarily a variant with a *different* core than *SEU* theory. Sheth (1973) combines evaluations and probabilities *additively*. His fundamental law is, in our notation (compare D10):

$$\text{D10 - (19')}: u''(k) = p_s(w) + v_s(e)$$
$$\text{D10 - (20')}: u'(k) = a \cdot (u''(k)) + b$$

The empirical conditions to be fulfilled in this theory (axioms of a two-dimensional additive conjoint structure - see Orth, 1974, p. 60) imply different preferences than the correspondent conditions for *SEU* theory. For a subject s it may hold: $p(w) = 0.7, v(e) = 1, p(w') = 0.3$ and $v(e') = 2$. According to the multiplicative rule we have

[15]For a more detailed discussion of the relation between attitudes, intention and behavior see Fishbein & Ajzen (1975).

[16]See, for example, Fishbein & Ajzen (1975, p. 30 f); Vroom (1964, p. 18).

$$w \otimes e \succ' w' \otimes e' \ (0.7 \cdot 1 > 0.3 \cdot 2),$$

however, according to the additive rule we have

$$w' \otimes e' \succ' w \otimes e \ (0.7 + 1 < 0.3 + 2).$$

Thereby, Sheth's theory constitutes a further differentiation of $AGUM$ which is different from SEU theory and which competes with the latter.

An even more radical deviation from the usual attitude theories is given if the attitude score is not conceptualized as the *sum* of attribute evaluations, which are weighted by the subjective probabilities (violation of D4 - (11)). Such non-additive attitude theories are required when the attributes are not (or cannot be) evaluated independently of each other. Roberts (1979, p. 219) gives several examples of such situations.

The relation between SEU and $AGUM$ is that of a differentiation, because for the theory elements

$$TE(SEU) = \langle\langle M_p(SEU), M(SEU), M_{pp}(SEU), r(SEU), C(SEU)\rangle, I(SEU)\rangle$$

and

$$TE(AGUM) = \langle\langle M_p(AGUM), M(AGUM), M_{pp}(AGUM), r(AGUM), C(AGUM)\rangle, I(AGUM)\rangle$$

it holds:

$$r(AGUM)(\langle S, H, K, \succ, \succ', \circ, u, u'\rangle) = \langle S, H, K, \succ, \succ', \circ, u\rangle$$
$$r(SEU(\langle S, H, K, W, E, \succ, \succ', \circ, \otimes, u, u', u'', p, v\rangle) = \langle S, H, K, W, E, \succ, \succ', \circ, \otimes, u, u'\rangle$$
$$re(SEU)(\langle S, H, K, W, E, \succ, \succ', \circ, \otimes, u, u'\rangle) = \langle S, H, K, \succ, \succ', \circ, u, u'\rangle$$
$$r\delta(SEU) = re(SEU)\ r(SEU)$$
$$(r\delta(SEU))^1(M(SEU)) \subset M(AGUM) \qquad \text{(via D10 - (19) and (20))}$$
$$(r\delta(SEU))^2(C(SEU)) \subset C(AGUM)$$
$$r\Delta(SEU) = r(AGUM)\ re(SEU)$$
$$(r\Delta(SEU))^2(I(SEU)) \subset I(AGUM).$$

This implies that

$$(r\Delta(SEU))^2[Ge(K(SEU))] \subset Ge(K(AGUM))$$

and

$$TE(SEU)\ \delta\ TE(AGUM).$$

With this, we have the following theory net:

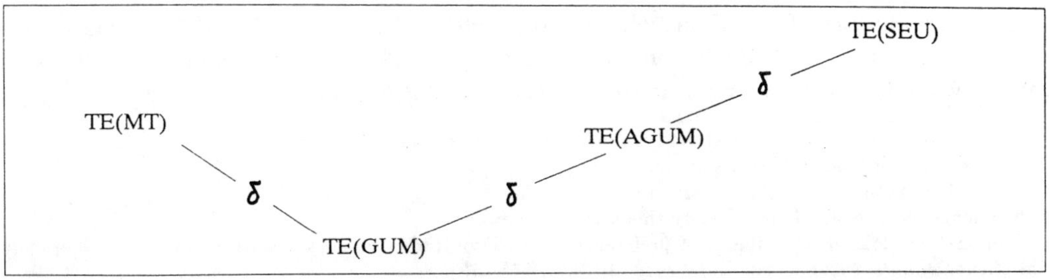

2.6 Prospect Theory (PT)

Kahneman & Tversky's so-called Prospect Theory[17] is a progressive development of *SEU* theory. Progress has been made in three respects: (1) The range of intended applications has been outlined sharply (choices between risky consequences ("prospects") with money as outcomes and objective winning probabilities), (2) the utility evaluation of the alternatives has been specified (the shape of the functions p and v has been determined), and (3) prior to the utility evaluation a phase of "editing" of the offered alternatives has been postulated in order to increase the empirical validity of the theory. The editing phase consists of six operations (coding, combination, segregation, cancellation, simplification, detection of dominance), which, however, deserve closer empirical investigation, in future research. For example, it is not clear to what extent they are intra- and interindividually stable and in which sequence they are applied. (The sequence of the operations is crucial for the preference order, as Kahneman & Tversky (1979, p. 275) show.) That means that it is usually not clear with which edited consequences the subject enters the phase of evaluation. In technical terms: The arguments of the functions p and v are not known in every case. Disregarding the editing phase for these reasons, Prospect Theory can be axiomatized as follows:

D13 $PT(x)$ iff
- (1) $SEU(x)$
- (2) $\forall s \in S,\ w \in W \subseteq [0,1]$:
  - a) p is differentiable and strictly monotone increasing ($p' > 0$) [18]
  - b) $p(r \cdot w) > r \cdot p(w)$, for $0 \leq r < 1$ and "small" w
  - c) $p(w) > w$, for "small" w
  - d) $p(w) + p(1-w) < 1$
  - e) $p(w \cdot r)/p(w) \leq p(w \cdot r \cdot q)/p(w \cdot q)$, for $0 < r, q < 1$
  - f) $p(0) = 0 \wedge p(1) = 1$
- (3) $\forall s \in S,\ e \in E \subseteq \mathbb{R}$:
  - a) $v''(e) < 0$, for $e > 0$ [19]
  - b) $v''(e) > 0$, for $e < 0$
  - c) $v'(e) < v'(-e)$, for $e > 0$
  - d) $v(0) = 0$

$M(PT) = \{x \ : \ PT(x)\}$

In D13 - (2), the subjective probability function is specialized in a sixfold manner. (2b) expresses that p is subadditive for "small"[20] objective probabilities, (2c) says that small probabilities are overestimated.

The subadditivity of p explains why $\langle 0.001 \otimes 6000$ Dollars $\rangle$ is preferred to $\langle 0.002 \otimes 3000$ Dollars $\rangle$, whereas $\langle 0.90 \otimes 3000$ Dollars $\rangle$ is preferred to $\langle 0.45 \otimes 6000$ Dollars $\rangle$.[21] Provided that the value function for profits is concave (D13 - (3a)), it follows:

---

[17] See Tversky & Kahneman (1974), and Kahneman & Tversky (1979).

[18] p' here is the first derivation of p.

[19] v" (v') here is the second (first) derivation of v.

[20] Kahneman & Tversky do not specify this term more exactly.

[21] This and the following examples of preferences, which contradict classical utility theory, are empirically valid phenomena - see Kahneman & Tversky (1979, p. 265-273).

$$p(0.001)/p(0.002) > 0.50 \text{ and } p(0.45)/p(0.90) < 0.50$$

or

$$p(0.50 \cdot 0.002) > 0.50 \cdot p(0.002)$$

and

$$p(0.50 \cdot 0.90) < 0.50 \cdot p(0.90).$$

This apparent anomaly is solved by the use of assumption (2b). An overestimation of small probabilities (see (2c)) is indicated by the fact that $\langle 0.001 \otimes 5000 \text{ Dollars} \rangle$ is preferred to $\langle 1.00 \otimes 5 \text{ Dollars} \rangle$.

(2d) says that the subjective probabilities of complementary events do not add up to 1.00. With the help of this assumption, some paradoxes of classical utility theory, which were pointed out by Allais (1953), can be solved. As an example, the complex consequence

$$\langle 0.33 \otimes 2500 \text{ Dollars} \circ 0.66 \otimes 2400 \text{ Dollars} \circ 0.01 \otimes 0 \text{ Dollars} \rangle$$

is less attractive than

$$\langle 1.00 \otimes 2400 \text{ Dollars} \rangle,$$

but

$$\langle 0.33 \otimes 2500 \text{ Dollars} \circ 0.67 \otimes 0 \text{ Dollars} \rangle$$

is more attractive than

$$\langle 0.33 \otimes 2400 \text{ Dollars} \circ 0.66 \otimes 0 \text{ Dollars} \rangle.$$

The first choice implies that

$$v(2400 \text{ Dollars}) > p(0.66) \cdot v(2400 \text{ Dollars}) + p(0.33) \cdot v(2500 \text{ Dollars}),$$

which means that

$$(1 - p(0.66)) \cdot v(2400 \text{ Dollars}) > p(0.33) \cdot v(2500 \text{ Dollars}),$$

whereas the second choice implies that

$$p(0.33) \cdot v(2500 \text{ Dollars}) > p(0.34) \cdot v(2400 \text{ Dollars}).$$

As a consequence, we have to assume $p(0.66) + p(0.34) < 1.00$. (2e) expresses the so-called subproportionality of the subjective probability function. This principle explains why $\langle 1.00 \otimes 3000 \text{ Dollars} \rangle$ is preferred to $\langle 0.80 \otimes 4000 \text{ Dollars} \rangle$, but at the same time $\langle 0.20 \otimes 4000 \text{ Dollars} \rangle$ is preferred to $\langle 0.25 \otimes 3000 \text{ Dollars} \rangle$.

These preferences imply

$$p(0.80)/p(1.00) < v(3000 \text{ Dollars})/v(4000 \text{ Dollars}) < p(0.20)/p(0.25),$$

from which it follows that

$$p(0.25)/p(1.00) < p(0.20)/p(0.80).$$

In this example we have $w = 1.00, r = 0.25$ and $q = 0.80$.
(2f) deserves no further explanation.

(3a) expresses that the value function v is concave for profits[22], and that v is convex for losses. Furthermore, v is generally steeper for losses than for profits (3c).

These special laws imply

$$M(PT) \subset M(SEU).$$

The potential and partial potential models of PT are identical to those of SEU:

D14 $PPT(x) \longleftrightarrow PSEU(x)$

$M_p(PT) = M_p(SEU)$

D15 $PPPT(x) \longleftrightarrow PPSEU(x)$

$M_{pp}(PT) = M_{pp}(SEU)$

Thus, we have

$$r(PT) = r(SEU).$$

Special constraints do not hold in PT. Since the outcomes are fixed amounts of money and the probability specifications are (quantitative) objective probabilities, it holds that

$$I(PT) \subset I(SEU).$$

As a result, $TE(PT)$ is a *specialization* of $TE(SEU)$, and the theory net is extended to

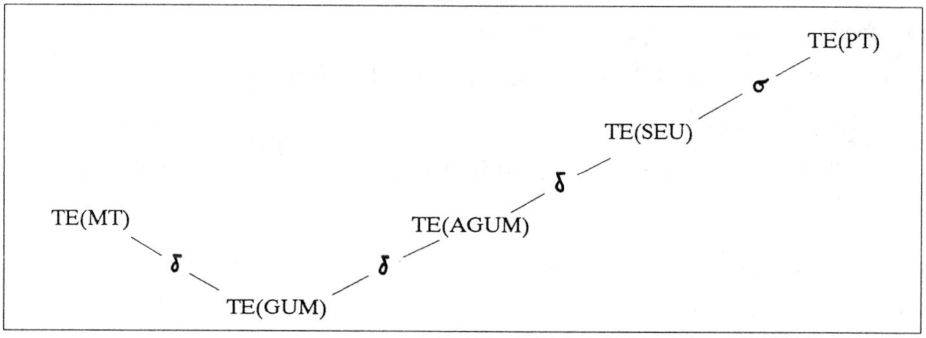

2.7 Theories of Objective Expected Utility (OEU) and of Subjective Expected Value (SEV)

Compared to SEU theory, the ranges of the functions p and v have been restricted considerably in Prospect Theory. There are three other theories which restrict these functions even stronger. One theory equates the subjective probabilities with objective probabilities and will be called Objective Expected Utility (OEU) Theory. Another theory equates the subjective values with objective (money) values and will be called Subjective Expected Value (SEV) Theory. A third theory, Objective Expected Value (OEV) Theory, replaces both subjective functions by objective ones. Schematically, these theories can be classified as follows:

[22]In Prospect Theory, "profits" and "losses" are conceptualized as being relative to a subjective point of reference.

		Probabilities subjective	Probabilities objective
Values	subjective	SEU	OEU
Values	objective	SEV	OEV

The following examples illustrate paradigmatic intended applications of these theories. The strictly rational player who wins and loses certain amounts of money with known objective probabilities will decide according to *OEV* theory.[23] - The investor who has clear ideas about profits and losses of possible investments, but who is forced to rely on subjective evaluations of the probabilities of these outcomes, should be a model of *SEV* theory. - The smoker who knows his statistical risk to become ill, but who makes subjective evaluations of the pleasure of smoking and of the anticipated suffering from the diseases, should be a model of *OEU*. Another model of *OEU* theory is the purchaser of an insurance (accident-, life- or household effects-insurance) who — if he calculated the utility of the insurance according to the same criterion as the insurance company does, namely according to the *OEV*-rule — would not conclude such an insurance. One possibility to integrate these theories into the hithero developed net is to conceive them as specializations of *SEU* theory in the following way:

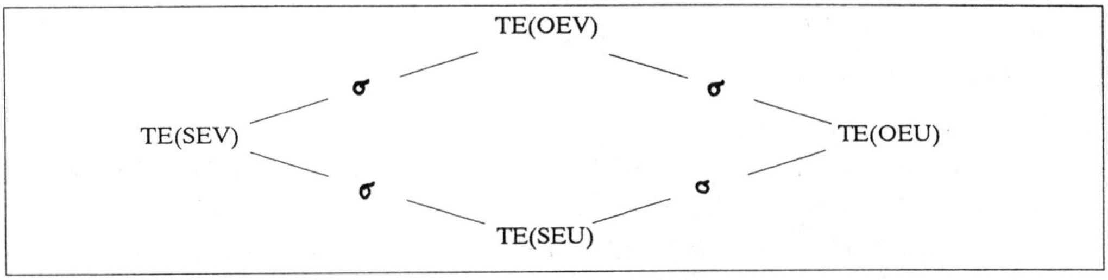

But this reconstruction ignores the fact that the character of the functions p and v changes drastically by these "specializations": They become determinable in a simple and straightforward way by the objective probabilities and values, without having to presuppose the validity of the theory. Consequently, they become non-theoretical functions. Furthermore, they are no longer subject-specific, which means another fundamental conceptual change. For these resons, de-theoretization is more adequate to describe their relation to the theory element *SEU*. In D16 and D19, the models of the predicates *OEU* and *SEV* are defined suitably.

D16 $OEU(x)$ iff there exist $S, H, K, \succ, \succ', \circ, W, E, \otimes, u, u', u'', v$ such that

(1) $x = \langle S, H, K, \succ, \succ', \circ, W, E, \otimes, u, u', u'', v \rangle$

(2) - (16) like D10 - (2) to (16)

(17) like D10 - (18)

(18) $\forall s \in S,\ (w, e, k) \in \otimes :$

$(w, e, k) \in \otimes \ \rightarrow\ u''_s(k) = w \cdot v_s(e)$

(19) like D10 - (20)

[23]Of course, he should only participate in games with positive expected values, which are, unfortunately, very rare in reality.

$M(OEU) = \{x \ : \ OEU(x)\}$

D17 $POEU(x)$ iff there exist $S, H, K, \succ, \succ', \circ, W, E, \otimes, u, u', u'', v$ such that
(1) - (17) like D16 - (1) to (17)

$M_p(OEU) = \{x \ : \ POEU(x)\}$

D18 $PPOEU(x)$ iff $PPSEU(x)$

$M_{pp}(OEU) = \{x \ : \ PPOEU(x)\}$

D19 $SEV(x)$ iff there exist $S, H, K, \succ, \succ', \circ, W, E, \otimes, u, u', u'', p$ such that
(1) $x = \langle S, H, K, \succ, \succ', \circ, W, E, \otimes, u, u', u'', p \rangle$
(2) - (17) like D10 - (2) to (17)
(18) $\forall s \in S, \ (w, e, k) \in \otimes :$
$\quad (w, e, k) \in \otimes \ \rightarrow \ u''_s(k) = p_s(w) \cdot e$
(19) like D10 - (20)

$M(SEV) = \{x \ : \ SEV(x)\}$

D20 $PSEV(x)$ iff there exist $S, H, K, \succ, \succ', \circ, W, E, \otimes, u, u', u'', p$ such that
(1) - (17) like D19 - (1) to (17)

$M_p(SEV) = \{x \ : \ PSEV(x)\}$

D21 $PPSEV(x)$ iff $PPSEU(x)$

$M_{pp}(SEV) = \{x \ : \ PPSEV(x)\}$

By $r\eta(OEU)$ the function p, and by $r\eta(SEV)$ the function v is eliminated from the potential models of SEU. The following relations hold:

$$M(OEU) \subset (r\eta(OEU))^1(M(SEU)) \qquad \text{(via D16 - (18))}$$
$$M(SEV) \subset (r\eta(SEV))^1(M(SEU)) \qquad \text{(via D19 - (18))}$$

For both theory cores the identity constraint for the remaining theoretical functions applies:

$$C(OEU) = (r\eta(OEU))^2(C(SEU))$$
$$C(SEV) = (r\eta(SEV))^2(C(SEU))$$

According to the above comments on the intended applications it follows:

$$I(SEV) \subset I(SEU) \supset I(OEU).$$

This leads to the partial theory net

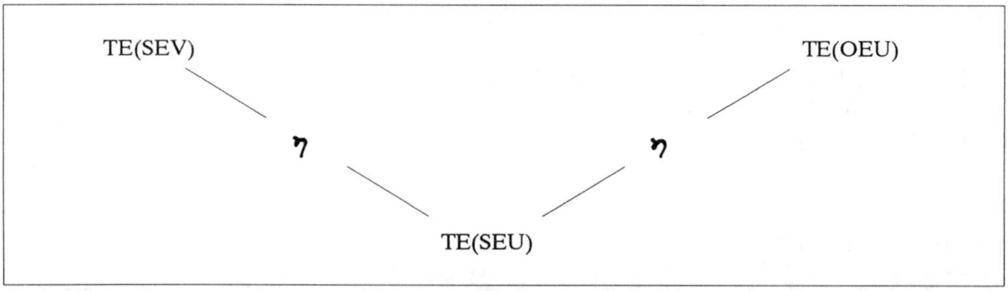

Tentatively, the OEV theory (with objective values and probabilities) is formalized in the following definition:

D22 $OEV(x)$ iff there exist $S, H, K, \succ, \succ', \circ, W, E, \otimes, u, u', u''$ such that
(1) $x = \langle S, H, K, \succ, \succ', \circ, W, E, \otimes, u, u', u'' \rangle$
(2) - (16) like D10 - (2) to (16)
(17) $\forall s \in S, \ (w, e, k) \in \otimes : \ (w, e, k) \in \otimes \rightarrow u''_s(k) = w \cdot e$

$M(OEV) = \{x \ : \ OEV(x)\}$

The theory element OEV could be interpretated formally as a de-theoretization of SEV as well as of OEU. The function p is replaced by w-values, and v by e-values. As a result, u'' is determined completely by non-theoretical functions and thus becomes non-theoretical, too. Indiretly, the functions u' and u are also determined by this procedure, so that a claim like "$x \in M(OEV)$" would have the character of a directly testable hypothesis. The truth value of D1 - (6) can be determined without any logical problems, because the utilities can be determined independently of the preferences.

Thereby, the theory element OEV differs substantially from the hithero reconstructed utility theories and should not be included in the theory net, which now looks as follows:

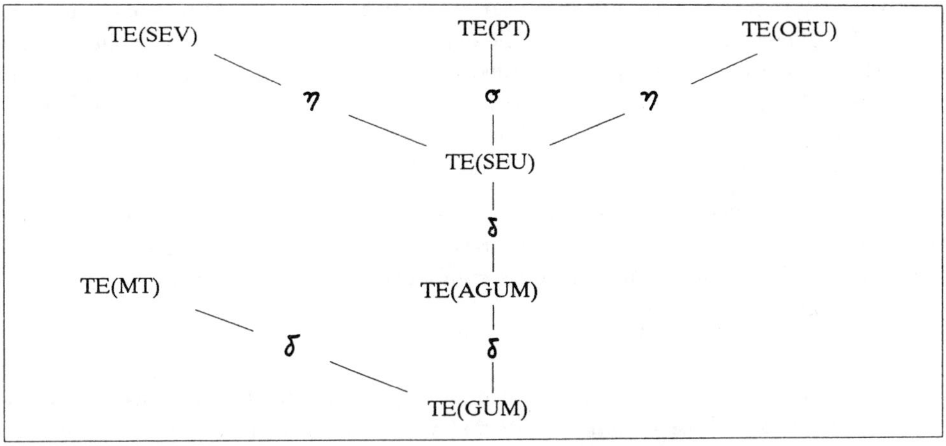

2.8 General Theory of Achievement Motivation (GAM)

Lewin's Resultant Valence Theory (RVT) and Atkinson's Risk Taking Theory (RTT) are predecessors of the Theory of Achievement Motivation as presented comprehensively by Atkinson & Birch (1970) and Heckhausen (1980).[24] Lewin's and Atkinson's (early) theories are usually considered as special cases of the "Expectancy-Valence" theory[25] which entered our reconstruction as the theory element SEU. A closer inspection, however, does not support this view, because two fundamental principles of SEU theory - the independence of subjective values from subjective probabilities and the independence of the risky consequences from each other - are violated by Lewin's and Atkinson's theories.

[24]Atkinson (1982) offers an informative retrospect on the development of his theory.
[25]See, for example, Atkinson (1975, p. 172 ff and 336 ff) or Heckhausen (1980, p. 386).

This becomes clear when considering the intended applications of the theories. The given behavioral alternatives are choices between difficulty levels of tasks of the same type. The difficulty levels are varied, for example, by different distances in ring toss games, by different time limits for arithmetic tasks or puzzles, etc. The subjects have to indicate (usually after a series of preliminary trials) which task (resp. difficulty level) they want to deal with next. The working on the task typically has two possible outcomes: success or failure. According to the theory, the subjects assign certain subjective probabilities and values to these outcomes, which they must feel to be dependent on their individual performance. The dependency between values and probabilities is expressed by Lewin's and Atkinson's hypothesis that success in a difficult task is valued more positively than success in an easy task, and, correspondingly, failure in an easy task is valued more negatively than failure in a difficult task.[26] In terms of the experimental technique this dependency becomes evident by the fact that the subjective success probability cannot be manipulated independently of the valuation of success. This, however, would be be indispensible for an adequate test of the multiplicative linkage between probability and values (compare the theory element SEU, particularly D10 - (19) and (20)).

The second kind of dependency also lies in the nature of the applications. The valuation of the utility of a risky consequence can never be made independently of the valuation of the utility of its complement. Each expectation of success (apart from surely expected success) goes along with the expectation of (and the fear of) failure. An adequate test of the additivity of the utilities of the consequences requires the experimental manipulability of these utilities, independently of each other (compare the theory element $AGUM$, particularly D4 - (11)). — Furthermore, this implies that the subjective success and failure probabilities depend on each other. Consequently, Lewin's and Atkinson's theories can neither be reconstructed as specializations nor as differentiations of SEU or of $AGUM$. —

Lewin et al. (1944) designate the difficulty levels (in the authors' terminology, "levels of activity") with $A^n, n = 1, 2, ...$ The "resultant valence", that is the attractiveness of a task of difficulty level n for an individual, which is symbolized by $^\circ Va(A^n)$ and given as

$$^\circ Va(A^n) = ^\circ Va(SucA^n) + ^\circ Va(FaiA^n) \tag{1}$$

$^\circ Va(SucA^n)$ and $Va(FaiA^n)$ are — in our terminology — the utilities of success and failure in this task. The task is chosen from the alternatives $A^1, A^2, ...$ which bears the the highest $^\circ Va(A^n)$-value. The difficulty level of the chosen task is called the "level of aspiration" (Lewin et al., 1944, p. 364). The choice of the level of aspiration, thus, is a special case of utility maximizing.

$^\circ Va(SucA^n)$ and $^\circ Va(FaiA^n)$ are conceptualized as the products of the subjective probabilities ($Prob(SucA^n)$ resp. $Prob(FaiA^n)$) and values ($Va(SucA^n)$ resp. $Va(FaiA^n)$) of the two possible outcomes:

$$^\circ Va(SucA^n) = Va(SucA^n) \circ Prob(SucA^n) \tag{2a}$$

[26] "Difficult" has a twofold meaning here: the high objective task difficulty (e.g. a great distance from which the rings are to be tossed) and the small subjective success probability. In the following formalization, the objective task difficulty is represented by the function d, the subjective success (resp. failure) probability by the function p^+ (resp. p^-). If d is high, p^+ is small and p^- is high. — The subjective values and probabilities depend on each other via d.

$$°Va(FaiA^n) = Va(FaiA^n) \circ Prob(FaiA^n), \tag{2b}$$

what leads to the fundamental law of the theory:

$$°Va(A^n) = Va(SucA^n) \cdot Prob(SucA^n) + Va(FaiA^n) \cdot Prob(FaiA^n) \tag{3}$$

As mentioned above, these functions are related in the following way:

a) $Prob(Suc)$ decreases monotonously with increasing task difficulty,
$Prob(Fai)$ increases, correspondingly.

b) $Va(Suc)$ increases monotonously with increasing task difficulty,
$Va(Fai)$ — because this is a negative force, which repells the subject from the task — increases, too. (Failure in easy tasks is harder to accept than in difficult tasks.)

The evaluations of success and failure are considered to be dependent not only on task difficulty, but also on the personality-specific tendencies to seek success and to avoid failure: "Great differences exist amoung people in regard to the degree to which they are ruled by the tendency to avoid failure or by the tendency to seek success. Some people appear very much afraid of failure and to them the possibility of failure is uppermost in their minds" (Lewin et al., 1944, p. 366). It can be derived from a numerical example[27] that a great fear of failure intensifies the (negative) valuation of failure $Va(Fai)$, and it can be assumed that the authors suggest a positive relation between $Va(Suc)$ and the tendency to seek success (although they do not give a numerical example for this relation):

c) $Va(Suc)$ increases monotonously with the tendency to seek success.
$Va(Fai)$ decreases monotonously with the tendency to avoid failure.

Without making use of a further assumption concerning the relation between $Prob(Suc)$ and $Prob(Fai)$ - which will be introduced later as a special law - the assumptions a) to c) are summerized in the following formal definition of a "General Theory of Achievement Motivation" (GAM):

D23 $GAM(x)$ iff there exist $S, H, d, \succ, m^+, m^-, u, p^+, p^-, v^+, v^-$ such that

(1) $x = \langle S, H, d, \succ, m^+, m^-, u, p^+, p^-, v^+, v^- \rangle$

(2) - (7) like D1 - (2) to (7)

(8) d is a function with $D_I(d) = H$ and $D_{II}(d) \subseteq \mathbb{N}$, such that

a) $d(h_i) > d(h_j)$ iff h_i is the more difficult task than h_j

b) $d(h_i) = a \longleftrightarrow d_i = a$

(9) m^+ is a function with $D_I(m^+) = S$ and $D_{II}(m^+) \subseteq \mathbb{R}^+$

(10) m^- is a function with $D_I(m^-) = S$ and $D_{II}(m^-) \subseteq \mathbb{R}^+$

(11) p^+ is a function with $D_I(p^+) = S \times H$ and $D_{II}(p^+) = [0,1]$, such that

$p^+(s,h) = a \longleftrightarrow p_s^+(h) = a$

(12) p^- is a function with $D_I(p^-) = S \times H$ and $D_{II}(p^-) = [0,1]$, such that

[27] Lewin et al. (1944, p. 365, Table IV)

$p^-(s,h) = a \longleftrightarrow p_s^-(h) = a$

(13) v^+ is a function with $D_I(v^+) = S \times H$ and $D_{II}(v^+) \subseteq \mathbb{R}^+$, such that

$v^+(s,h) = a \longleftrightarrow v_s^+(h) = a$

(14) v^- is a function with $D_I(v^-) = S \times H$ and $D_{II}(v^-) \subseteq \mathbb{R}^-$, such that

$v^-(s,h) = a \longleftrightarrow v_s^-(h) = a$

(15) $\forall h_i, h_j \in H,\ s \in S:$
$(d_i > d_j) \rightarrow (p_s^+(h_i) \leq p_s^+(h_j))$

(16) $\forall h_i, h_j \in H,\ s \in S:$
$(d_i > d_j) \rightarrow (p_s^-(h_i) \geq p_s^-(h_j))$

(17) $\forall h_i, h_j \in H,\ s \in S:$
$(d_i > d_j) \rightarrow (v_s^+(h_i) \geq v_s^+(h_j))$

(18) $\forall h_i, h_j \in H,\ s \in S:$
$(d_i > d_j) \rightarrow (v_s^-(h_i) \geq v_s^-(h_j))$

(19) $\forall s_i, s_j \in S,\ h \in H:$
$(m^+(s_i) > m^+(s_j)) \rightarrow (v_{si}^+(h) \geq v_{sj}^+(h))$

(20) $\forall s_i, s_j \in S,\ h \in H:$
$(m^-(s_i) > m^-(s_j)) \rightarrow (v_{si}^-(h) \leq v_{sj}^-(h))$

(21) $\forall s \in S,\ h \in H:$
$u_s(h) = p_s^+(h) \cdot v_s^+(h) + p_s^-(h) \cdot v_s^-(h)$

$M(GAM) = \{x\ :\ GAM(x)\}$

Compared to the General Theory of Utility Maximizing, this predicate has been extended by the three GAM-non-theoretical functions d, m^+ and m^- and by the four GAM-theoretical functions p^+, p^-, v^+ and v^-. d attaches to each task an integer which indicates the task's difficulty level. The subjective probabilities of success and failure (p^+ resp. p^-) and the subjective valuations of success and failure (v^+ resp. v^-) depend on d in the described way. (D23 - (15) to (20) formalize the assumptions listed under points a) to c) above, D23 - (21) represents the fundamental law (3) of GAM.)

The tendencies to seek success (m^+) and to avoid failure (m^-) have been reconstructed as non-theoretical terms, because methods of measurement for these tendencies have been developed, which do not presuppose the validity of the theory of achievement motivation. These methods are based on a psychoanalytically inspired projection theory, according to which people ascribe their experiences and behavior dispositions to other - fictive or real - persons under certain circumstances. The Thematic Apperception Test (Murray, 1943), for instance, on which some methods of measurement for the achievement motive are founded (e.g. McClelland et al., 1953; Heckhausen, 1963), tries to assess these dispositions by analyzing phantasy stories which the subjects are asked to tell about a series of pictures. What these methods have in common is the hypothesis that the desires and motives ascribed to the actors in the stories give information about the desires and motives of the teller of the stories. As problematic as this hypothesis may be - the crucial point for the non-theoretical status of m^+ and m^- is the fact that their measurement makes no use of the laws D23 - (15) to (21).

The potential models result from the models by omitting exactly these laws:

D24 $PGAM(x)$ iff there exist $S, H, d, \succ, m^+, m^-, u, p^+, p^-, v^+, v^-$
such that
(1) to (14) like D23 - (1) to (14)

$M_p(GAM) = \{x : PGAM(x)\}$

As mentioned above, u, p^+, p^-, v^+, v^- are understood as GAM-theoretical functions. This leads to the following definition of the partial potential models:

D25 $PPGAM(x)$ iff there exist $S, H, d, \succ, m^+, m^-$
such that
(1) $x = \langle S, H, d, \succ, m^+, m^- \rangle$
(2) - (5) like D25 - (2) to (5)
(6) - (8) like D25 - (8) to (10)

$M_{pp}(GAM) = \{x : PPGAM(x)\}$

This means that

$r(GAM)(\langle S, H, d, \succ, m^+, m^-, u, p^+, p^-, v^+, v^- \rangle) = \langle S, H, d, \succ, m^+, m^- \rangle$

and

$re(GAM = (\langle S, H, d, \succ, m^+, m^- \rangle) = \langle S, H, \succ \rangle.$

The identity of the functions p^+, p^-, v^+, v^- in different applications is formulated as a constraint. Let X be a set of potential models of GAM, and let x_i and x_j be two elements from this set:

$$x_i = \langle S_i, H_i, d_i, \succ_i, m_i^+, m_i^-, u_i, p_i^+, p_i^-, v_i^+, v_i^- \rangle$$
$$x_j = \langle S_j, H_j, d_j, \succ_j, m_j^+, m_j^-, u_j, p_j^+, p_j^-, v_j^+, v_j^- \rangle.$$

Then the constraint reads as follows:

$X \in C(GAM) \longleftrightarrow \forall (x_i, x_j) \in X^2$:
a) $(s \in S_i \cap S_j \ \wedge \ h \in H_i \cap H_j) \rightarrow (p_i^+(s,h) = p_j^+(s,h) \ \wedge \ p_i^-(s,h) = p_j^-(s,h))$
b) $(s \in S_i \cap S_j \ \wedge \ (h, h') \in H_i^2 \cap H_j^2) \rightarrow$
$(v_i^+(s,h)/v_i^+(s,h') = v_j^+(s,h)/v_j^+(s,h') \ \wedge \ v_i^-(s,h)/v_i^-(s,h') = v_j^-(s,h)/v_j^-(s,h'))$

There is a double "overlapping" between the models: between persons and between tasks. In different applications, the subjects have to assess the probabilities and values of the outcomes independently of the "context"; this means here independently of the social context and independently of the difficulties of the other tasks.

With this discussion, the components of the theory core GAM have been described:

$$K(GAM) = \langle M_p(GAM), M(GAM), M_{pp}(GAM), r(GAM), C(GAM) \rangle$$

The above characterization of the intended applications of this theory element showed that it deals with a very specific type of choices, namely choices between difficulty levels of similar tasks. Success and failure have to be perceived of as dependent on one's own performance.

With

$$r\Delta(GAM) = r(GUM) \ re(GAM)$$

it follows for the intended applications of GAM and GUM:

$$(r\Delta(GAM))^2(I(GAM)) \subset IGUM.$$

According to D23 - (15) to (21) with

$$r\delta(GAM) = re(GAM)\ r(GAM)$$

it follows for the models of GAM and GUM:

$$(r\delta(GAM))^1(M(GAM)) \subset M(GUM).$$

The constraints of GAM, too, are severer than those of GUM:

$$(r\delta(GAM))^2(C(GAM)) \subset C(GUM).$$

Consequently, the empirical content of GAM is greater than that of GUM:

$$(r\Delta(GAM))^2[(r(GAM))^2[Pot(M(GAM)) \cap C(GAM)]] \subset$$

$$(r(GUM))^2[Pot(M(GUM)) \cap C(GUM)],$$

which can also be expressed as

$$(r\Delta(GAM))^2[Ge(K(GAM)) \subset Ge(K(GUM))]$$

This means that $TE(GAM)$ can be regarded as a *differentiation* of $TE(GUM)$:

$$TE(GAM)\ \delta\ TE(GUM).$$

2.9 Resultant Valence Theory (RVT)

In contrast to GAM, Lewin's Resultant Valence Theory (RVT) is characterized by the specific assumption of complementary subjective probabilities of the outcomes "success" and "failure":

D26 $RVT(x)$ iff
(1) $GAM(x)$
(2) $\forall s \in S,\ h \in H : p^+(s,h) = 1 - p^-(s,h)$

$M(RVT) = \{x\ :\ RVT(x)\}$

$M_p(RVT) = M_p(GAM)$

$M_{pp}(RVT) = M_{pp}(GAM)$

The range of intended applications of RVT is the same as the one of GAM, and special constraints do not hold in RVT. According to D26 - (2) it holds that

$$M(RVT) \subset M(GAM).$$

Thus, RVT enters the theory net as a specialization of GAM:

$$TE(RVT)\ \sigma\ TE(GAM).$$

2.10 Risk-Taking Theory (RTT)

Atkinson's Risk-Taking Theory (*RTT*) can be conceived of as a specialization of Lewin's theory. In Atkinson's notation the fundamental law reads[28] :

$$T = M_S \cdot I_S \cdot P_S + M_F \cdot I_F \cdot P_F \text{ [29]} \tag{4}$$

As in Lewin's theory, the tendency T to work on a certain task is equal to the sum of the products resulting from the valuation of success ($M_S \cdot I_S$) and its subjective probability (P_S) as well as the valuation of failure ($M_F \cdot I_F$) and its subjective probability (P_F). Furthermore, Atkinson also assumes that the subjective probabilties of the two possible outcomes add up to 1.00:

$$P_S = 1 - P_F. \tag{5}$$

However, Atkinson's conception of the determinants of the valuation of success and failure is more elaborate and empirically more significant than Lewin's. Firstly, Atkinson provides exact methods of measurement for the variables m^+ and m^- (in Atkinson's notation: M_S and M_F), secondly, he specifies the task dependent component of the valuation as "incentive value" of success (I_S) and of failure (I_F), respectively, finally, he specifies the mathematical connection between these variables. He equates the incentive value of success with the probability of failure:

$$I_S = 1 - P_S \tag{6}$$

Correspondingly, the (negative) "incentive" value of failure is equal to the negatively signed probability of success:

$$I_F = -P_S \,. \tag{7}$$

So the total motivation results in:

$$\begin{aligned} T &= (M_S \cdot (1 - P_S)) \cdot P_S + (M_F \cdot (-P_S)) \cdot (1 - P_S) \\ &= (P_S - P_S^2) \cdot (M_S - M_F) \,. \end{aligned} \tag{8}$$

If $M_S > M_F$ holds, (8) leads to the well known ∩-shaped relation between total motivation and objective task difficulty: Subjects whose motive to seek success is stronger than their motive to avoid failure will prefer tasks with medium difficulty over very easy or very difficult ones. On the other hand, subjects whose motive to avoid failure preponderates ($M_F > M_S$), will avoid tasks with medium difficulty, but prefer extreme (high or low) levels of difficulty. For those subjects we find a ∪-shaped relation between total motivation and task difficulty.

The following definition summarizes the above mentioned assumptions of Atkinson's theory:

D27 $RTT(x)$ iff
(1) $RVT(x)$
(2) $v^+(s,h) = m^+ \cdot (1 - p^+(s,h))$
(3) $v^-(s,h) = m^- \cdot (-p^+(s,h))$

$M(RTT) = \{x \ : \ RTT(x)\}$

---

[28] The extrinsic motivation (compare Atkinson, 1975, p. 422 ff) is not considerated here.
[29] The subscripts "S" und "F" indicate "Success" and "Failure".

$M_p(RTT) = M_p(RVT)$

$M_{pp}(RTT) = M_{pp}(RVT)$

The constraints and the intended applications of RTT are assumed to be the same as in RVT.

With

$$M(RTT) \subset M(RVT) \qquad \text{(via D27 - (2) and (3))}$$

we get

$$TE(RTT) \; \sigma \; TE(RVT).$$

The three theory elements concerning achievement motivation are related to the General Theory of Utility Maximizing as follows:

$$TE(RTT) \; \sigma \; TE(RVT) \; \sigma \; TE(GAM) \; \delta \; TE(GUM).$$

This completes the net of the presently reconstructed utility theories, which now looks as follows:

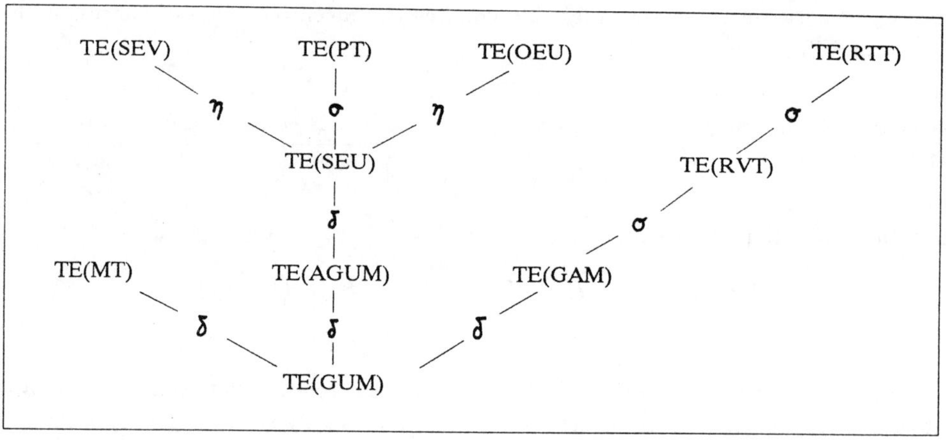

2.11 Testability of Achievement Motivation Theories

Let us conclude this paragraph with some comments on the testability of the achievement motivation theories considered here. GAM is certainly the hardest theory to test, because the theoretical functions in D23 - (21) are very weakly connected with the non-theoretical function d. Although Lewin restricts the functions p^+ and p^-, he does not specify the mathematical relation between incentive value and motive strength. Only Atkinson's theory seems to be testable in a strict sense, namely in the framework of conjoint measurement theory. Today, conjoint measurement is the one and only theory which enables us to solve simultanously the two fundamental problems of testing pychological laws. The first problem is to demonstrate the *measurability* of the quantities in question on the necessary scale level, and the second problem is to substantiate empirically the postulated *mathematical connection* between these quantities. Most of the numerous empirical studies on risk-taking theory have disregarded these problems, and therefore they cannot be considered as tests of these theories in a strict sense.

Conjoint measurement as a methodology of testing Atkinson's theory has been proposed by Krantz & Tversky (1971) and Krantz et al. (1971), this proposal, however, has not been realized yet (to my knowledge). Krantz and Tversky comment on Atkinson's law (4) that "this is a simple polynomial in six variables" (1971, p. 154). At first glance, this conception seems to be plausible. However, in order to test the axioms of polynomial conjoint structures, all cells of the completely crossed factorial design must be experimentally realizable. This means in the present case: The six variables M_S, I_S, P_S, M_F, I_F and P_F have to be varied independently of each other. As we have seen (at the beginning of Paragraph 8), this is not possible. But is it possible to test the simplified law (8)

$$T = (P_S - P_S^2) \cdot (M_S - M_F) ,$$

which was deducted from the special assumptions (5) to (7)?

This would be possible under two conditions. On the one hand, the theory of polynomial conjoint measurement would have to be extended in order to find sufficient qualitative conditions for the representation of non-simple polynomials. Hithero, the representation problem has been solved only for simple polynomials[30], with one exception.

This exeption is Huang (1975), who proves a representation theorem for the simplest case of a non-simple polynomial:

$$y = x_1 \cdot x_2 + x_1 \cdot x_3 .$$

However, the laws to be tested in theories of achievement motivation are more complicated cases of non-simple polynomials. (8) would have the form

$$y = (x_1 - x_1^2) \cdot (x_2 - x_3) = x_1 \cdot x_2 - x_1 \cdot x_3 - x_1^2 \cdot x_2 + x_1^2 \cdot x_3 ,$$

Lewin's law (3) would have the form (assuming that $Prob(Suc) = 1 - Prob(Fai)$):

$$y = x_1 \cdot x_2 + x_3 \cdot (1 - x_1) = x_1 \cdot x_2 - x_2 \cdot x_3 + x_3 .$$

As long as testable axioms for such non-simple polynomials are not known, one could try to test (8) alternatively by means of the axioms of distributive conjoint measurement (see Krantz et al., 1971, p. 345ff). With $P = P_S - P_S^2$, equation (8) can be simplified to

$$T = P \cdot (M_S - M_F) .$$

This was noticed by Krantz & Tversky (1971, p. 154). Two tests would now be necessary, one for $P_S \geq 0.50$ and the other for $P_S < 0.50$. Unfortunately, this brings us to a dilemma. In order to conduct the splitting of the subjective success probabilities, one has to know them in advance. But the subjective probabilities are available only as a result of a measurement precedure, which would have to be carried out most adequately just as non-simple polynomial conjoint measurement. Thus, we are thrown back to the initial problem, namely to find axioms for the representation of (8).

---

[30]Simple polynomials can be separated step by step, until the sums and products do not have in common any variable any more.

On the other hand, the subjective character of the probability- and value-functions, originally emphasized by the theorists of achievement motivation, should be taken more seriously again. Usually, aggregated data have been (and are) analyzed in order to corroborate or to refute the theory. The sample of subjects is splitted on the basis of the medians of the M_F- and M_S-values, and the extreme groups (subjects with high M_S-values and low M_F- values vs. subjects with low M_S-values and high M_F-values) are compared with respect to their risk-taking behavior or other dependent variables. Apart from the fact that the M_F- and M_S- values are mere index measurements, the scale type and empirical meaning of which are unknown (only Kuhl (1978), applying the Rasch-model[31] to the measurement of M_F and M_S, makes a laudable exception from this measurement-theoretical naivety), and apart from the fact that the comparison of extreme groups is a very weak test of the theory (for the theory deals with the whole range of $(M_S - M_F)$-differences[32]), the level of aggregated data analysis disregards the subjective character of the functions. The conclusion from the behavior of an "average subject" to the individual behavior is legitimate only under the "assumption of identical subjects". This means in the present context that all subjects would use the same probabilities and values. (It is easy to formulate this assumption as a specialization of *RTT*.) An adequate test of the theory would have to analyse individual data. Only this level of data analysis permits the calculation of *subjective* probabilities and values. As a matter of fact, such a methodology would demand - aside from individual paired comparisons between a sufficient number of task difficulties - that the variables M_S and M_F could be manipulated (independently of each other) in an experiment. In order to do so, it is indispensible that the motives of success and failure are stimulated, e.g. according to the procedures used by McClelland et al. (1953). This previously developed method for an experimental manipulation of the motives of success and failure could be utilized again for a more adequate testing of the theories of achievement motivation.

3 Concluding Discussion

The essentials of the preceding reconstruction are summerized. Starting from a rather general theory element as a basis, a considerable complex net of psychological theories, belonging to different sub-disciplines, has been spun together by differentiations, specializations and de-theoretizations. This has enabled us to describe more precisely the relations between theories of utility (in the narrow sense), attitude and achievement motivation than it was previously possible. This reconstruction makes a widespread opinion concerning the relationship between theories of achievement motivation and *SEU* theory untenable. Thus, it is illustrated that the explication of intertheoretical relations can be a rather profitable enterprise, even for the object science.

Furthermore, it becomes evident that the relation between (psychological) theory elements is often more complicated than was hithero supposed by structuralist philosophers of science. The conjecture raised by Balzer and Sneed (1977, p. 200), "that there are three such relations which are complete in the sense that all other interesting relations among theories can be expressed in terms of them", namely theoretization, specialization and reduction, has not

[31]This probabilistic measurement model and its developments are discussed extensively in Fischer (1974).

[32]If the differences $M_S - M_F$ should be taken seriously in the mathematical sense, first of all these variables had to be measured on the appropriate scale level.

been confirmed. In particular, the analysis of theories from the social sciences has shown that the conceptual apparatus of the elements of a theory net is not constant. Frequently, a theory element is enriched by theoretical as well as by *non-theoretical* components. Non-theoretical enrichments of theory elements have been found by Diederich (1981) in his (partial) reconstruction of Marx' economical theory and by Westermann (1987) in his reconstruction of the theory of cognitive dissonance (see also his contribution in this volume). Moreover, the present reconstruction demonstrates that the theoretical and non-theoretical extensions of a theory element frequently are carried out *simultanously*. This phenomenon (which may turn out as being particularly characteristic for theories of the social sciences) has been accounted for by the introduction of the differentiation-relation between theory elements. Differentiation is a rather general intertheoretical relation, from which specialization, theoretization and (non-theoretical) extension can be derived as special cases. The generality of that relation may also prove useful for reconstructive work in other disciplines.

The analysis of the empirical content of psychological utility theories has two substantial results: First, only the Ramsey-substitutes of claims like "$y \in M$" turn out to be testable without running into a logical circle or infinite regress. The empirical content of these Ramsey-sentences can be expressed by the testable axioms of corresponding measurement structures. However, the relation between the problem of theoretical terms and the results of representation theory of measurement, which is touched upon by our approach, needs further investigation.[33] Second, the study of the empirical content reveals a desideratum of psychological methodology. The fundamental laws of Lewin's and Atkinson's theories of achievement motivation are not adequately testable, because these laws represent types of non-simple polynomials which are not yet covered by the theory of polynomial conjoint measurement.

Finally, the reconstruction brought to light a certain divergence-artifact in the course of theory testing. The theory to be tested is not always identical with the theory actually being tested. Theories of achievement motivation usually are tested on an aggregated data level which ignores the subject-specific status of the assessment of probabilities and values of success and failure.

4 Technical Appendix

We treat here only those intertheoretical relations which are used in the preceding theory net. Stegmüller (1979, 1986a, 1986b) and Balzer et al. (1987) offer comprehensive presentations of the technical apparatus of structuralism. The most significant applications of the structuralist metatheory to non-physical theories up to 1985 are summarized in Stegmüller (1986c).

4.1 Specialization (σ)

D28 T' is a *specialization* of T ($T' \sigma T$) iff there exist theory elements
$T' = \langle\langle M_p', M', M_{pp}', r', C'\rangle, I'\rangle$ and
$T = \langle\langle M_p, M, M_{pp}, r, C\rangle, I\rangle$ such that:

[33]This research seems to be quite urgent, for at least one of the formal criteria for theoreticity, which was proposed recently (Balzer, 1985a), leads to the paradoxical result that *all terms* of a theory of fundamental (!) measurement are *theoretical* terms.

(1) $M'_{pp} = M_{pp}$
(2) $M'_p = M_p$
(3) $r' = r$
(4) $M' \subseteq M$
(5) $C' \subseteq C$
(6) $I' \subseteq I$

A theory is specialized by adding special laws to the fundamental law(s). The conceptual apparatus of the theory remains unchanged. This is guaranteed by (1) to (3). (4) expresses that the special laws say "more" than the fundamental law(s). (5) takes into account special constraints in T'. (6) says that the special laws are postulated only for a subset of the intended applications of T.

4.2 De-Theoretization (η)

A theory element is de-theorized if at least one theoretical term is transformed to a non-theoretical term. This can be done by equalizing a theoretical term with a non-theoretical term or by substituting a theoretical term with a function of one or more non-theoretical terms. Thereby, the theoretical function becomes uniquely determinable in non-theoretical term(s) and thus loses its theoretical status.

D29 T' is a de-theoretization of T ($T' \, \eta \, T$) iff for the theory elements
$T' = \langle\langle M'_p, M', M'_{pp}, r', C'\rangle, I'\rangle$ and
$T = \langle\langle M_p, M, M_{pp}, r, C\rangle, I\rangle$
there exist $r\eta$ and $k, q, q' \in \mathbb{N}$ with $q' > q$
such that:
(1) $M'_{pp} = M_{pp}$
(2) $r\eta$ is a function with $D_I(r\eta) = M_p$ and $D_{II}(r\eta) = M'_p$,
such that
$r\eta(\langle n_1, ..., n_k, t_1, ..., t_q, t_{q+1}, ..., t_{q'}\rangle) = \langle n_1, ..., n_k, t_1, ..., t_q\rangle$
(3) $M' \subseteq r\eta^1(M)$
(4) $C' \subseteq r\eta^2(C)$
(5) $I' \subseteq I$

r cuts off the T-theoretical terms $t_1, ..., t_{q'}$ from the potential models of T, r' cuts off the T'-theoretical terms $t_1, ..., t_q$ from the potential models of T'. $r\eta$ eliminates from the potential models of T those theoretical terms $t_{q+1}, ..., t_{q'}$ which are transformed to non-theoretical terms. This means that r consists of the concatenation of $r\eta$ and r':

$$r = r' \, r\eta \, .$$

The "empirical" terms are the same in both theory elements, see D29 - (1). (3) expresses the restriction of the "latitude" of the models caused by the de-theoretization, and (4) permits special constraints for T'. Consequently, the empirical content of T' is stronger than that of T:

$$Ge(K') \subseteq Ge(K) \, .$$

Usually, the substitutability of theoretical by non-theoretical terms will be confined to a subset of the intended applications of the orininal theory T. This is expressed in (5).

4.3 Differentiation (δ)

Differentiation is a combination of theoretical and non-theoretical extension of an existing theory element T. If a T-theoretical term t is conceptualized in a new theory T' as a function of two (or more) new theoretical terms t'_i and t'_j, that is

$$t = f(t'_i, t'_j) \,,$$

then T' is the more differentiated theory. T' uses more concepts than T, and usually imposes additional restrictions on the function t, whereby the empirical content increases. The introduction of new theoretical terms often is accompanied by the employment of additional non-theoretical terms. This property distinguishes differentiation from theoretization.

D30 T' is a *differentiation* of T ($T' \;\delta\; T$) iff for the theory elements
$T' = \langle\langle M'_p, M', M'_{pp}, r', C'\rangle, I'\rangle$ and $T = \langle\langle M_p, M, M_{pp}, r, C\rangle, I\rangle$
there exist $re', r\delta, r\Delta$ and $k, k', q, q' \in \mathbb{N}$ with $k' > k$ and $q' > q$ such that:
(1) r is a function with $D_I(r) = M_p$ and $D_{II}(r) = M_{pp}$ such that
$r(\langle n_1, ..., n_k, t_1, ..., t_q\rangle) = \langle n_1, ..., n_k\rangle$
(2) re' is a function with $D_I(re') = M'_{pp}$ and $D_{II}(re') = M_p$
such that
$re'(\langle n_1, ..., n_k, n_{k+1}, ..., n_{k'}, t_1, ..., t_q\rangle) = \langle n_1, ..., n_k, t_1, ..., t_q\rangle$
(3) r' is a function with $D_I(r') = M'_p$ and $D_{II}(r') = M'_{pp}$
such that
$r'(\langle n_1, ..., n_k, n_{k+1}, ..., n_{k'}, t_1, ..., t_q, t_{q+1}, ..., t_{q'}\rangle) =$
$\langle n_1, ..., n_{k'}, t_1, ..., t_q\rangle$
(4) $r\delta = re'\; r'$
(5) $r\delta^1(M'_p) = re'^1(M'_{pp}) = M_p$
(6) $r\delta^1(M') \subseteq M$
(7) $r\delta^2(C') \subseteq C$
(8) $r\Delta = r\; re'$
(9) $r\Delta^2(I') \subseteq I$

r cuts off the T-theoretical terms $t_1, ..., t_q$ from the potential models of T, r' cuts off the T'-theoretical terms $t_{q+1}, ..., t_{q'}$ from the potential models of T'. re' eliminates the non-theoretical terms $n_{k+1}, ..., n_{k'}$ (which have been added in T') from the partial potential models of T'. $r\delta$ symbolizes the concatenation of the restriction functions r' and re' (in this order). (5) has been included in the definition for reasons of clearness; actually it is a consequence of (1) to (4). (6) allows special laws, (7) allows special constraints in T'. In order to make both theory elements "empirically" comparable (i.e. comparable on the T-non-theoretical level), $r\Delta$ is introduced in (8), which shortens the partial potential models of T' to partial potential models of T. (9) says that the range of intended applications of T' usually is smaller than that of T. It follows from these definitions that the empirical content of T' (from which the new non-theoretical terms have been eliminated) is a subset of the empirical content of T, thus, T' says "more about less":

$$r\Delta^2[Ge(K')] \subseteq Ge(K).$$

Specialization, theoretization and non-theoretical extension are special cases of the differentiation-relation. In non-theoretical extension, the non-theoretical concepts are enriched, but the theoretical concepts remain the same (r' is empty). In theoretization, new theoretical terms are added, but the non-theoretical terms remain unchanged (re' is empty). In specialization, neither non-theoretical terms (re' is empty) nor theoretical terms (r' is empty) are added.

5 References

Allais, M. (1953). Le comportement de l'homme rationnel devant le risque. Critique des postulats et axioms de l'ecole americaine. *Econometrica*, **21**, 503-546.

Atkinson, J.W. (1975). *Einführung in die Motivationsforschung.* Stuttgart: Klett.

Atkinson, J.W. (1982). Old and new conceptions of how expected consequences influence actions. In Feather (1982, pp. 17-52).

Atkinson, J.W., & D. Birch (1970). *A dynamic theory of action.* New York: Wiley.

Balzer, W. (1985a). On a new definition of theoreticity. *Dialectica*, **39**, 127-145.

Balzer, W., & J. Sneed (1977). Generalized net structures of empirical theories. Part I. *Studia Logica*, **36**, 195-211.

Balzer, W., & J. Sneed (1978). Generalized net structures of empirical theories. Part II. *Studia Logica*, **37**, 167-194.

Balzer, W., C.-U. Moulines & J. Sneed (1987). *An architectonic for science. The structuralist program.* Dordrecht: Reidel.

Diederich, W. (1981). *Strukturalistische Rekonstruktionen. Untersuchungen zur Bedeutung, Weiterentwicklung und interdisziplinären Anwendung des strukturalistischen Konzepts wissenschaftlicher Theorien.* Braunschweig: Vieweg.

Feather, N.T. (Ed.) (1982). *Expectations and actions.* New York: Wiley.

Fischer, G. (1974). *Einführung in die Theorie psychologischer Tests.* Bern: Huber.

Fishbein, M. (1963). An investigation of the relationship between beliefs about an object and the attitude toward that object. *Human Relations*, **16**, 233-240.

Fishbein, M., & I. Ajzen (1975). *Belief, attitude, intention and behavior. An introduction to theory and research.* Reading (Mass.): Addison-Wesley.

Gadenne, V. (1984). *Theorie und Erfahrung in der psychologischen Forschung.* Tübingen: Mohr.

Gadenne, V. (1985). Theoretische Begriffe und die Prüfbarkeit von Theorien. *Zeitschrift für allgemeine Wissenschaftstheorie*, **16**, 19-24.

Gigerenzer, G. (1981). *Messung und Modellbildung in der Psychologie.* München: Reinhardt.

Hays, W.L. (1973). *Statistics for the social sciences.* London: Holt, Rinehart and Winston.

Heckhausen, H. (1963). *Hoffnung und Furcht in der Leistungsmotivation.* Meisenheim: Hain.

Heckhausen, H. (1980). *Motivation und Handeln: Lehrbuch der Motivationspsychologie.* Berlin: Springer.

Herrmann, T. (1976). *Die Psychologie und ihre Forschungsprogramme.* Göttingen: Hogrefe.

Huang, L. (1975). A nonsimple conjoint measurement model. *Journal of Mathematical Psychology*, **12**, 437-448.

Hucklenbroich, P. (1982). Epistemological reflections on the structuralist philosophy of science. *Metamedicine*, **3**, 279-296.

Hunt, J.McV. (Ed.) (1944). *Personality and the behavior disorders. Vol. I.* New York: Roland Press.

Kahneman, D., & A. Tversky (1979). Prospect theory: An analysis of decision under risk. *Econometrica*, **47**, 263-291.

Krantz, D.H., & A. Tversky (1971). Conjoint measurement analysis of composition rules in psychology. *Psychological Review*, **78**, 151-169.

Krantz, D.H., R.D. Luce, P. Suppes, & A. Tversky (1971). *Foundations of measurement. Vol. I: Additive and polynomial representations.* New York: Academic Press.

Kuhl, J. (1978). Situations-, reaktions- und personenbezogene Konsistenz des Leistungsmotivs bei der Messung mittels des Heckhausen TAT. *Archiv für Psychologie*, **130**, 37-52.

Lakatos, I. (1974). Falsifikation und die Methodologie wissenschaftlicher Forschungsprogramme. In Lakatos & Musgrave (1974, pp. 89-190).

Lakatos, I., & A. Musgrave (Eds.) (1974). *Kritik und Erkenntnisfortschritt.* Braunschweig: Vieweg.

Lewin, K., T. Dembo, L. Festinger, & P.S. Sears (1944). Level of aspiration. In Hunt (1944, pp. 333-378).

Lynch, J.G., & J.L. Cohen (1978). The use of subjective expected utility theory as an aid to understanding variables that influence helping behavior. *Journal of Personality and Social Psychology*, **36**, 1138-1151.

McClelland, D., J.W. Atkinson, R. Clark, & E. Lowell (1953). *The achievement motive.* New York: Appelton-Century-Crofts.

Murray, H.A. (1943). *Thematic apperception test manual.* Cambridge: Harvard University Press.

Orth, B. (1974). *Einführung in die Theorie des Messens.* Stuttgart: Kohlhammer.

Popper, K.R. (1974). Die Normalwissenschaft und ihre Gefahren. In Lakatos & Musgrave (1974, pp. 51-58).

Popper, K.R. (1984). *Logik der Forschung. (Achte Auflage).* Tübingen: Mohr. (Erstausgabe 1935, Wien: Springer.)

Ramsey, F.P. (1931). *The foundations of mathematics and other logical essays.* New York: Harcourt.

Roberts, F.S. (1979). *Measurement theory with applications to decisionmaking, utiliy, and the social sciences.* Reading (Mass.): Addison-Wesley.

Rosenberg, M.J. (1956). Cognitive structure and attitudinal affect. *Journal of Abnormal and Social Psychology*, **53**, 367-372.

Rosenberg, M.J. (1960). An analysis of affective-cognitive consistency. In Rosenberg et al. (1960, pp. 15-64).

Rosenberg, M.J., & R.P. Abelson (1960). An analysis of cognitive balancing. In Rosenberg et al. (1960, pp. 112-163).

Rosenberg, M.J., C.I. Hovland, W.J. McGuire, R.P. Abelson, & J.W. Brehm (Eds.) (1960). *Attitude organization and change.* New Haven: Yale University Press.

Rotter, J.B. (1954). *Social learning and clinical psychology.* Englewood Cliffs: Prentice Hall.

Sheth, J.N. (1973). Brand profiles from beliefs and importances. *Journal of Advertising Research*, **13**, 37-42.

Sneed, J. (1971). *The logical structure of mathematical physics.* Dordrecht: Reidel.

Sneed, J. (1979). *The logical structure of mathematical physics. (Second Edition, Revised).* Dordrecht: Reidel

Stegmüller, W. (1969). *Probleme und Resultate der Wissenschaftstheorie und analytischen Philosophie. Band I: Wissenschaftliche Erklärung und Begründung.* Berlin: Springer.

Stegmüller, W. (1970). *Probleme und Resultate der Wissenschaftstheorie und analytischen Philosophie. Band II: Theorie und Erfahrung.* Berlin: Springer.

Stegmüller, W. (1973). *Probleme und Resultate der Wissenschaftstheorie und analytischen Philosophie. Band II, 2. Halbband: Theorienstrukturen und Theoriendynamik.* Berlin: Springer.

Stegmüller, W. (1973a). *Probleme und Resultate der Wissenschaftstheorie und analytischen Philosophie. Band IV: Personelle und statistische Wahrscheinlichkeit.* Berlin: Springer.

Stegmüller, W. (1979). *The structuralist view of theories.* Berlin: Springer.

Stegmüller, W. (1980). *Neue Wege der Wissenschaftsphilosophie.* Berlin: Springer.

Stegmüller, W. (1986a). *Probleme und Resultate der Wissenschaftstheorie und analytischen Philosophie. Band II: Theorie und Erfahrung. Teil F: Neuer intuitiver Zugang zum strukturalistischen Theorienkonzept, Theorie-Elemente, Theoriennetze, Theorienevolutionen.* Berlin: Springer.

Stegmüller, W. (1986b). *Probleme und Resultate der Wissenschaftstheorie und analytischen Philosophie. Band II: Theorie und Erfahrung. Teil G: Strukturspezies, T-Theoretizität, Approximation, verallgemeinerte intertheoretische Relationen, Inkommensurabilität.* Berlin: Springer.

Stegmüller, W. (1986c). *Probleme und Resultate der Wissenschaftstheorie und analytischen Philosophie. Band II: Theorie und Erfahrung. Teil H: Realismus und Strukturalismus, Anwendungen: Tauschwirtschaft, Entscheidungstheorie, Neurosenlehre, Kapital- und Mehrwerttheorie.* Berlin: Springer.

Stephan, E. (1989). *Zur logischen Struktur psychologischer Theorien. Eine Untersuchung im Rahmen der strukturalistischen Wissenschaftstheorie.* Berlin: Springer.

Tversky, A. (1967). Utility theory and additivity analysis of risky choices. *Journal of Experimental Psychology*, **75**, 27-36.

Tversky, A. (1967a). Additivity, utility, and subjective probability. *Journal of Mathematical Psychology*, **4**, 175-201.

Tversky, A., & D. Kahneman (1974). Judgement under uncertainty: Heuristics and biases. *Science*, **185**, 1124-1131.

Vroom, V.H. (1964). *Work and motivation.* New York: Wiley.

Werbik, H. (1978). *Handlungstheorien.* Stuttgart: Kohlhammer.

Westermann, R. (1987). *Strukturalistische Theorienkonzeption und empirische Forschung in der Psychologie. Eine Fallstudie.* Berlin: Springer.

Westmeyer, H. (1977). Psychologie und Wissenschaftstheorie: Einige Überlegungen aus analytischer Sicht. In K.A. Schneewind (Hg.) (1977). *Wissenschaftstheoretische Grundlagen der Psychologie.* München: Reinhardt, pp. 71-92.

Wiswede, G. (1988). Umrisse einer integrativen Lerntheorie sozialen Verhaltens. *Zeitschrift für Sozialpsychologie*, **19**, 17-30.

Chapter 5

Anderson's Theory of Cognitive Architecture (ACT*)

Towards a Structuralist Reconstruction of some Important Theory-Elements

Elke Heise and Rainer Westermann

University of Göttingen

Abstract

*ACT** is the most recent version of J.R. Anderson's theory of higher-level cognition. This chapter presents some first results of a structuralist reconstruction of *ACT**. They may be used to eliminate terminological and conceptual ambiguities of the verbal formulation, to specify the links to other theories in cognitive psychology or artificial intelligence and to clarify the implications of the theory for empirical research.

*ACT**'s fundamental processes, which are summarized by Anderson in 14 basic assumptions, are reconstructed as a central theory element. It pertains both to the declarative and the procedural component of memory. The basic element of the theory net is a simplification of the central element. It represents the fundamental law concerning the relationships between activation of declarative memory nodes on the one hand and activation and test rate in procedural memory on the other hand.

For the various domains of applications the basic element must be enlarged by new terms and substantial axioms. The whole *ACT**-theory consists of two parts, comprising memory for facts and procedural learning, respectively. For the first subnet the most important theory-elements are sketched and it is shown how they are connected by intra-theoretical relations like enlargement and specialization.

As an example of *ACT**'s intended applications an experimental study from the fact-retrieval paradigm is analyzed. A theory-element is introduced that can be considered as the direct theoretical reference point of this research. As a result we can describe a specialization path through the theory-net from the basic and central elements down to one of the highly specific experimental elements. A comparison of the complex central element and the specific application elements clearly shows that only rather small and simple parts of the complete *ACT**-theory have so far been used to derive empirically testable hypotheses.

In his book "The Architecture of Cognition" J.R. Anderson (1983) presents *ACT**, the most recent version of his theory of cognitive architecture. *ACT** (Adaptive Control of Thought) is intended to be a *unitary theory of higher-level cognition.*

> The most deeply rooted preconception guiding my theorizing is a belief in the unity of human cognition, that is, that all the higher cognitive processes, such as memory, language, problem solving, imagery, deduction, and induction, are different manifestations of the same underlying system. (Anderson, 1983, p. 1)

The theory combines a *declarative* and a *procedural* component of memory, each dominating a certain domain of applications. The declarative component refers to memory for facts and consists of a *long-term memory* and a *working memory.*

> Working memory contains the information that the system can currently access, consisting of information retrieved from long-term declarative memory as well as temporary structures

deposited by encoding processes and the action of productions. Basically, working memory refers to declarative knowledge, permanent or temporary, that is in an active state. (pp. 19-20)

For declarative memory Anderson chooses a *semantic network* notation with spreading activation, following the tradition of Quillian (1969), Collins & Loftus (1975) and McClelland & Rumelhart (1981). The domain of those intended applications which mainly emphasize the declarative part of memory comprises fact retrieval (Anderson, 1974; Reder & Ross, 1983), priming- effects (Neely, 1977), and elaborative processing (Bradshaw & Anderson, 1982).

*ACT**'s procedural memory has been developed within the *production system* framework (Newell & Simon, 1972), i.e. Anderson assumes that human cognition is based on a set of productions that operate on the declarative knowledge. Each production consists of a condition-action-pair. When the condition is sufficiently satisfied by data elements of working memory, the corresponding production is selected and applied, i.e. its action adds a temporary structure to working memory. Procedural memory processes are primarily involved in the acquisition of cognitive skills. Empirical research has mainly concentrated on the acquisition of programming skills (Anderson, Farrell & Sauers, 1984), proof generation in geometry (Anderson, 1984), and prototype formation (Elio & Anderson, 1981).

The *ACT*-framework has attracted considerable interest in cognitive psychology and *ACT** is a good example of a topical theory in a lively area of psychological research. For that reason it seems worthwile to reconstruct *ACT** in terms of the *structuralist view* of scientific theories (Sneed, 1979; Stegmüller, 1976, 1986; Balzer, Moulines & Sneed, 1987).

Especially the results of an earlier reconstruction of the theory of cognitive dissonance (Westermann, 1987) have lead us to expect that the whole *ACT**-theory can be reconstructed only as a rather complex net of theory-elements which is built upon a distinct basic element.

In the first section of this article we derive axiomatic definitions of the sets of models and potential models for this basic theory-element (*ACT*-B*) from which all other elements of the *ACT** theory-net can be obtained by specialization. For empirical applications *ACT*-B* must be enlarged by introducing new terms and substantial axioms. This will be exemplified in the second section by the reconstruction of a theory-element (FR-74) which directly underlies an experiment from the fact- retrieval paradigm (Anderson, 1974). In the third section, we introduce a central theory-element *ACT*-C* to reconstruct the 14 basic assumptions in which Anderson (1983, pp. 22-23) summarizes his theory. In the final section, a preliminary sketch of a more complete *ACT** theory-net is given.

1 The Basic Element

1.1 The Potential Models of ACT*-B

We begin with the definition of the set of potential models of the basic element *ACT*-B*. In the definitions of this chapter, verbal labels will be used to give first characterizations of the *intended interpretations* of the terms and relationships. More detailed explanations and some illustrative citations from Anderson's (1983) book are always given afterwards.

D1 x is a potential model of *ACT*-B*, $x \in M_p(ACT^*\text{-}B)$,
if and only if there are

$\mathbb{R}, T, El, Cnd, Acn, Cu, Gu, DM, WM, DL,$
$CCnd, AAcn, N, PL, >_N, Sub, Sup, Comp, Top, Prd, Grf, M, a, a_0, s, r, sc,$
$in, s_N, a_N, a_{N0}, exc, g, g_0, pt, pc, tr$
such that
(a) $x = \langle \mathbb{R}, T, El, Cnd, Acn, Cu, Gu, DM, WM, DL,$
$a, a_0, s, r, sc, in, CCnd, AAcn, N, PL, >_N, Sub, Sup, Comp,$
$Top, Prd, Grf, M, s_N, a_N, a_{N0}, exc, g, g_0, pt, pc, tr\rangle$, and
(b) the following conditions B1 to B21 are satisfied.

B1 T is a real interval (points of time)
El is a non-empty set (declarative cognitive elements).

B2 $Cu \subseteq Po(El)$ (declarative cognitive units)
with $0 < |c_i| \leq 5$.

B3 $Gu \subseteq Cu$ (immediate goals of current behavior).

B4 $DM \subseteq Cu \times T$ (long-term declarative memory units);
$WM \subseteq Cu \times T$ (working memory units).

B5 $DL \subseteq (DM \cup WM) \times (DM \cup WM)$
(directly connected cognitive units)
with $(c_{it}, c_{ju}) \in DL$ only if $t = u$.

B6 $a : (DM \cup WM) \Longrightarrow \mathbb{R}^{0+}$ (activation),
$a_0 : T \Longrightarrow \mathbb{R}^{0+}$ (threshold for activation),
$s : (DM \cup WM) \Longrightarrow \mathbb{R}^{+}$ (strength),
$r : Cu \times Cu \times T \Longrightarrow \mathbb{R}^{0+}$ (relative link strength)
with

(a) $$r(i,j,t) = \frac{s(j,t)}{\sum_k s(k,t)}$$

(with the summation over all c_{kt} for which $(c_{it}, c_{kt}) \in DL$)
if $(c_{it}, c_{jt}) \in DL$, and

(b) $$r(i,j,t) = 0$$

otherwise.

B7 $sc : (DM \cup WM) \Longrightarrow \mathbb{R}^{0+}$ (source activation),
$in : (DM \cup WM) \Longrightarrow \mathbb{R}^{+}$ (input) with

$$in(i,t) = sc(i,t) + \sum_j r(j,i,t)a(j,t)$$

(with the summation over all c_{jt} for which $(c_{jt}, c_{it}) \in DL$).

B8 Cnd is a non-empty set (conditions),
Acn is a non-empty set (actions).

B9 $CCnd \subseteq Po(Cnd)$ (combined conditions),
$AAcn \subseteq Po(Acn)$ (combined actions).

B10 $N \subseteq CCnd \times T$ (pattern nodes).

B11 $PL \subseteq N \times N$ (directly connected pattern nodes)
with $(n_{pt}, n_{qu}) \in PL$ only if $t = u$.

B12 $>_N \subseteq N \times N$ is a strict partial order relation on N
with $n_{pt} >_N n_{qu}$ only if $t = u$.

B13 $Sub \subseteq PL$ (subpatterns)
with $(n_{pt}, n_{qt}) \in Sub$ if and only if
$n_{pt} >_N n_{qt}$;

B14 $Sup \subseteq PL$ (superpatterns)
with $(n_{pt}, n_{qt}) \in Sup$ if and only if
$n_{qt} >_N n_{pt}$;

B15 $Comp \subseteq N \times N$ (competitors)
with $(n_{pt}, n_{qu}) \in Comp$ if and only if
$t = u$ and there is one $n_{rt} \in N$
such that $(n_{pt}, n_{rt}) \in Sub$ and $(n_{qt}, n_{rt}) \in Sub$.

B16 $Top \subseteq N$ (top nodes)
with $n_{pt} \in Top$ if and only if
there is no $n_{qt} \in N$ with $n_{qt} >_N n_{pt}$,
$Prd \subseteq Top \times AAcn$ (productions).

B17 $s_N : N \Longrightarrow \mathbb{R}^+$ (strength of pattern nodes),
$a_N : N \Longrightarrow \mathbb{R}^{0+}$ (activation of pattern nodes),
$a_{N0} : T \Longrightarrow \mathbb{R}^+$ (activation threshold).

B18 $exc : AAcn \Longrightarrow Cu$ (execution).

B19 $Grf \subseteq Cnd \times Gu$ (goal-reference),
$M \subseteq WM \times N$ (matching)
with $(c_{it}, n_{pu}) \in M$ only if $t = u$.

B20 $g : M \Longrightarrow \mathbb{R}$ (degree of match),
$g_0 : T \Longrightarrow \mathbb{R}$ (threshold for g).

B21 $pt : N \Longrightarrow \mathbb{N}$ (number of pattern tests to be performed),
$pc : N \Longrightarrow \mathbb{N}$ (number of already completed pattern tests)
with $pc(p,t) \leq pt(p,t)$ for all n_{pt},
$tr : N \Longrightarrow \mathbb{R}^{0+}$ (test-rate).

The expressions $\mathbb{R}$, $\mathbb{R}^+$, $\mathbb{R}^{0+}$, and $\mathbb{N}$denote the auxiliary base sets of real numbers, positive real numbers, non-negative real numbers, and natural numbers, respectively. In B1 we introduce a time interval T and a set El of declarative cognitive elements. In B2 the set Cu of cognitive units is defined as a subset of the power set of El.

> Knowledge comes in chunks or *cognitive units* as they are called in ACT* ... each ... cognitive unit encodes a set of elements in a particular relationship. Chunks contain no more than five elements. More complex structures can be created by hierarchical structures, such as a sentence's phrase structure or a proposition embedded in another. In such cases one cognitive unit appears as an element of another. (Anderson, 1983, p. 23)

The cognitive units can be represented as the nodes of a network which are interconnected by links.

> The interconnections of these structures and elements can define a network structure ..., referred to as a *tangled hierarchy*, which is pieced together from cognitive units joining sets of elements. The resulting network can be relatively complex because of the various ways cognitive units can be combined. For instance, a unit can serve as an element in another unit, and the units can be joined when the same element occurs in several of them. It is useful to think of the knowledge structure so formed as a simple network in which all elements or units are *nodes* and the connections among them are *links*. This network structure will prove useful in understanding spreading activation, for instance. (p. 25)

Since each element of a cognitive unit can be another cognitive unit, there seems to be no clear conceptual distinction between cognitive elements and units. As will be seen below, the storage and activation processes of ACT^* refer exclusively to cognitive units. Nevertheless the composition of cognitive units has important consequences, because it determines the interconnections between the nodes. For instance, the probability that two cognitive units are directly linked increases when they have at least one element in common.

As cognitive units representing immediate behavioral goals are of special importance (see below), a subset Gu of *goal units* is introduced in B3.

Long-term declarative memory and working memory are defined as subsets of the cartesian product of Cu with time (B4). When an element c_{it} of $Cu \times T$ is also an element of the subset DM, this means that the cognitive unit c_i is present in the declarative network at time t. When c_{ju} is an element of WM, this means that c_j is in working memory at time u. In order to reconstruct the network of nodes and links, we need a relation DL of those pairs of cognitive units that are directly connected (B5).

One of the key concepts in ACT^* is *activation*:

> Activation controls the rate of information processing. It is the 'energy' that runs the 'cognitive machinery.' Activation spreads through the declarative network along paths from original sources to associated concepts. (p. 86)

In B6 we introduce a real-valued function a for the level of activation of each declarative and working memory unit.

> Activation serves the function in ACT of an associative relevancy heuristic. That is, activation measures how closely associated a piece of information is to information currently used, and it is a heuristic assumption that associated information is most likely to be needed to guide processing. To simply have two levels of activation (*on* and *off*) severely limits the value of activation as a relevancy heuristic. The value is maximized when activation can take on a continuous range of levels. There are neurophysiological arguments for a continuously varying level of activation. At some level of abstraction it is reasonable to identify activation with rate of neural firing (although nodes probably do not correspond to simple neurons ...). Since the rate of neural firing varies continuously, it follows that activation should do so also. (p. 27)

The function s is introduced in B6 for the *strength* of cognitive units.

> Each node in declarative memory has an associated strength, which is basically a function of the frequency of use of that cognitive unit or element ... With the concept of node strength, it is possible to define the relative strength of association between nodes... These relative strengths are important in the spread of activation ..., because more activation flows down stronger paths. (p. 27)

As shown is B6, this relative *link strength* $r(i, j, t)$ from the cognitive unit c_{it} to the unit c_{jt} is proportional to the strength of c_{jt} which is divided by the sum of the strengths of all nodes c_{kt} that are directly connected to c_{it}.

The *source activation sc* of a declarative element (B7) is greater than zero if the element is a source node from which activation spreads throughout the network. In all other cases the source activation equals zero. At any time t the input to a node in the declarative network is defined as the sum of its source activation and the sum of the activation levels of all other nodes connected to it, weighted by their respective relative link strengths.

B8 to B16 refer to the procedural component of memory. In *ACT* procedural knowledge* is constituted by productions.

> Production system theories have gradually increased in prominence in psychology over the past decade. Their basic claim is that underlying human cognition is a set of condition-action pairs called productions. The condition specifies some data patters, and if elements matching these patterns are in working memory, then the production can apply. The action specifies what to do in that state. The basic action is to add new data elements to working memory. (pp. 5-6)

Since each production is an ordered pair of a condition- and an action component, we introduce a set Cnd of conditions and a set Acn of actions as fundamental concepts. As complex combinations of these are required for the creation of productions, two sets $CCnd$ and $AAcn$ are defined as subsets of the power sets of Cnd and Acn, respectively.

The procedural network is constituted by the so-called *pattern nodes* and the connections between them (Anderson, 1983, pp. 30-33). Each pattern node corresponds to one condition or a combination of conditions. Therefore, we introduce a set N of pattern nodes which is defined as a subset of the cartesian product of the set of combined conditions with time (B10), and a relation PL comprising those pairs of pattern nodes that are directly linked (B11, cf. the corresponding relation DL in declarative memory). Since the pattern network is conceived of as hierarchically ordered, we also define a strict partial order relation $>_N$ (B12). In terms of the partial order relation $>_N$ we define sets of subpatterns, superpatterns, and competitors (B13- B15, cf. the substantial axiom B27 below).

Among the pattern nodes those on the highest level in the network are of special importance, because productions are formed by combining these *top nodes* with action-components (cf. the example of a data-flow network in Anderson, 1983, pp. 30-33). Thus, the set Prd of productions is defined as a subset of the cartesian product of the set Top with the set $AAcn$ (B16).

Just like declarative cognitive units each pattern node has an associated strength and a level of activation (B17). The process of production application can be expressed by the execution function exc which associates each combined action with a declarative cognitive unit (B18).

Productions can specify goals in their conditions. For that reason we introduce a goal-reference relation Grf (B19). The decision about which production to apply is made on the basis of *pattern matching processes* which operate in a parallel fashion (Anderson, 1983, pp. 30-33). Starting from the bottom of the network the features specified in the condition clause of each node are tested to see whether they match elements in working memory until compatible instantiations of top nodes are found. This matching can be represented by a subset M of the cartesian product of the declarative cognitive units in working memory with the pattern nodes N.

In B20 a function g for the quantitative *degree of match* is defined on the set M, because a production can be applied even if its condition is only partially matched by the contents of working memory.

> The pattern-matching process permits productions to apply even if their conditions are not completely matched. If a productions's condition is the best interpretation of the available data and enough pieces of the patterns are available to get the pattern above threshold, that production will apply ... Many errors in performance of a skill ... can be explained by such partial matching. For instance, use of a related but incorrect word in speaking (and) ... the *word superiority* effect ... (pp. 32-33).

Depending on the complexity of its condition component, each pattern node has to perform a certain number of tests (pt in B21); how many tests it has already finished, is denoted by pc. The last function, *tr*, expresses the test rate of each node, i.e. the number of tests which can be performed per time unit.

1.2 The Models of ACT*-B

D2 x is a model of *ACT*-B*, $x \in M(ACT^*\text{-}B)$, if and only if
(a) x is a potential model of *ACT*-B* according to D1 and
(b) the following conditions B22 to B28 are satisfied.

B22 For all $c_{it} \in (DM \cup WM)$
(a) if $c_i \notin Gu$, then $\dfrac{da(i,t)}{dt} = \beta \cdot in(i,t) - \alpha \cdot a(i,t)$ $\quad (\alpha, \beta \in \mathrm{I\!R}^{0+})$
(b) if $c_i \in Gu$, then $\dfrac{da(i,t)}{dt} = \beta \cdot in(i,t)$ $\quad (\beta \in \mathrm{I\!R}^{0+})$

B23 For all $c_{it} \in DM$,
if $a(i,t) > a_0(t)$, then $c_{it} \in WM$.

B24 For all $c_i \in Cu$ and for all $t \in T$:
If $c_{it} \in WM$, then there is a $n_{pt} \in N$ such that $(c_{it}, n_{pt}) \in M$.

B25 For all $t \in T$, there is at most one $c_i \in Gu$ with $c_{it} \in WM$.

B26 For all $prd_{ptb} = (n_{pt}, aacn_b) \in Prd$
with $n_{pt} = (ccnd_p, t) \in Top$
and for all $c_i = exc(aacn_b)$:
If $pc(p,t)/pt(p,t) = 1$ and $a_N(p,t) > a_{NO}(t)$ and
(a) there is no $c_{jt} \in WM$ with $c_j \in Gu$ or
(b) there is a $c_{jt} \in WM$ with $c_j \in Gu$ and
$(cnd_m, c_j) \in Grf$ with $cnd_m \in ccnd_p$ and
there is no $prd_{qtc} = (n_{qt}, aacn_c) \in Prd$
with $n_{qt} = (ccnd_q, t) \in Top$,
such that $(cnd_n, c_j) \in Grf$ with $cnd_n \in ccnd_q$ and
$pc(q,t)/pt(q,t) = 1$ and $a_N(q,t) > a_N(p,t)$,
then there is a $v \in T$ with $v > t$,
such that for all $u \in T$ with $v > u \geq t$

$c_{iu} \in WM$ and
$(c_{ku}, n_{pu}) \notin M$ for all c_k with $(c_{kt}, n_{pt}) \in M$.

B27 For all $(n_{pt}, n_{qu}) \in N \times N$:
If $a_N(n_{pt}) > a_N(n_{qu})$,
then $tr(n_{pt}) > tr(n_{qu})$.

B28 For all $(n_{pt}, n_{qu}) \in N \times N$:
if $(c_{it}, n_{pt}), (c_{ju}, n_{qu}) \in M$
and (ceteris paribus)
(a) $g(i,t,p,t) > g(j,u,q,u)$ or
(b) $s_N(p,t) > s_N(q,u)$ or
(c) $a(i,t) > a(j,u)$ or
(d) $\sum_r a_N(r,t) > \sum_s a_N(s,u)$
with the summation over all n_{rt}, n_{su} for which
$(n_{pt}, n_{rt}), (n_{qu}, n_{su}) \in Sup$ or
(e) $\sum_r a_N(r,t) > \sum_s a_N(s,u)$
with the summation over all n_{rt}, n_{su} for which
$(n_{pt}, n_{rt}), (n_{qu}, n_{su}) \in Sub$ or
(f) $\sum_r a_N(r,t) < \sum_s a_N(s,u)$
with the summation over all n_{rt}, n_{su} for which
$(n_{pt}, n_{rt}), (n_{qu}, n_{su}) \in Comp$
then $a_N(p,t) > a_N(q,u)$.

To describe the *spread of activation* over the declarative network and its rapid decay Anderson (1983, p. 22) presents a differential equation which we have reformulated in axiom B22. In this equation β and α are proportionality parameters for the amount of input and the exponential decay process, respectively. Note, that only non-goal elements are subject to automatic decay, whereas goal-related elements stay active until they are explicitly turned off.

Working memory is defined by means of the continuous activation variable a.

> Activation measures the likelihood that a particular piece of knowledge will be useful at a particular moment ... Spreading activation is a parallel mechanism for spreading measures of associative relevance over the network of knowledge. These measures are used to decide how to allocate resources to later, more time-consuming processes, such as pattern matching, that operate on the knowledge ... In the standard terminology of cognitive psychology, spreading activation defines working memory for ACT. Because there are degrees of activation, ACT's concept of working memory is one of degrees. (Anderson, 1983, pp. 87-88).

If we took these words literally, we could not define working memory as a set. Since this would lead to considerable conceptual difficulties and contradictions, we try to give Anderson's notion a precise and consistent meaning by introducing a threshold function a_0 (cf. B6 above). A declarative cognitive unit c_{it} is defined to be an element of working memory if its level of activation $a(i,t)$ exceeds $a_0(t)$, the momentary threshold at time t (B23).

As soon as a declarative cognitive unit is active in working memory, it is combined with at least one pattern node and thereby enters the matching process (B24).

B25 states that at any particular moment only one current goal can be active in the system.

> When a current goal is satisfied, attention shifts to the next goal in the goal stack. Productions that refer to the current goal take precedence over productions that might otherwise apply because of strength or specificity ... It is interesting to speculate on why the system should be restricted to a single current goal and hence restricted to serial processing of what is most important. This may be a response to the limited capacity of system resources such as working memory and to the seriality of effectors, for example, hands. It is important that the system be able to assign as many resources as possible to the most important task ... It would have been an evolutionary disaster if humans, in using their hands to protect themselves, could have a competing production grab control of their hands to wipe the sweat from their brow. (pp. 136-137)

In B26 the process of *production execution* is reconstructed. If a top node has completed its tests and its level of activation is above threshold, the corresponding production fires, i.e. its action component adds a cognitive unit to working memory. If there is a goal active in the system and the production refers to it, it can only be applied, if there is no other highly activated production referring to the same current goal. This has to be demanded, because productions that specify a goal in their condition can never be applied in parallel. This is *goal dominance*, one of ACT^*'s principles of conflict resolution (Anderson, 1983, p. 136). In B 26 and other substantial axioms different indices (i.e. c_{it} and c_{ju}, prd_{ptb} and prd_{qtc}, etc.) denote different elements of the same set, i.e. we always presuppose that $i \neq j$ and/or $t \neq u$, etc.

The most important part of the ACT^*-system is the activation-based, data-flow *pattern matcher*, which has been developed by Anderson (1983, pp. 137-156) on the basis of previous work by Forgy (1979), McClelland & Rumelhart (1981), and Rumelhart & McClelland (1982).

> Pattern matching is the mechanism that decides which productions will apply. A fundamental claim of the production system architecture is that pattern matching underlies all varieties of cognition, providing its data-driven quality ... It is assumed that each top node ... is ... decomposed into nodes representing subpatterns ... Only the top nodes in the network correspond to productions; the subpattern nodes are shared by multiple productions. ... Pattern matching is achieved by combining tests up from the bottom of such a network. Tests are performed to determine what elements in working memory match the primitive features at the bottom nodes. Supernodes combine the test results to determine if they are compatible. (Anderson, 1983, pp. 30-31)

The pattern matcher also achieves the various kinds of conflict resolution, if the degree of match is sufficiently large for more than one top node at the same time (cf. Anderson, 1983, pp. 132-137).

The rate at which a pattern node can perform its tests is a monotone-increasing function of its level of activation (B28).

> Because the process of performing tests at a node takes considerable time, evidence for a match at a node will gradually build up or decrease with time. The node's level of activation, which reflects the system's current confidence that the node will result in a match, determines the speed of pattern matching. (p. 32)

The last axiom, B28, comprises all those factors that have an influence on the activation of a pattern node.

> The level of activation of each node in the pattern network is a positive function of the strength of the node, the level of activation of the data structures being matched, and the degree of match

> to these structures. It is a negative function of the level of activation of competing patterns matching to the same data. (p. 23)

In contrast to declarative memory, spread of activation in production memory is not only excitatory, but also inhibitory.

> Subpatterns of a node send positive activation to the node. This positive activation is referred to as *bottom-up excitatory influence*. ... Alternate interpretations ... of the same subpatterns compete by means of *lateral inhibitory influences*. Finally, patterns support the activation of their subpatterns by *top-down excitatory influences*. ... These computations on activation are designed to achieve the *data refractoriness* principle, the idea that each data structure will be matched to a single pattern. This phenomenon is ubiquitous in perception ... and similar phenomena also exist at higher levels of cognition. (p. 32)

In B28 (d) to (f) this is reformulated by means of the terms that have been introduced in B13 to B15 above.

2 An Experimental Element

The original fact-retrieval (FR) experiment is reported in Anderson (1974) as Experiment 1. As it is a simple and typical representative of *ACT**'s intended applications in the domain of *memory for facts*, the experimental paradigm shall briefly be described.

During a learning phase subjects are presented with simple sentences of the form 'A person is in the location'. The person and location components vary according to the number of sentences in which they occur (1-3). After a subject has commited the sentences to memory, he or she is shown a test stimulus of the same form and has to judge whether it belongs to the study set.

According to *ACT** it is expected, that sentences and their main components are represented as interconnected nodes (especially propositional nodes) in a semantic network. On the basis of the postulated spreading-activation mechanism it can be predicted that the mean reaction times for judging a probe will increase as the number of sentences which share the components of the probe increases. The effect is expected to show no difference for the person and the location dimensions.

The structuralist analysis of this experimental situation yields a special corresponding theory-element which we call FR-74. Since the basic element is hypothesized to underly all intended applications of the theory, only those expressions and laws which are not already part of *ACT*-B* will be characterized below.

2.1 The Potential Models of FR-74

D3 x is a potential model of FR-74, $x \in Mp(FR\text{-}74)$,
if and only if there are
$\mathbb{R}, T, El, Cnd, Acn, Cu, Gu, DM, WM, DL,$
$CCnd, AAcn, N, PL, >_N, Sub, Sup, Comp, Top, Prd, Grf, M, Ps, Lo, E_s,$
$PE_s, B, PB, Ch, Lc, Plp, Cu_b, a, a_0, s, r, sc, in, s_N, a_N, a_{N0}, exc, g, g_0,$
pt, pc, tr, sec, per, rt
such that
(a) $x = \langle \mathbb{R}, T, El, Cnd, Acn, Cu, Gu, DM, WM, DL, CCnd, AAcn, N, PL, AAcn, N,$

$PL, >_N, Sub, Sup, Comp, Top, Prd, Grf, M, Ps, Lo,$
$E_s, PE_s, B, PB, Ch, Lc, Plp, Cu_b, a, a_0, s, r, sc, in, s_N, a_N,$
$a_{N0}, exc, g, g_0, pt, pc, tr, sec, per, rt\rangle$,

(b) $\langle \mathbb{R}, T, El, Cnd, Acn, Cu, Gu, DM, WM, DL, a, a_0, s, r, sc, in, CCnd,$
$AAcn, N, PL, >_N, Sub, Sup, Comp, Top, Prd, Grf, M,$
$s_N, a_N, a_{N0}, exc, g, g_0, pt, pc, tr\rangle \in Mp(ACT^*\text{-}B)$
according to D1, and

(c) the following conditons FR1 to FR3 are satisfied.

FR1 Ps is a non-empty set (person components),
Lo is a non-empty set (location components)
with $Ps \cap Lo = \emptyset$.
$E_s \subseteq Ps \times Lo$ (external sentence stimuli),
$PE_s \subseteq E_s \times T$ (present external sentence stimuli),
B is a non-empty set (open behaviors),
$PB \subseteq B \times T$ (present open behaviors).

FR2 $Ch \subseteq El$ (character nodes),
$Lc \subseteq El$ (location nodes)
with $Ch \cap Lc = \emptyset$ and $Ch \times Lo \subseteq Cu$
$Plp \subseteq Ch \times Lc$ (person-location propositions),
$Cu_b \subseteq Cu$ (behavior-tagged cognitive units)

FR3 $sec : E_s \Longrightarrow Plp$ (sentence encoding),
$per : Cu_b \Longrightarrow B$ (performance),
$rt : PE_s \Longrightarrow \mathbb{R}^+$ (reaction time).

In FR1 and FR2, sets comprising the stimulus material and the corresponding internal representations as well as elementary behavioral units are defined and characterized. Although ACT^* postulates three representational types, only the propositional code is used in most memory experiments; therefore we do not define subsets for temporal strings or spatial images at this point. FR3 introduces three functions which are essential for the reconstruction of some special laws.

2.2 The Models of FR-74

D4 x is a model of FR-74, $x \in M(FR\text{-}74)$,
if and only if
(a) x is a potential model of FR-74 according to D3 and
(b) the following conditions FR4 to FR10 are satisfied.

FR4 For all $e_i \in E_s$:
If $e_{it} \in PE_s$,
then $c_{it} \in WM$ with $c_i = sec(e_i)$.

FR5 For all $c_{it} \in WM$:
if $c_{it} \notin DM$,
then with probability p:
there is a $v \in T$ with $v > t$,

such that for all $u \in T$ with $v > u > t$
$c_{iu} \in DM$ and $s(i,u) = 1$.

FR6 For all $c_{it} \in WM$:
if $c_{it} \in DM$,
then there is a $v \in T$ with $v > t$,
such that for all $u \in T$ with $v > u > t$
$c_{iu} \in DM$ and $s(i,u) = s(i,t) + 1$.

FR7 For all $c_i = (ch_i, lc_i) \in Plp$:
If $c_{it} \in (DM \cup WM)$,
then $c_{jt} = (\{ch_i\}, t), c_{kt} = (\{lc_i\}, t) \in (DM \cup WM)$ and
$(c_{it}, c_{jt}), (c_{it}, c_{kt}), (c_{jt}, c_{it}), (c_{kt}, c_{it}) \in DL$.

FR8 For all $c_i \in Cu_b$:
If $c_{it} \in WM$,
then $b_{it} \in PB$ with $b_i = per(c_i)$.

FR9 For each pair $e_i = (ps_i, lo_i), e_j = (ps_j, lo_j) \in E_s$:
If $e_{it}, e_{ju} \in PE_s$ and
$|\{lo_x : (ps_i, lo_x) \in E_s\}| > |\{lo_x : (ps_j, lo_x) \in E_s\}|$ or
$|\{ps_x : (ps_x, lo_i) \in E_s\}| > |\{ps_x : (ps_x, lo_j) \in E_s\}|$,
then $rt(e_{it}) > rt(e_{ju})$.

FR10 For each quadruple $e_i = (ps_i, lo_i), e_j = (ps_j, lo_j)$,
$e_k = (ps_k, lo_k), e_l = (ps_l, lo_l) \in E_s$:
If $e_{it}, e_{ju}, e_{kv}, e_{lw} \in PE_s$ and (ceteris paribus)
$|\{lo_x : (ps_i, lo_x) \in E_s\}| - |\{lo_x : (ps_j, lo_x) \in E_s\}|$
$= |\{ps_x : (ps_x, lo_k) \in E_s\}| > |\{ps_x : (ps_x, lo_l) \in E_s\}|$,
then $rt(e_{it}) - rt(e_{ju}) = rt(e_{kv}) - rt(e_{lw})$.

The axioms FR4 to FR10 represent the special laws of *FR*-74, which unlike the fundamental laws of *ACT*-B* are expected to be satisfied only in a certain subset of *ACT**'s applications.

FR4 describes the encoding of a present external sentence into working memory. The following axioms FR5 and FR6 are formalizations of *ACT**'s *storage* and *strengthening* mechanisms in declarative (long-term) memory.

> If a temporary cognitive unit is created in working memory, there is a probability p that a copy of it will be created in declarative long-term memory. If a copy is created, it will have one unit strength. If a cognitive unit is created in working memory and a copy already exists in long-term memory, its long-term strength will increase by one unit. (Anderson, 1983, p. 30)

When a cognitive unit has been strengthened at t, it will keep its new strength for a certain time interval following t. The validity of these axioms, although not explicitly stated in FR-74, is necessary to assure that the facts to be learned are represented in the semantic network when the test phase begins.

If an abstract proposition, which in this special case consists of a character and a location component, is part of declarative memory, then its constituents are represented as nodes in declarative memory, too. The proposition node and its corresponding concept nodes are interconnected, so that activation can spread between them in both directions (FR7).

Axiom FR8 connects the cognitive system with its environment. As soon as a cognitive unit which is tagged as behavioral is present in working memory, it results in the performance of a corresponding unit of behavior.

FR9 and FR10 are formalizations of two empirical predictions, which are put to test in Anderson (1974, Experiment 1). For each test sentence, the more sentences in the learning set include the same person or location as the given sentence, the longer it will take a subject to classify it as studied or not studied (FR9). This effect is expected to be of equal size for person and location components (FR10).

In order to define the sets of models and potential models for *FR*-74 the theory-element has to be completed by B1 to B28 from the basic element. In case of *FR*-74 the sets comprise domain-specific elements. For instance, there is only one specific goal ('sentence recognition') needed in Gu, and Prd contains a number of productions for sentence recognition.

The fundamental laws of *ACT*-B* are needed to explain the empirically testable phenomena by the theory. On the theoretical level the effect of the intersection in person and location components (FR9) is reflected by the so-called fan effect. 'Fan' refers to the number of facts connected to a particular component. As Anderson (1983) writes,

> Pattern matching will take longer with high-fan probes, those whose elements appear in multiple study sentences. The fan from an element reduces the amount of activation that can go to any propositional trace or to the probe encoding it. Pattern matching for targets is a function of the activation of the propositional trace and the probe. (pp. 110-111)

The axioms B22 to B28 together with the special laws FR4 to FR8 constitute the theoretical frame for the explanation of the experimental effect.

3 The Central Element

Anderson (1983, pp. 22-23) summarizes the fundamental processes of his theory in 14 *basic assumptions*. Our exemplaric analysis of the fact-retrieval experiment in the proceeding section clearly shows that the terms and assumptions are not completely used in every empirical application of *ACT**. Thus, Anderson's basic assumptions do not correspond to the basic element of *ACT**, but to a terminologically and substantially much richer theory-element. We call it the central theory-element, *ACT*-C*. As *ACT*-C* is a specialization (in the general sense) of *ACT*-B*, we can presuppose the basic element and will only introduce the new terms and laws of *ACT*-C*.

3.1 The Potential Models of ACT*-C

D5 x is a potential model of *ACT*-C*, $x \in Mp(ACT^*\text{-}C)$,
if and only if there are
$\mathbb{R}, T, El, Cnd, Acn, Cu, Gu, Pr, Im, St, DM, WM, DL, Sgo, Acp, PE,$
$Enc, CCnd, AAcn, N, PL, >_N, Sub, Sup, Comp, Top, Prd, Prg, Prs,$
$Grf, M, Ret, Seq, MM, a, a_0, s, s_0, r, sc, in, s_N, s_{NOd}, s_{NOp},$
$a_N, a_{NO}, exc, g, g_0, pt, pc, tr, gm, gm_0, fdb$
such that
(a) $x = \langle \mathbb{R}, T, El, Cnd, Acn, Cu, Gu, Pr, Im, St, DM, WM, DL, Sgo,$

$Acp, PE, Enc, CCnd, AAcn, N, PL, >_N, Sub, Sup, Comp,$
$Top, Prd, Prg, Prs, Grf, M, Ret, Seq, MM, a, a_0, s, s_0,$
$r, sc, in, s_N, s_{NOd}, s_{NOp}, a_N, a_{NO}, exc, g, g_0,$
$pt, pc, tr, gm, gm_0, fdb\rangle,$

(b) $\langle \mathbb{R}, T, El, Cnd, Acn, Cu, Gu, DM, WM, DL, a, a_0, s, r, sc, in,$
$CCnd, AAcn, N, PL, >_N, Sub, Sup, Comp, Top, Prd, Grf, M, s_N$
$a_N, a_{NO}, exc, g, g_0, pt, pc, tr\rangle \in Mp(ACT^*\text{-}B)$
according to D1, and

(c) the following conditions C1 to C6 are satisfied.

C1 $Pr \subseteq Cu$ (propositions),
$Im \subseteq Cu$ (spatial images),
$St \subseteq Cu$ (temporal strings)
with $St \cap Pr = \emptyset$, $Im \cap Pr = \emptyset$, $St \cap Im = \emptyset$.

C2 $Sgo \subseteq Gu \times Gu$ (subgoals),
$Acp = \{acn^+, acn^-\} \subseteq Acn$ (goal-popping actions),
$PE \subseteq E \times T$ (present external stimuli),
$Enc \subseteq PE \times Cu$ (encoding),
$s_0 : T \Longrightarrow \mathbb{R}^+$ (threshold for strength).

C3 $Prg \subseteq Prd$ (general productions),
$Prs \subseteq Prd$ (domain specific productions)
with $Prs \cup Prg = Prd$ and $Prs \cap Prg = \emptyset$.

C4 $Ret \subseteq CCnd \times Cu$ (retrieval),
$Seq \subseteq Prd \times Prd$ (sequence)
with $(prd_{ptb}, prd_{quc}) \in Seq$ only if $t < u$.

C5 $MM \subseteq Top \times Top$ (meta-matching)
with $(n_{pt}, n_{qu}) \in MM$ only if $t = u$,
$gm : MM \Longrightarrow \mathbb{R}$ (degree of meta-match),
$gm_0 : T \Longrightarrow \mathbb{R}$ (threshold for gm).

C6 $s_{NOd} : T \Longrightarrow \mathbb{R}^+$ (discrimination threshold for s_N),
$s_{NOp} : T \Longrightarrow \mathbb{R}^+$ (proceduralization threshold for s_N),
$fdb : \{c_{it} : c_{it} \in WM \text{ and } c_i = exc(aacn_b)\} \longrightarrow \{0, 1\}$ (feedback).

ACT^* uses at least three different kinds of cognitive units. The corresponding subsets of Cu are called Pr, St, and Im (C1).

> Cognitive units can be such things as propositions (for example, (*hate*, *Bill*, *Fred*)), strings (*one*, *two*, *three*), or spatial images (a triangle above a square). (Anderson, 1983, p. 23)
>
> These types differ in their representational assumptions and hence they are called *representational* types. More generally, I claim that the cognitive system has evolved many different representational types, each intended to facilitate a certain type of computation. (p. 26)

The relation Sgo in C2 is needed to reconstruct the *hierarchical goal structures* which control cognitive processing in ACT^*.

> ACT*'s productions can create and transform a hierarchical goal structure that reflects the current plan of action ... ACT* focuses attention on a goal by making it a strong source of activation. It can shift focus of attention within this goal structure. For instance, when a goal

> is achieved it is popped, and attention is shifted to the next goal ... The goal structure is a principled construction with a clear semantics. That is, subgoals are asserted as necessary and sufficient conditions for achieving the goal. (p. 33)

If a pair (c_i, c_j) of goals is an element of Sgo, this means that c_j is a subgoal of c_i. A goal can be popped either after successful or unsuccessful processing. Thus, the set Acp consists of two elements acn^+ and acn^- ("popping with success" and "popping with failure"). These ***goal-popping actions*** can be considered as standard actions which are responsible for a shift in the goal structure the system is currently attending to. Goal-popping actions play an important role in the process of production composition (see C13 below). C2 further introduces a set PE of those external stimuli with which the cognitive system is actually confronted at a certain time and an encoding relation Enc which combines these present environmental stimuli with internal representations. The threshold function for strength will be needed in the substantial axioms below.

Especially in knowledge compilation *ACT** differentiates general productions with a wide range of applicability from ***domain-specific productions*** which are suited to a particular task. Both sets are introduced as subsets of Prd (C3).

There are certain production conditions referring to cognitive units which have to be retrieved from long-term memory. On the basis of the relation Ret (C4) this retrieval process can be reconstructed. The relation Seq comprises pairs of productions that follow each other in a problem-solving process and may therefore be subject to knowledge composition (see C13). As Anderson (1983, p. 238) emphasizes, this sequence is not determined by temporal but by logical contiguity.

The condition clauses of productions can be compared with regard to their degree of similarity. For this ***meta-matching*** we define the relation MM and a corresponding function gm, again permitting partial matches (C5).

The two threshold functions from C6 are necessary in the formalization of the corresponding learning mechanisms. After a production has been executed the cognitive system will receive feedback, indicating success or failure of the application.

> There are two basic ways in which ACT can identify that a production application is in error and determine the correct action ... In the external feedback situation the learner may be directly told that his behavior is in error or he may infer this by comparing his behavior to an external referent ... In the internal computation case the learner must identify that a fact is contradictory, that a goal has failed, or that there is some other failure to meet internal norms. In either case the feedback is only indirectly about the production. It is directly about the action of the production that entered into working memory. (pp. 248-249)

The function fdb is introduced to describe this mechanism. Its range consists of only two values, because

> in principle, a production application could be characterized as being in one of three states - known to be incorrect, known to be correct, or correctness unknown. However, the mechanisms we have implemented for ACT do not distinguish between the second and third states. If a production applies and there is no comment on its success, it is treated as if it were a successful application. (p. 248)

3.2 The Models of ACT*-C

D6 x is a model of *ACT*-C*, $x \in M(ACT^*\text{-}C)$, if and only if

(a) x is a potential model of $ACT^*\text{-}C$ according to D5 and
(b) the following conditions C7 to C21 are satisfied.

C7 For all $(c_{it}, c_{ju}) \in WM \times WM$ with $sc(i,t), sc(j,u) > 0$:
If $s(i,t) < s(j,u)$, then $sc(i,t) < sc(j,u)$.

C8 = FR5

C9 = FR6

C10 If $c_{it} \in WM$ with $c_i \in Gu$
and there is no $prd_{ptb} = (n_{pt}, aacn_b) \in Prs$
with $n_{pt} = (ccnd_p, t) \in Top$,
such that $g(i,t,p,t) > g_0(t)$
and there is a $prd_{qtc} = (n_{qt}, aacn_c) \in Prg$
with $n_{qt} = (ccnd_q, t) \in Top$,
such that $g(i,t,q,t) > g_0(t)$
and $s(j,t) > s_0(t)$ for $c_{jt} \in DM$ with $(ccnd_q, c_j) \in Ret$,
then there is a $v \in T$ with $v > t$
such that for all $u \in T$ with $v \geq u > t$
$c_{iu}, c_{ju} \in WM$ and $(c_{jv}, n_{qv}), (c_{iv}, n_{qv}) \in M$.

C11 For all $prd_{ptb} = (n_{pt}, aacn_b) \in Prd$
with $n_{pt} = (ccnd_p, t) \in Top$:
$a_N(p,t) > a_{N0}(t)$ only if
$g(i,t,p,t) > g_0(t)$
for at least one $c_{it} \in WM$ with $(c_{it}, n_{pt}) \in M$.

C12 For all $prd_{ptb} = (n_{pt}, aacn_b) \in Prg$
with $n_{pt} = (ccnd_p, t) \in Top$:
$a_N(p,t) > a_{N0}(t)$ only if
$(c_{it}, n_{pt}) \in M$ for all c_i with $(ccnd_p, c_i) \in Ret$.

C13 For each pair $prd_{ptb} = (n_{pt}, aacn_b) \in Prd$
with $n_{pt} = (ccnd_p, t) \in Top$
and $prd_{quc} = (n_{qu}, aacn_c) \in Prd$
with $n_{qu} = (ccnd_q, u) \in Top$:
If $(prd_{ptb}, prd_{quc}) \in Seq$ and
$c_{it} \in WM$ with $c_i \in Gu$ and
$(c_{it}, n_{pt}) \in M$ and
$(cnd_m, c_i) \in Grf$ with $cnd_m \in ccnd_p$ and
$pc(p,t)/pt(p,t) = 1$ and
$a_N(p,t) > a_{N0}(t)$
and
(a) $c_{iu} \in WM$ and
$(c_{iu}, n_{qu}) \in M$
$(cnd_n, c_i) \in Grf$ with $cnd_n \in ccnd_q$ and
$pc(q,u)/pt(q,u) = 1$ and
$a_N(q,u) > a_{N0}(u)$
or

(b) $c_{ju} \in WM$ with $c_j \in Gu$ and $c_j = exc(aacn_b)$ and
$(c_i, c_j) \in Sgo$ and
$(c_{ju}, n_{qu}) \in M$ and
$(cnd_n, c_j) \in Grf$ with $cnd_n \in ccnd_q$ and
$pc(q,u)/pt(q,u) = 1$ and
$a_N(q,u) > a_{N0}(u)$ and
$acn^+ \in aacn_c$,
then (with probability p) for all $v > u$:
there is a $prd_{rvd} = (n_{rv}, aacn_d) \in Prd$
with $n_{rv} = (ccnd_r, v) \in Top$ and
$ccnd_r = ccnd_p \cup (ccnd_q/\{cnd_n\})$ and
$aacn_d = aacn_c/\{acn^+\}$, such that:
if $(c_{iv}, n_{rv}) \in M$, then $g(i,v,r,v) > g_0(v)$.

C14 If $c_{it} \in WM$ with $c_i \in Gu$
and there is a $prd_{ptb} = (n_{pt}, aacn_b) \in Prg$
with $n_{pt} = (ccnd_p, t) \in Top$,
such that $a_N(p,t) > a_{N0}(t)$ and
$s(j,t) > s_0(t)$ for all $c_{jt} \in DM$
with $(ccnd_p, c_j) \in Ret$
and $s_N(p,t) > s_{N0p}(t)$,
then for all $u > t$:
there is a $prd_{quc} = (n_{qu}, aacn_c) \in Prs$
with $n_{qu} = (ccnd_q, u) \in Top$, such that:
if $(c_{iu}, n_{qu}) \in M$, then $g(i,u,q,u) > g_0(u)$.

C15 For all $prd_{pub} = (n_{pu}, aacn_b) \in Prs$
with $n_{pu} = (ccnd_p, u) \in Top$:
If $prd_{ptb} \notin Prs$ for all $t < u$,
then $(n_{pu}, n_{qu}) \in MM$ for all $n_{qu} \in Top$
with $p \neq q$ and $(n_{qu}, aacn_c) = prd_{quc} \in Prs$.

C16 For each pair $prd_{ptb} = (n_{pt}, aacn_b) \in Prs$
with $n_{pt} = (ccnd_p, t) \in Top$ and
$prd_{qtc} = (n_{qt}, aacn_c) \in Prs$
with $n_{qt} = (ccnd_q, t) \in Top$:
If $(n_{pt}, n_{qt}) \in MM$ and
$gm(p,t,q,t) > gm_0(t)$,
then for all $u > t$:
there is a $prd_{rud} = (n_{ru}, aacn_d) \in Prs$
with $n_{ru} = (ccnd_r, u) \in Top$
such that
$g(i,u,r,u) > g_0(u)$ for all $c_{iu} \in WM$
for which $g(i,u,p,u) > g_0(u)$ or $g(i,u,q,u) > g_0(u)$.

C17 For all $prd_{ptb} = (n_{pt}, aacn_b) \in Prs$
with $n_{pt} = (ccnd_p, t) \in Top$:
If $c_{it} \in WM$ with $c_i \in Gu$ and

$(cnd_m, c_i) \in Grf$ with $cnd_m \in ccnd_p$ and
$pc(p,t)/pt(p,t) = 1$ and
$a_N(p,t) > a_{N0}(t)$ and
there is no $prd_{qtc} \in Prd$
with $n_{qt} = (ccnd_q, t) \in Top$,
such that $(cnd_n, c_i) \in Grf$ with $cnd_n \in ccnd_q$ and
$pc(q,t)/pt(q,t) = 1$ and
$a_N(q,t) > a_N(p,t)$
and $s_N(p,t) > s_{N0d}(t)$
and $c_{ju} \in WM$ with $c_j = exc(aacn_b)$ and $u > t$
and $fdb(j,u) = 0$,
then for all $v > u$:
there is a $prd_{rvd} = (n_{rv}, aacn_d) \in Prs$
with $n_{rv} = (ccnd_r, v) \in Top$,
such that
$g(k,v,p,v) > g_0(v)$ for all $c_{kv} \in WM$,
for which $g(k,v,r,v) > g_0(v)$ and
$not(g(k,v,r,v) > g_0(v)$ for all $c_{kv} \in WM$,
for which $g(k,v,p,v) > g_0(v))$.

C18 For all $n_{pu} = (ccnd_p, u) \in Top$
with $(n_{pu}, aacn_b) = prd_{pub} \in Prd$:
If $prd_{ptb} \notin Prd$ for all $t < u$,
then $s_N(p,u) = 1$.

C19 For all pairs of $n_{pt} = (ccnd_p, t) \in Top$
with $(n_{pt}, aacn_b) = prd_{ptb} \in Prd$ and $n_{qt} = (ccnd_q, t) \in Top$
with $(n_{qt}, aacn_c) = prd_{qtc} \in Prd$
for which $(g(i,t,q,t) > g_0(t)$ for all $c_{it} \in WM$ with $g(i,t,p,t) > g_0(t))$:
If $pc(p,t)/pt(p,t) = 1$
and $a_N(p,t) > a_{N0}(t)$
and there is no $prd_{rtd} = (n_{rt}, aacn_d) \in Prd$
with $n_{rt} = (ccnd_r, t) \in Top$,
for which $(cnd_n, c_k) \in Grf$ with $cnd_n \in ccnd_r$
and $a_N(r,t) > a_N(p,t)$
and $c_{ju} \in WM$ with $c_j = exc(aacn_b)$ and $u > t$
then there is a $v \in T$ with $v > t$,
such that for all $u \in T$ with $v > u > t$
(a) $s_N(p,u) = s_N(p,t) + 1$ and
$s_N(q,u) = s_N(q,t) + 1$
if $fdb(j,u) = 1$, and
(b) $s_N(p,u) = 0.25 \cdot s_N(p,t)$ and
$s_N(q,u) = 0.25 \cdot s_N(q,t)$.
if $fdb(j,u) = 0$.

C20 For all $c_{iu} \in WM$:
If and only if

(a) $(e_{ju}, c_i) \in Enc$
for at least one $e_{ju} \in PE$ or
(b) $c_i \in Gu$ or
(c) $c_i = exc(aacn_b)$ for at least one
$prd_{ptb} = (n_{pt}, aacn_b) \in Prd$
with $n_{pt} = (ccnd_p, t) \in Top$,
such that $a_N(p,t) > a_{N0}(t)$ with $t < u$
and there is no $prd_{qtc} = (n_{qt}, aacn_c) \in Prd$
with $n_{qt} = (ccnd_q, t) \in Top$,
such that $a_N(q,t) > a_N(p,t)$
and there is no $prd_{rxd} = (n_{rx}, aacn_d) \in Prd$
with $n_{rx} = (ccnd_r, x) \in Top$,
such that $a_N(r,x) > a_{N0}(x)$
with $t < x \leq u$,
then there is a $w \in T$ with $w > u$, such that for all $v \in T$
with $w > v \geq u$:
$sc(i,u) > 0$.

C21 For all $c_i \in Gu$ with $c_{it} \in WM$:
If $a_N(p,t) > a_{N0}(t)$ and
$pc(p,t)/pt(p,t) = 1$ and
$(cnd_m, c_i) \in Grf$ with $cnd_m \in ccnd_p$
for at least one $prd_{ptb} = (n_{pt}, aacn_b) \in Prd$
with $n_{pt} = (ccnd_p, t) \in Top$ and $Acp \cap aacn_b \neq \emptyset$
and there is no $prd_{qtc} = (n_{qt}, aacn_c) \in Prd$
with $n_{qt} = (ccnd_q, t) \in Top$, such that
$(cnd_n, c_i) \in Grf$ with $cnd_n \in ccnd_q$ and
$pc(q,t)/pt(q,t) = 1$ and
$a_N(q,t) > a_N(p,t)$,
then there is a $v \in T$ with $v > t$,
such that for all $u \in T$ with $v > u > t$: $c_{iu} \notin WM$.

For each cognitive unit that is a source node the amount of *source activation sc* is a monotone-increasing function of its strength s (C7; Anderson, 1983, pp. 22, 174). The central axioms for the long-term storage and *strengthening* of declarative cognitive units have been introduced as FR5 and FR6 in the reconstruction of the fact-retrieval experiment above.

When there is no domain-specific production available that matches the current goal in working memory,

> general problem-solving procedures can take the declarative information ... and interpret it to produce coherent and domain-appropriate behavior. (p. 219).

Axiom C10 describes this interpretive application of a *general problem-solving procedure.* Before a general production can fire, declarative knowledge has to be retrieved from long-term memory into working memory from where it enters the pattern matcher. A declarative cognitive unit can only be retrieved if it has a strength value above the threshold.

A production's level of activation can only be high enough for application, if the *degree of match* between its condition and a declarative structure in working memory exceeds some threshold value (Anderson, 1983, p. 32). Thereby the system, although permitting partial matches, avoids production execution when there is insufficient correspondence between the declarative and the procedural knowledge (C11). Compared to knowledge-specific productions, that do not require any retrieval processes, the application of general productions is considerably slower. They can only achieve a level of activation above threshold, if the condition component is matched to the long-term declarative knowledge it refers to (C12).

With respect to the *acquisition of new information* there is a significant difference between declarative memory and production memory. As Anderson (1983) explains,

> the acquisition of productions is unlike the acquisition of facts or cognitive units in the declarative component. It is not possible to simply add a production in the way it is possible to simply encode a cognitive unit. Rather, procedural learning occurs only in executing a skill; one learns by doing. This is one of the reasons why procedural learning is a much more gradual process than declarative learning. (p. 215)

Since the interpretive application of general productions requires a lot of working memory capacity, it is more advantageous for the system to generate domain-specific productions.

> They are acquired gradually and with caution because productions do control behavior rather directly. Gradual creation of a set of task-specific productions makes it more likely that errors will be detected in the learning process before the system has totally relinquished control to the new production set. (p. 34)

In *ACT**,

> new productions can be created from the trace of production application. Composition collapses a sequence of productions into a new one. Proceduralization builds new productions that eliminate the long-term memory retrievals of old ones. (p. 23)
>
> According to ACT*, all knowledge initially comes in declarative form and must be interpreted by general procedures. However, by performing a task, *proceduralization* gradually replaces the interpretive application with productions that perform the behavior directly. ... This proceduralization process is complemented by a *composition* process that can combine a sequence of productions into a single production. Proceduralization and composition, which together are called knowledge compilation, create task-specific productions through practice. Knowledge compilation is the means by which new productions enter the system. (p. 34)

In C13 and C14 we have reformulated proceduralization and composition (see Anderson, 1983, chapter 6, for more details). The composition mechanism operates on a pair of productions that are logically contiguous in solving a particular problem and collapses them into a single *macroproduction*. The initial productions are either so-called *brother productions*, i.e. they refer to a common goal, or the first production sets a subgoal which is successfully processed by the second. The composed production has the effect of the sequence, whereas the process of subgoal setting and return is eliminated. If a general production has been applied in goal-directed processing, an attempt will be made to generate a domain-specific production that will match the same data structure more rapidly in the future. For proceduralization only general productions with a sufficiently high strength, indicating a certain history of successful applications, will be chosen.

C15 refers to the *meta-matching process* which operates on every new specific production in the system.

> That is, whenever a production is formed, an attempt is made to compare it to other existing productions to see if a potential generalization exists. (p. 244).

Generalization (C16) and discrimination (C17) are so-called *tuning mechanisms* that operate on task-specific procedures, further improving their adaptivity within the domain.

> Once a production set has been created, it can be tuned for a domain. Productions accumulate strength according to their history of success. Generalization and discrimination processes search for problem features that are predictive of the success of a particular method. Composition continues to collapse frequently repeated sequences of productions into single productions. These various learning processes produce the gradual, continued improvement in skill performance that has been noted by many researchers. (pp. 34-35).

For generalization, a pair of productions which have been identified as similar by metamatching is taken in order to create a new one with a wider range of application comprising all those cases to which the former apply. As a complementary process to generalization the discrimination mechanism restricts a production's range of application. It is especially designed to correct overgeneralizations that have led to unsuccessful applications and negative feedback. Again a minimum level of strength is required to protect the system from perseverating discriminations of wrong rules (Anderson, 1983, p. 247).

Another important mechanism for tuning productions and eliminating unsuccessful ones is *strengthening*.

> When first created, a production has a strength of 1. Each time it applies, its strength increases by 1. However, when a production applies and receives negative feedback, its strength is reduced by 25 percent. (p. 251)

Strengthening and reduction of strength do not only pertain to the applied production but also to all of its generalizations. We have formalized these postulates in C18 and C19.

The last two axioms refer to working memory structures. According to Anderson (1983, p. 89)

> there are three ways in which an element can become a source of activation in working memory. First, an element that encodes an environmental stimulus will become a source. For example, if a word is presented, its memory representation will be activated. Second, when a production executes, its actions build structures that become sources of activation. Third, a production can focus the goal element on a structure in working memory, and the elements of such a focused structure can become sources of activation. (p. 89)

The internal representation of an environmental stimulus will stay active as a source as long as the stimulus is present. A cognitive unit resulting from a production execution becomes a source node for a certain period of time. The current goal, however, supplies the system with activation until it is changed. Since goal structures are not subject to rapid decay (cf. B1 above), they have to be turned off by goal-popping actions when the cognitive system shifts its focus of attention.

4 A Preliminary Theory-Net

*ACT**'s two main domains of applications are *memory for facts* and *procedural learning.* According to this distinction the complete theory-net consists of two parts with the common basic element *ACT*-B*. Our central element *ACT*-C* also belongs to both parts, because its laws pertain to both domains.

In Figure 1 the special net for memory for facts is preliminarily sketched. From the top to the bottom of the net the theory-elements are developed by successive *specializations* (in

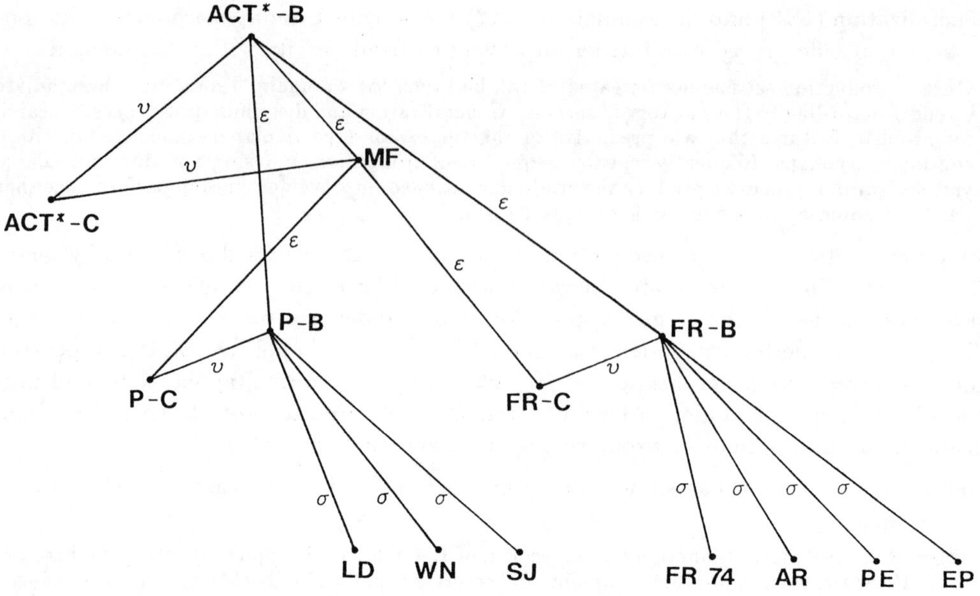

Figure 1: *A preliminary ACT*-net for memory for facts*

Note.
Abbreviations for theory-elements:

*ACT**-B :	basic element
*ACT**-C :	central element
MF :	memory for facts
P-B :	"special basic" element for priming
P-C :	"special central" element for priming
FR-B :	"special basic" element for fact retrieval
FR-C :	"special central" element for fact retrieval
LD :	lexical decision
WN :	word naming
SJ :	sensibility judgment
FR-74 :	fact retrieval (1974)
AR :	associative relatedness
PE :	practice effects
EP :	elaborative processing

Abbreviations for intra-theoretical relations

ε :	enlargement
σ :	strict specialization
υ :	simplification

the general sense). Their left-to-right order approximately corresponds to their temporal or logical relationships (cf. Westermann (this volume) for a more detailed explanation of the intra-theoretical relations). The experimental element *FR*-74, which was developed in section 2 above, is a general specialization of both the basic and the central element.

When we start with *ACT*-C*, which represents Anderson's 14 basic assumptions, the basic element is obtained by simplification. If the basic element is enlarged by those terms and relationships that should be given in all applications of *ACT** with respect to memory for facts, we get the element *MF*. Viewed from the central element on the other hand, *MF* is generated by simplification, because it does not contain any terms or substantial axioms referring to ACT^*'s learning mechanisms. Compared to MF, the theory-elements which dominate research in priming and fact retrieval are enlarged by further substantial axioms while at the same time other laws are omitted. Therefore, we differentiate ***special central*** theory-elements (P-C, FR-C) from ***special basic*** theory-elements (P-B, FR-B) for the two domains, respectively. Strict specializations of these elements then result in the more specific theoretical reference points of corresponding empirical research. One of these elements on the lowest level of the net is our FR-74.

The element AR refers to judgments of associative relatedness (Reder, 1982; Reder & Ross, 1983). In corresponding empirical studies the subjects' task is to judge if a certain fact is thematically consistent with previously learned facts. An ACT^* explanation of the effects can easily be given if the special representational assumptions described by Reder & Ross (1983) are taken into account.

PE comprises special laws which describe the improvement of fact retrieval as a function of extensive practice (cf. Anderson, 1983, pp. 182-189). Empirical studies concerning the elaborative processing of declarative material (Bradshaw & Anderson, 1982; Reder, 1979; Reder & Anderson, 1982) are subsumed under the theory-element EP. ACT^*'s explanation of so-called "depth of processing" effects in memory for facts is based on this element.

In our reconstruction we distinguish between three main kinds of *priming* studies to which ACT^* has been applied. In the priming paradigm subjects are presented with a prime which is followed by the target stimulus to which they have to respond. The judgment of the target can be facilitated or inhibited, depending on the prime-to-target relationship. All theory-elements in this domain of applications have special representational assumptions in common. Whereas in word naming tasks (WN) the presented stimulus has simply to be read, in lexical decision tasks (LD) an item has to be classified as a word or a nonword (Neely, 1977). The priming experiment which was conducted by Reder (1983) can be viewed as an exemplaric application of SJ. Reder used sentence stimuli which had to be classified as sensible or nonsensical. We expect that the special net for procedural learning can be constructed in a similar fashion.

In the course of the development of a complete theory-net for ACT^* we will get a better understanding of the *empirical content* of the theory-elements, and we will then be able to give a well- founded identification of the ***ACT*-theoretical terms***. At the moment, we can only conjecture that terms such as WM (working memory), a (activation), M (matching), g (degree of match), and tr (test rate) will turn out to be ACT^*-theoretical according to the informal criterion of theoreticity (see Sneed, 1979; Balzer, Moulines & Sneed, 1987). Terms like T (points of time), Cu (cognitive units), DM (declarative memory), DL (directly linked), E (outside stimuli), N (pattern nodes), and Prd (Productions) are likely to be ACT^*-non-theoretical. In addition, those terms that have been introduced for the experimental element FR-74 (E_s, B, and rt, for instance) can be characterized as ACT^*-non-theoretical.

Moreover, *constraints* which connect overlapping applications will be defined. According to Balzer, Moulines & Sneed (1987, p.46), ***"...constraints single out certain admissible combinations of potential models"***. Objects which occur in more than one potential model within such a combination satisfy certain requirements. If, for instance, in two information-processing systems the same combination of conditions is realized as a pattern node, a reasonable constraint will be the claim that the node should have an equal *"number of pattern tests to be performed"* in both systems, i.e. the corresponding functions *pt* and *pt'* in the two systems are required to have the same values for the node.

A comprehensive and successful structuralist reconstruction of *ACT** will not only help to eliminate the terminological and conceptual ambiguities of the verbal formulation of the theory; it will also lead to a specification of the *intertheoretical links* to other theories of cognition, emotion, motivation, and action control, to a better understanding of the connections to more general frameworks (such as the general information processing approach reconstructed by Ueckert, 1983), and to a clarification of the *implications of the theory for empirical research.* The last point seems to be of special importance, since most applications of the theory are post-hoc explanations of observations by the results of *ACT** computer simulations. There is a considerable lack of experimental studies planned to be valid tests of empirical hypotheses derived from the theory.

5 References

Anderson, J.R. (1974). Retrieval of propositional information from long-term memory. *Cognitive Psychology*, **6**, 451-474.

Anderson, J.R. (1983). *The architecture of cognition.* Cambridge, MA: Harvard University Press.

Anderson, J.R. (1984). Acquisition of proof skills in geometry. In R.S. Michalski, J.G. Carbonell & T.M. Mitchell (Eds.), *Machine learning.* New York: Springer-Verlag.

Anderson, J.R., Farrell, R., & Sauers, R. (1984). Learning to program in LISP. *Cognitive Science*, **8**, 87-129.

Balzer, W., Moulines, C.U., & Sneed, J.D. (1987). *An architectonic for science.* Dordrecht: Reidel.

Bradshaw, G.L., & Anderson, J.R. (1982). Elaborative encoding as an explanation of levels of processing. *Journal of Verbal Learning and Verbal Behavior*, **21**, 165-174.

Collins, A.M., & Loftus, E.F. (1975). A spreading-activation theory of semantic processing. *Psychological Review*, **82**, 407- 428.

Elio, R., & Anderson, J.R. (1981). Effects of category generalizations and instance similarity on schema abstraction. *Jornal of Experimental Psychology: Human Learning and Memory*, **7**, 397-417.

Forgy, C.L. (1979). *On the efficient implementation of production systems.* Unpublished Ph.D. dissertation. Carnegie- Mellon University, Pittsburgh.

McClelland, J.L., & Rumelhart, D.E. (1981). An interactive activation model of context effects in letter perception: pt.1. An account of basic findings. *Psychological Review*, **88**, 375-407.

Neely, J.H. (1977). Semantic priming and retrieval from lexical memory: roles of inhibitionsless spreading activation and limited-capacity attention. *Journal of Experimental Psychology: General*, **106**, 226-254.

Newell, A., & Simon, H.A. (1972). *Human problem solving.* Englewood Cliffs, NJ: Prentice-Hall.

Quillian, M.R. (1969). The teachable language comprehender. *Communications of the ACM*, **12**, 459-476.

Reder, L.M. (1979). The role of elaborations in memory for prose. *Cognitive Psychology*, **11**, 221-234.

Reder, L.M. (1982). Plausibility judgments versus fact retrieval: Alternative strategies for sentence verification. *Psychological Review*, **89**, 250-280.

Reder, L.M. (1983). What kind of pitcher can a catcher fill? Effects of priming in sentence comprehension. *Journal of Verbal Learning and Verbal Behavior*, **22**, 189-202.

Reder, L.M., & Anderson, J.R. (1982). Effects of spacing and embellishment on memory for the main points of a text. *Memory & Cognition*, **10**, 97-102.

Reder, L.M., & Ross, B.H. (1983). Integrated knowledge in different tasks: the role of retrieval strategy on fan effects. *Journal of Experimental Psychology: Learning, Memory, and Cognition*, **9**, 55-72.

Rumelhart, D.E., & McClelland, J.L. (1982). An interactive activation model of context effects in letter perception: pt. 2. The contextual enhancement effect and some tests and extensions of the model. *Psychological Review*, **89**, 60-94.

Sneed, J.D. (1979). *The logical structure of mathematical physics* (2nd ed.). Dordrecht: Reidel.

Stegmüller, W. (1976). *The structure and dynamics of theories.* Berlin: Springer-Verlag (Original work published 1973).

Stegmüller, W. (1986). *Theorie und Erfahrung: Dritter Teilband. Die Entwicklung des neuen Strukturalismus seit 1973 (Probleme und Resultate der Wissenschaftstheorie und Analytischen Philosophie, Band II).* Berlin: Springer-Verlag.

Ueckert, H. (1983). Computer-Simulation. In J. Bredenkamp & H. Feger (Hrsg.), *Hypothesenprüfung. (Enzyklopädie der Psychologie, Serie Forschungsmethoden der Psychologie: Band 5,* S. 530-616). Göttingen: Hogrefe.

Westermann, R. (1987). *Strukturalistische Theorienkonzeption und empirische Forschung in der Psychologie.* Berlin: Springer-Verlag.

Chapter 6

Structuralism as a Method of Theory Construction

The Example of the Social Psychological Role Conflict Theory[1]

Martti Kuokkanen

University of Helsinki

Abstract

Resting on the ideas of Gross, Mason and McEachern (1958) a generalized theory on role expectation conflicts is formulated and it is proved that their original theory is a special case of this generalization. It is shown that role conflict theory is adequately presentable as a theory-net precisely in the sense of structuralism. The generalized theory is formulated using specialization- and theoretization-relations as methodological means.

Some General Methodological Notes

The theory of Gross, Mason and McEachern (1958) states the creating of an informative, exact and simple system of prediction and explanation is its target, a theory with these features is very rare in social psychological theorizing. The theory is extremely simple when it is looked at logically. However, this theory is methodologically and philosophically very interesting because it is a "real" theory of the social realm, and it really seems to have some explanatory and predictive power. However, I intend to consider the empirical adequacy of the theory not at all. I will concentrate on the analysis of the theory from the point of view of the structuralist theory of science. The analysis supports very strongly the philosophical and methodological views of structuralism. In particular, the example of role conflict theory indicates that structuralism may serve as a method of theory construction. Consequently, structuralism is more than a philosophy of reconstruction of scientific theories.

The Role Conflict Theory

The potential application area of the theory of Gross, Mason and McEachern consists of rather typical every-day situations in which the social environment generates incompatible expectations for individuals, and so individuals are faced with role conflict situations. The role conflict theory is rather idealizing in the sense that it can conceptually handle only situations with two incompatible role expectations.

[1]Many thanks to Carol Norris and John Calton for correcting my English. The final version was written in Munich, June 1989. Thanks are due to Deutsche Forschungsgemeinschaft and to the Academy of Finland for a grant of the scientific exchange programme. Special thanks are due to Auli Kaipainen for excellent text processing and to Hans Westmeyer and Wolfgang Balzer for fruitful comments.

Denote the two incompatible role expectations with symbols A and B. The role conflict theory allows four different alternative ways to behave: First, individuals may notice the expectation A and behave in a way which satisfies the expectation A. Second, the same may happen with respect to the expectation B. Third, individuals may notice both of the expectations and behave in such a way that both of the expectations are (partially) satisfied, i.e. individuals try to seek a compromise. Finally the theory allows the possibility that individuals don't do (can't do) anything relevant in order to satisfy the expectations, i.e. they escape from the conflict situation.

The role conflict theory has rather strong targets from the point of view of the philosophy of science. The theory tries to give an explanatory account why individuals in a social situation of a given type behave in just the way they behave. The core of the theory is that individuals in a social role conflict situation structurize and evaluate the situation according to definite internalized principles, and these principles in turn determine without any residual the behavior of individuals. According to the role conflict theory there is an internal ("theoretical" or "psychological") dimension which functions as a central conceptual instrument for structurizing and evaluating the conflict situation. It is relevant to take into account whether none, one or both of the incompatible expectations are socially legitimated or not, on the other hand it is also relevant to see whether none, one or both of the expectations are socially sanctioned or not.

The theory can conceptually handle only such situations in which individuals structurize the expectations with appropriate actions either completely legitimated or completely not-legitimated. Hence, the theory can't take into account at all the degree of legitimation; this surely would be interesting and important at least theoretically. Individuals' view of both the sanction aspect of the expectations and appropriate actions is also dichotomized. The expectations with appropriate actions are either negatively sanctioned or not sactioned at all, i.e. omitting an action which is appropriate to satisfy a sanctioned expectation leads to punishment by society. Conceptually it is possible to introduce a function for degrees of legitimation and sanction, and in fact I will below revise the role conflict theory such that different degrees of legitimation and sanction are taken into account.

Next I represent the basic assumptions and axioms of the role conflict theory in a formally precise way. The theory needs no less than 34 axioms in order to handle conflict situations with only two incompatible expectations and four different ways of behavior. So, though the theory is really extremely uneconomic, it is, in any case, systematic.

The Effects of Legitimation of Expectations on Behavior

The basic assumption concerning the effect of legitimation of expectations on individuals' behavior is very simple. The theory proposes that if a person structurizes and evaluates the expectations of himself as legitimated he takes the expectations seriously into account and hence tries to act a way which satisfies these legitimated expectations. On the other hand, if a person doesn't structurize and evaluate an expectation, the case of A as legitimated is itself irrelevant according to the theory. Such cases have relevance relative only to the other expectation B. The same also holds in the case of sanction, so, the cases of non-legitimation and/or non-sanction of expectations have relevance only relative to each other. It is also worthy of note that the theory doesn't make a difference between the cases of legitimation, unlegitimation and indifference, or sanction, unsanction and indifference.

As above, denote the incompatible role expectations by symbols A and B and the relevant action alternatives as follows. Let a denote the type of action or an action token which satisfies expectation A; b denotes the type of action or an action token which satisfies expectation B; c denotes a compromise action (type), i.e. c satisfies partially both expectation A and expectation B. And finally let d denote the action alternative in which individuals escape from the conflict situation without being able to do anything relevant.

Moreover, let the symbol $L(A)$ denote the case where an individual structurizes and evaluates the expectation A as legitimated, and the symbol $\neg L(A)$ denote the case in which $L(A)$ doesn't hold. The symbols $L(B)$ and $\neg L(B)$ have the same meanings with respect to expectation B.

According to the role conflict theory if a person applies to the solution of a role conflict situation only the legitimation aspect, i.e. he/she structurizes and evaluates the legitimation aspect as the only relevant one, then his/her behavior is determined by the following assumptions or axioms:

L1 if $L(A)$ and $L(B)$ then c.
L2 if $L(A)$ and $\neg L(B)$ then a.
L3 if $\neg L(A)$ and $L(B)$ then b.
L4 if $\neg L(A)$ and $\neg L(B)$ then d.

The assumptions of legitimation on behavior are very simple. If the person structurizes and evaluates both of the expectations as legitimated, compromise-like behavior follows. If both of the expectations are non-legitimated, then the person escapes the situation. And finally the person's behavior satisfies the legitimated expectation if exactly one of the expectations is legitimated.

The Effects of Sanction of Expectations on Behavior

The basic assumption concerning the sanction of alternative behaviors is as follows. If a person believes that in a role conflict situation the neglecting of some role expectation leads to a rather strong execution of sanctions or punishment, then the person tends to behave in a way which satisfies the role expectation in order to avoid the sanctions.

Let the symbol $S(A)$ denote the case where an individual structurizes and evaluates the expectation A as sanctioned, i.e. neglecting the behavior token (the behavior of type) a generates a rather strong punishment, and $\neg S(A)$ refers to the case in which $S(A)$ doesn't hold. The symbols $S(B)$ and $\neg S(B)$ have the same meanings with respect to expectation B. Now the basic assumption concerning the effects of sanction on behavior are as follows:

S1 if $S(A)$ and $S(B)$ then c.
S2 if $\neg S(A)$ and $S(B)$ then b.
S3 if $S(A)$ and $\neg S(B)$ then a.

According to the theory, persons behave in a compromise-like way in situations in which they believe that both of the relevant role expectations and action tokens are sanctioned. And if persons believe that only one of the two expectations is sanctioned they tend to behave in a way to satisfy this expectation. The theory gives no behavior prediction if persons believe that expectations with associated action tokens are not at all sanctioned.

The Compound Effects of Legitimation and Sanction on Behavior

The considerations above differentiate between the effects of legitimation and sanction. However, the theory assumes very realistically that in order to solve the role expectation conflict situation persons apply both of these principles at the same time. On the other hand, the theory assumes prima facie a little unrealistically that the concepts of legitimation and sanction are independent of each other, and so there are no less than 16 different situations to consider. In seven of these 16 cases it is assumed that both of the principles can be applied without any qualifications. According to the theory these seven cases are adequately captured by the following axioms which generate appropriate behavior predictions as follows (cf. Gross, Mason & McEachern, 1958, pp. 281 - 318):

A1	if	$L(A)$,	$S(A)$,	$L(B)$	and	$S(B)$	then	c.
A4	if	$L(A)$,	$\neg S(A)$,	$L(B)$	and	$\neg S(B)$	then	c.
A7	if	$L(A)$,	$S(A)$,	$\neg L(B)$	and	$\neg S(B)$	then	a.
A8	if	$L(A)$,	$\neg S(A)$,	$\neg L(B)$	and	$\neg S(B)$	then	a.
A10	if	$\neg L(A)$,	$\neg S(A)$,	$L(B)$	and	$S(B)$	then	b.
A12	if	$\neg L(A)$,	$\neg S(A)$,	$L(B)$	and	$\neg S(B)$	then	b.
A16	if	$\neg L(A)$,	$\neg S(A)$,	$\neg L(B)$	and	$\neg S(B)$	then	d.

In the situation referred to by axiom $A1$ a person behaves in a compromise- like way because he/she structurizes and evaluates both expectations as both legitimated and sanctioned. Axiom $A4$ gives a special case of the situation of $A1$. $A7$ refers to the situation in which a person structurizes and evaluates expectation A as both legitimated and sanctioned, while expectation B is neither legitimated nor sanctioned; therefore an action type satisfying A follows. $A8$ refers to the situation which is a special case of the situation of $A7$. Axioms $A10$ and $A12$ both handle the situations with respect to the expectation B. In the situation of $A16$ the theory predicts escape-type behavior because in such a situation a person structurizes and evaluates neither expectation as legitimated or sanctioned.

According to the theory the following situations are problematic, and the principles of legitimation and sanction can't be applied together without qualification. First if a person structurizes and evaluates one of the expectations as sanctioned but not legitimated and the other one as not sanctioned but legitimated, the theory needs qualifications. Second, if there are two legitimated expectations sanctioned in the opposite way with respect to each other the theory gives no behavior predictions without qualifications. And third, a situation with non-legitimated expectations which are sanctioned in the opposite way is problematic.

The notion of *orientation of expectation* is introduced into the theory in order to handle these problematic situations. The basic idea is as follows: A person's orientation of expectation determines a person's fundamental attitude to the resolution of the role conflict situation. A person exemplifies *a moral orientation of expectation* if he/she structurizes and evaluates the conflict situation primarily in respect to its legitimation aspect of expectations. Thus, the behavior of a morally oriented person depends primarily on whether the role expectations are legitimated or not. In ethical terms, such a person's behavior might be seen as exemplifying deontic principles.

If a person structurizes and evaluates the conflict situation primarily depending upon whether the expectations are sanctioned or not then he/she is exemplifying *an expedient orientation of expectation.* In a role conflict situation, the behavior of an expedient oriented person thus depends primarily on whether the expectations are sanctioned or not. In ethical terms, such a person's behavior exemplifies utilitarian principles.

The role conflict theory introduces also a third, "mixed" type of orientation of expectation. A *"morally-expedient"* or *"mixed orientation"* person combines appropriately both the legitimation aspect and the sanction aspect in order to resolve the problematic role conflict situation.

The theory may be qualified to handle also these troublesome situations, if the theory assumes that the assumptions $A1, A4, A7, A8, A10, A12$ and $A16$ and consequently the notions of legitimation and sanction in suitable situations are independent of the notion of orientation of expectation. The orientation of expectation thus has no methodologically relevant role at all with respect to the behavior of persons in these seven cases, though according to the theory in the other nine cases this concept has a very central explanatory role.

The Pure Moral Orientation of Expectation

The basic assumptions concerning the behavior of a person with a pure moral orientation of expectation are the following. A person who structurizes and evaluates only one of the two role expectations as legitimated behaves so as to satisfy legitimated expectation and to avoid the behavior which satisfies the expectation not structurized and evaluated as legitimated. Sanction thus has no role at all if the person exemplifies a moral orientation of expectation. Applied to the rest of possible situations this assumption therefore generates the following axioms:

MoA2	if	$L(A)$,	$\neg S(A)$,	$L(B)$	and	$S(B)$	then c.
MoA3	if	$L(A)$,	$S(A)$,	$L(B)$	and	$\neg S(B)$	then c.
MoA5	if	$L(A)$,	$S(A)$,	$\neg L(B)$	and	$S(B)$	then a.
MoA6	if	$L(A)$,	$\neg S(A)$,	$\neg L(B)$	and	$S(B)$	then a.
MoA9	if	$\neg L(A)$,	$S(A)$,	$L(B)$	and	$S(B)$	then b.
MoA11	if	$\neg L(A)$,	$S(A)$,	$L(B)$	and	$\neg S(B)$	then b.
MoA13	if	$\neg L(A)$,	$S(A)$,	$\neg L(B)$	and	$S(B)$	then d.
MoA14	if	$\neg L(A)$,	$\neg S(A)$,	$\neg L(B)$	and	$S(B)$	then d.
MoA15	if	$\neg L(A)$,	$S(A)$,	$\neg L(B)$	and	$\neg S(B)$	then d.

If there are two legitimated role expectations (MoA2, MoA3) then a person exemplifying a moral orientation of expectation makes a compromise between these expectations by his/her action. If there is no legitimated role expectation (MoA13, MoA14 and MoA15), a person exemplifying such an orien- tation of expectation escapes the conflict situation. In the rest of the cases a morally oriented person satisfies the role expectation which he/she structurizes and evaluates as legitimated (MoA5, MoA6, MoA9 and MoA11).

The Pure Expedient Orientation of Expectation

A person exemplifying an expedient orientation of expectation structurizes and evaluates expectations depending on whether or not the expectations are sanctioned. The basic assumption is that such a person tries to avoid any behavior which produces sanctions. The sanctioned consequences of action alternatives and role expectations thus are relevant factors which determine the behavior of a person exemplifying an expedient orientation of expectation. The axioms are as follows:

EA2	if	$L(A)$,	$\neg S(A)$,	$L(B)$	and	$S(B)$	then	b.
EA3	if	$L(A)$,	$S(A)$,	$L(B)$	and	$\neg S(B)$	then	a.
EA5	if	$L(A)$,	$S(A)$,	$\neg L(B)$	and	$S(B)$	then	c.
EA6	if	$L(A)$,	$\neg S(A)$,	$\neg L(B)$	and	$S(B)$	then	b.
EA9	if	$\neg L(A)$,	$S(A)$,	$L(B)$	and	$S(B)$	then	c.
EA11	if	$\neg L(A)$,	$S(A)$,	$L(B)$	and	$\neg S(B)$	then	a.
EA13	if	$\neg L(A)$,	$S(A)$,	$\neg L(B)$	and	$S(B)$	then	c.
EA14	if	$\neg L(A)$,	$\neg S(A)$,	$\neg L(B)$	and	$S(B)$	then	b.
EA15	if	$\neg L(A)$,	$S(A)$,	$\neg L(B)$	and	$\neg S(B)$	then	a.

If an expedient oriented person structurizes and evaluates only one of the role expectations as sanctioned he/she tends to satisfy the sanctioned expectation (EA2, EA3, EA6, EA11, EA14 and EA15). In the rest of the cases both of the expectations are sanctioned, so the expedient person makes a compromise (EA5, EA9 and EA13). Next, consider the third type of orientation, the moral-expedient or mixed orientation.

The Mixed Orientation of Expectation

The basic assumption here is that the behavior of a mixed oriented person in a conflict situation is determined by both the legitimation aspect and the sanction aspect. The mixed oriented person structurizes and evaluates the conflict situation using disjunctively both of these aspects. So the axioms concerning the behavior of a mixed oriented person are as follows:

MiA2	if	$L(A)$,	$\neg S(A)$,	$L(B)$	and	$S(B)$	then	b.
MiA3	if	$L(A)$,	$S(A)$,	$L(B)$	and	$\neg S(B)$	then	a.
MiA5	if	$L(A)$,	$S(A)$,	$\neg L(B)$	and	$S(B)$	then	a.
MiA6	if	$L(A)$,	$\neg S(A)$,	$\neg L(B)$	and	$S(B)$	then	c.
MiA9	if	$\neg L(A)$,	$S(A)$,	$L(B)$	and	$S(B)$	then	b.
MiA11	if	$\neg L(A)$,	$S(A)$,	$L(B)$	and	$\neg S(B)$	then	c.
MiA13	if	$\neg L(A)$,	$S(A)$,	$\neg L(B)$	and	$S(B)$	then	c.
MiA14	if	$\neg L(A)$,	$\neg S(A)$,	$\neg L(B)$	and	$S(B)$	then	b.
MiA15	if	$\neg L(A)$,	$S(A)$,	$\neg L(B)$	and	$\neg S(B)$	then	a.

If two expectations are to the same "degree" legitimated and/or sanctioned, a person with a mixed orientation tends to make a compromise (MiA6, MiA11, MiA13). The rest of the cases illustrate the situation in which one of the two expectations is "more" legitimated and/or sanctioned than the other, so the person with a mixed orientation tends to satisfy such an expectation by his/her behavior.

The Applications of the Role Conflict Theory

Gross, Mason and McEachern applied their theory to the role conflict situations of school superintendents in Massachusetts. The superintendents were classified into the three categories of orientation of expectation by their answers to a questionnaire. Then relevant behavior predictions were formulated using the theory. The role conflict theory predicted the role conflict resolution correctly in 264 of the 291 (91 percent) role conflict cases of different types. Later the theory was applied to the resolution of role conflict of four different groups: two groups of business executives, a group of company training directors, and a group of labor leaders. The overall accuracy of the predictive ability of the theory was 71 percent. The theory was also applied in studies of police officers and police trainees with roughly the same accuracy of predictions as above. Hence, the theory might be evaluated as a rather succesful explanatory and predictive account especially relative to its structural and conceptual simplicity.

The Generalization of the Role Conflict Theory

The Gross, Mason and McEachern theory is rather interesting in many respects from the point of view of the philosophy of science. The explanatory concepts of the theory are the categories of legitimation and sanction and the notion of orientation of expectation. The notion of orientation of expectation is explicitly definable in the theory using terms of application of legitimation and sanction, i.e. the notion of orientation of expectation is irrelevant from the logical point of view of deductive systematization.

The central concepts of the role conflict theory are not theoretical in the modern pragmatico-semantical sense, but rather in the classical positivist sense (cf. Balzer, Moulines & Sneed, 1987, and Tuomela, 1973, for discussion of theoreticity). It is clear that neither the use of the notions of orientation of expectation, legitimation and sanction nor the empirical fixation of the type of orientation of expectation, legitimation and sanction presuppose the assumption of the truth of the theory in its applications. Rather, from the methodological point of view, some kind of conceptual certainty of the applicability of the conceptual machinery of the theory is sufficient and adequate. It is no surprise, therefore, that one of the main tasks of theoretical and methodological work with the role theory approach has been the creation of a theory-independent language or conceptual framework. This aspect has been one central methodological problem especially in the theoretical discussion concerning roles (see as typical examples, Gross, Mason & McEachern, 1958, pp. 3 - 75; Biddle & Thomas, 1966, pp. 3 - 63; Secord & Backman, 1964, pp. 449 - 520; and Sarbin & Allen, 1968). The notion of orientation of expectation is of special interest in this respect. This notion then, i.e. a way to classify individuals according to their "orientation" to certain given social situations, is theoretical in the modern pragmatico-semantical sense - not relative to the role conflict theory, but to the questionnaire (cf. 2.7) with its statistical techniques which furnishes criteria by which to classify persons into those relevant orientation types presupposed by the entire theory.

A Generalized Version of the Role Conflict Theory

The role conflict theory has one very restrictive feature. Conceptually it can only take account of the social conflict situations in which there exist exactly two incompatible role expectations with four four types of action or tokens. The following proposal represents a generalization of the role conflict theory. This generalized theory allows the number of incompatible role expectations with associated action alternatives to increase without any practical limit, i.e. the generalized theory can conceptually handle n incompatible role expectations with $n+2$ actions (n for any finite number).

Denote by the symbols $E_1, ...E_n$ the n incompatible role expectations and let $a_1, ...a_n$ denote the actions which satisfy the appropriate expectations, i.e. each a_i satisfies its appropriate role expectation E_i. Let c and d denote respectively compromise behavior and escape behavior as above. Hence, $E = \{E_1, ...E_n\}$ denotes the finite set of mutually incompatible role expectations and $A = \{a_1, ...a_n, c, d\}$ denotes the relevant finite set of actions.

Consider next a finite set
$X = E \times A = \{\langle E_1, a_1\rangle, \langle E_1, a_2\rangle, ...\langle E_2, a_1\rangle, \langle E_2, a_2\rangle, ...\langle E_n, c\rangle, \langle E_n, d\rangle\}$.
The set X yields all possible combinations of mutually incompatible role expectations and alternative actions.

Now let us introduce the principles of legitimation and sanction and the principle of combined legitimation and sanction using exact set-theoretical means, i.e. functions. Consider a function $f_L : E \Rightarrow \{0, 1\}$ which satisfies the following conditions:

$$(1) \qquad f_L(E_i) = \begin{cases} 0 & \text{iff a person recognizes role} \\ & \text{expectation } E_i \text{ as non-legitimated;} \\ 1 & \text{iff a person recognizes role} \\ & \text{expectation } E_i \text{ as legitimated.} \end{cases}$$

Hence, $D_I(f_L) = E, D_{II}(f_L) = \{0, 1\}$. We can simply call function f_L a legitimation function. Completely analogously, we define a sanction function as follows : A sanction function is of form $f_S : E \Rightarrow \{0, 1\}$ which satisfies the following conditions:

$$(2) \qquad f_S(E_i) = \begin{cases} 0 & \text{iff a person recognizes role} \\ & \text{expectation } E_i \text{ as non-sanctioned;} \\ 1 & \text{iff a person recognizes role} \\ & \text{expectation } E_i \text{ as sanctioned.} \end{cases}$$

So, sanction function f_S is formally completely analogous to legitimation function f_L; $D_I(f_S) = E = D_I(f_L)$ and $D_{II}(f_S) = \{0, 1\} = D_{II}(f_L)$. However, their contents are intuitively different as they should be. Finally, we define a derived concept, a justification function using legitimation and sanction functions. A justification function is of the form $f : E \Rightarrow \{0, 1, 2\}$ which satisfies the following conditions:

$$(3) \qquad f(E_i) = \begin{cases} 0 & \text{if } f_L(E_i) + f_S(E_i) = 0; \\ 1 & \text{if } f_L(E_i) + f_S(E_i) = 1; \\ 2 & \text{if } f_L(E_i) + f_S(E_i) = 2. \end{cases}$$

Later we shall have a proof that the concepts defined above are really adequate to capture the content of the Gross-Mason-McEachern theory on role expectation conflicts. Next we can construct a generalized theory on role expectation conflicts using essentially the formal means and terms of structuralist philosophy of science. First, we identify the set of partial possible models for the generalized theory as set M_{pp},

(4) $M_{pp} = \{X : X \in Po(E \times A), X \neq \emptyset, E = \{E_1, ...E_n\}$ is a finite set of mutually incompatible role expectations and $A = \{a_1, ...a_n, c, d\}$ is a finite set of related actions$\}$.

Next the set of possible models for the generalized theory is identified as set M_p,

(5) $M_p = \{\langle X, f_L^X, f_S^X, f^X \rangle\}$

in which component X is as defined by clause (4) above and components f_L^X, f_S^X and f^X are restrictions of functions f_L, f_S and f relative to X.

The set of models for the generalized theory is identified as a set M, $M \subseteq M_p$,

(6) $M = \{\langle X^*, f_L, f_S, f \rangle : X^* \in M_{pp}$ and the following conditions are satisfied with respect to X^* :
1) $X^* = \{x^*\} = \{\langle E_i, a_i \rangle\}$ if there exists an $E_i \in E$ such that $f(E_i) > f(E_j)$ for any $E_j \in E, i \neq j$;
2) $X^* = \{\langle E_i, c \rangle, ...\langle E_j, c \rangle\}$ if there are $E_i, ...E_j \in E, i \neq ... \neq j$ such that $f(E_i) = ... = f(E_j) > 0$;
3) $X^* = \{\langle E_1, d \rangle, \langle E_2, d \rangle, ...\langle E_n, d \rangle\}$ if $f(E_i) = 0$ for any $E_i \in E\}$.

The set of models for the generalized theory, M contains precisely the elements of the set of possible models, M_p which satisfy the axioms 1) - 3) of definition (6) above. These axioms have the following intuitive content: Axiom 1) says that if E contains one expectation which is more justified than the other ones then this expectation is registered and persons try to satisfy this expectation by performing the relevant action (type) a_i. Axiom 2) says that if in E there are several expectations which are justified to the same extent then all of them are registered and a compromise follows. Finally, axiom 3) says that if none of the expectations in E are justified then escape behavior follows.

Next we turn to the problem of the existence of constraints for the generalized theory. There clearly is at least one candidate for a constraint. It is at least in some types of role conflict situations very natural and methodologically important to require that the legitimation function, the sanction function and the justification function are conservative. This requirement has the following content:

Consider $y_1 = \langle X^1, f_L^1, f_S^1, f^1 \rangle$ and $y_2 = \langle X^2, f_L^2, f_S^2, f^2 \rangle, y_1, y_2 \in M_p$. Let $X^1 \cap X^2 \neq \emptyset$. Then it follows from the definitions of functions f_L, f_S and f that $E^* = E_1 \cap E_2$, the intersection of the domains of functions f_L^1 and f_L^2, functions f_S^1 and f_S^2 and functions f^1 and f^2 is non-empty. Then it is very natural to require that the role expectations in E^* should be legitimated/sanctioned or non-legitimated/non-sanctioned to the same extent by a person. If such a requirement is not satisfied then the justification of a role expectation may depend rather heavily on the context, i.e. on the (justification of) the other expectations which are included in E_1 and E_2. Then varying E_1 and E_2 may yield different justification for the one and the same role expectation E_i in E^*. Such a case seems to be rather realistic, too, in some situations. Hence, a conservative constraint for the generalized theory really is methodologically extremely important, because accepting/ rejecting it yields completely different types for the resolution of role conflicts.

The related restrictive conditions read as follows:

$$(7)\quad \begin{cases} (a) & \text{for any } y_i, y_j \in Y, Y \subseteq M_p : \\ & \text{if } E_i \in D_I(f_L^i) \cap D_I(f_L^j) \text{ then } f_L^i(E_i) = f_L^j(E_i) \\ (b) & \text{for any } y_i, y_j \in Y, Y \subseteq M_p : \\ & \text{if } E_i \in D_I(f_S^i) \cap D_I(f_S^j) \text{ then } f_S^i(E_i) = f_S^j(E_i) \\ (c) & \text{for any } y_i, y_j \in Y, Y \subseteq M_p : \\ & \text{if } E_i \in D_I(f^i) \cap D_I(f^j) \text{ then } f^i(E_i) = f^j(E_i) \end{cases}$$

Note that clause (7c) is redundant in the sense that clauses (7a and b) together imply clause (7c). This follows from the fact that functions f_L and f_S completely define, or determine function f.

Consider now a constraint for the generalized theory which is identified as set C,

(8) $C = \{Y : Y \subseteq M_p, Y \neq \emptyset$ and for any $y_i, y_j \in Y$:
if $E_i \in D_I(f_L^i) \cap D_I(f_L^j)$ then $f_L^i(E_i) = f_L^j(E_i)$ and
if $E_i \in D_I(f_S^i) \cap D_I(f_S^j)$ then $f_S^i(E_i) = f_S^j(E_i)\}$.

Next we show that set C, defined by formula (8) and clauses (7a,b) really satisfies the defining conditions of constraints. A "transitive" constraint $C \subseteq Po(M_p)$ should satisfy the following conditions (cf. Balzer, Moulines & Sneed, 1987):

(i) $\emptyset \notin C$,
(ii) if $y \in M_p$ then $\{y\} \in C$ and
(iii) if $Y, Y' \in Po(M_p), Y, Y' \neq \emptyset, Y' \subseteq Y$ and $Y \in C$ then $Y' \in C$.

That a C, defined in formula (8), is a constraint is shown only relative to condition (7a). The proof relative to condition (7b) is completely analogous. And finally conditions (7a,b) together yield the related constraint for f.

Claim 1 : $\emptyset \notin C$. This follows immediately from definition (8).
Claim 2 : if $y \in M_p$ then $\{y\} \in C$. Consider $y_i, y_j \in M_p$. Let $i = j$. Then condition (7,a) is automatically satisfied in particular, because $f_L^i = f_L^j$.
Claim 3 : Let $Y \in C$, $Y' \subseteq Y$. Then $Y' \in C$. Consider an arbitrary $Y = \{y_1, ...y_n : y_1, ...y_n \in M_p\}$. Let $Y \in C$. First, assume that for any $y_i, y_j \in Y, i \neq j$ it holds that : $D_I(f_L^i) \cap D_{II}(f_L^j) = \emptyset$. Then $y_i \in C$ and $y_j \in C$ which was shown in claim 2 above. Second, assume that for arbitrary $y_i, y_j \in Y, i \neq j$ it holds that : $D_I(f_L^i) \cap D_I(f_L^j) \neq \emptyset$. Then it follows from condition (7a) that if $E_i \in D_I(f_L^i) \cap D_I(f_L^j)$ then $f_L^i(E_i) = f_L^j(E_i)$. On the other hand, condition (7a) in no way restricts parts $f_L^i \backslash f_L^i \cap f_L^j$ and $f_L^j \backslash f_L^i \cap f_L^j$ of functions f_L^i and f_L^j. But then $\{y_i\} \in C$, $\{y_j\} \in C$ and in particular $\{y_i, y_j\} \in C$.

Finally, consider the set of intended applications I for the generalized theory. The only adequate candidate for intended applications is a non-empty part of M_{pp}. Hence, we can identify intended applications by the following clause

(9) $I \subseteq M_{pp}$.

In the above we have defined all the relevant components of the structuralist concepts of a theory-core and a theory-element for the generalized theory. We then arrive at the point where

(10) $G = \langle M_p, M, M_{pp}, C\rangle$

is the theory-core of the generalized role conflict theory and

(11) $GRCT = \langle G, I\rangle$

is the related theory-element of the generalized role conflict theory. Finally, the theory-claim of the generalized theory reads as follows:

(12) All elements $x_1 = \langle E_1, a_1\rangle, ...x_m = \langle E_m, a_m\rangle \in I$ are expandable to structures $y_1 = \langle X^1, f_L^1, f_S^1, f^1\rangle, ...y_m = \langle X^m, f_L^m, f_S^m, f^m\rangle$ such that $y_1, ...y_m \in Po(M) \cap C$.

Two notes are in order. First, in order to achieve a more detailed formulation for the generalized theory of role conflicts, a finite set of persons, $P = \{p_1, ...p_m\}$ should be taken into account. If "personal differences" relative to resolutions of role conflicts would be incorporated then the definitions above should be slightly modified. We then had instead of the domains of functions f_L, f_S and f (see definitions 1, 2 and 3) the following: $D_I(f_L) = D_I(f_S) = D_I(f)$ would be set $P \times E$. Technically it is convenient to introduce this modification into the components of elements of M_p as an extra index p for persons. However, for simplicity this is not done.

Second, according to the conventions of structuralism, our formulation of the generalized role conflict theory indicates that role expectations and actions, or tokens are the non-theoretical components whilst the legitimation function, the sanction function and the justification function are the theoretical components. But this is not at all obvious. Structuralists have shown that there exist several adequate criteria of theoreticity (cf. Balzer, Moulines & Sneed, 1987). So, it is not claimed that the legitimation function, the sanction function and the justification function are theoretical components and the other ones are non-theoretical. The theoreticity problem should be studied in more detail in a broader context of application of the theory. On the other hand, if we consider the methodological roles of the concepts of the generalized role conflict theory from the point of view of scientific explanation, then the legitimation function, the sanction function and the justification function clearly work as the ***explanatory concepts*** of the theory. Consider the question "Why did p do a_i in such and such a situation?". The answer would be that p recognized the role expectation E_i as justified whilst the other expectations were not justified.

A Theory-Net for GRCT

In this section we study the relationship between the generalized theory and the theory of Gross, Mason and McEachern. In particular, we show that the latter theory contains three partially incompatible theory-elements in the structuralist sense, and each of these three theory-elements is a specialization of the generalized theory in that sense. Let M stand for the set of models of the generalized theory-element $GRCT$, let M_1 stand for the set of models of the Gross-Mason-McEachern theory-element with mixed orientation, let M_2 stand for the set of models of the Gross-Mason-McEachern theory-element with moral orientation and finally let M_3 stand for the set of models of the Gross-Mason-McEachern theory-element with expedient orientation. We will show that the following relations hold between these sets of models:

(13a) $M_1 \subset M, M_2 \subset M$ and $M_3 \subset M$;
(13b) $M_2 \cap M_3 \neq \emptyset, M_2 \cap M_1 \neq \emptyset$ and $M_3 \cap M_1 \neq \emptyset$.

The following figure illustrates the related theory-net:

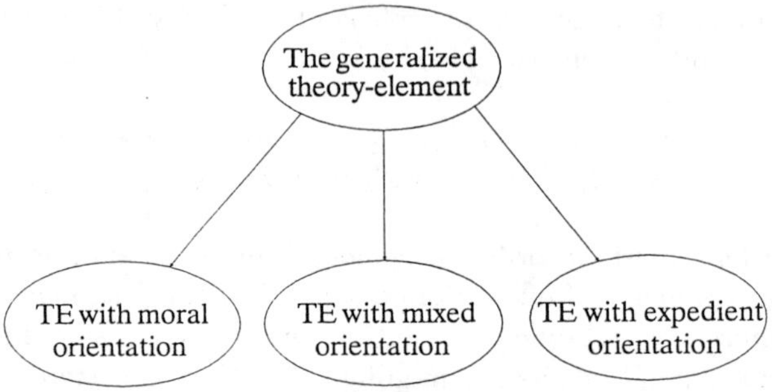

Here the arrows indicate the specialization-relation of structuralism.

Start with the set of models for $GRCT$ which was identified as set $M = \{\langle X^*, f_L, f_S, f\rangle\}$. The elements $\langle X^*, f_L, f_S, f\rangle$ of M satisfy the following conditions:

0) $X^* \in M_{pp}$;

1) $X^* = \{x^*\} = \{\langle E_i, a_i\rangle\}$ if there exists an $E_i \in E$ such that $f(E_i) > f(E_j)$ for any $E_j \in E, i \neq j$;

2) $X^* = \{\langle E_i, c\rangle, ...\langle E_j, c\rangle\}$ if there are $E_i, ...E_j \in E, i \neq j$ such that $f(E_i) = ... = f(E_j) > 0$;

3) $X^* = \{\langle E_1, d\rangle, \langle E_2, d\rangle, ...\langle E_n, d\rangle\}$ if $f(E_i) = 0$ for any $E_i \in E$.

Restrict the functions f_L, f_S and consequently the function f in $y \in M$ by the following two clauses:

(14a) $D_I(f_L^1) = \{E_1, E_2\} = E^1, D_I(f_L^1) \subset D_I(f_L)$
(14b) $D_I(f_S^1) = \{E_1, E_2\} = E^1, D_I(f_S^1) \subset D_I(f_S)$.

Then the domains of functions f_L and f_S reduce to $\{E_1, E_2\}$. Consequently $f_L^1 \subset f_L$, $f_S^1 \subset f_S$ and $f^1 \subset f$.

Restricting A to $A^1 = \{a_1, a_2, c, d\}$ yields set $X^1 = E^1 \times A^1$ with $X^1 = \{\langle E_1, a_1\rangle, \langle E_1, a_2\rangle, \langle E_2, a_1\rangle, \langle E_2, a_2\rangle, \langle E_1, c\rangle, \langle E_2, c\rangle, \langle E_1, d\rangle, \langle E_2, d\rangle\}$. Then $X^1 \in M_{pp}$. Finally, consider the set of intended applications of the new theory-core. It is evident that $I_1 \subseteq E^1 \times A^1 \subseteq I$. Hence, $I_1 \subseteq I$.

In the above we have constructed a new theory-element $RCT_1 = \langle G_1, I_1\rangle$ in which G_1, the related theory-core, is the structure $\langle M_p, M_1, M_{pp}, C\rangle$. Here M_1 is defined by assumptions 1)

- 3) of the theory-core G of the generalized role conflict theory plus the restrictive special assumptions (14a,b). Hence, $M_1 \subseteq M$ holds. The other components of theory-core G_1 are precisely the same as the related components of theory-core G. Finally, noting that $I_1 \subseteq I$, justifies the theory-element RCT_1 as a specialization of theory-element $GRCT$.

It is interesting to note that the specialization above is yielded purely by restricting the interpretations of the concepts. From a model theoretical point of view this relation is the sub-model/extension relation $y' \sqsubset y$, i.e. if $y' = \langle D'_1, ...D'_m, f'_1, ...f'_k \rangle$ and $y = \langle D_1, ...D_m, f_1, ...f_k \rangle$ then $D'_i \subseteq D_i, f'_j \subseteq f_j, D'_i \neq \emptyset, f'_j \neq \emptyset$ for any $i = 1, ...m$ and for any $j = 1, ...k$. However, a methodologically more interesting specialization may be yielded by adding some extra laws, i.e. some extra assumptions on the interdependency of interpretations of the concepts of a theory.

Next it is shown that the set of models M_1 of theory-element RCT_1 is adequate to capture the content of Gross', Mason's and McEachern's role conflict theory in the sense that M_1 contains precisely the models for axioms A1, A4, A7, A8, A10, A12, A16, Mia2, MiA3, MiA5, MiA6, MiA9, MiA11, MiA13, MiA14 and MiA15.

Let E^1 and A^1 be as follows: $E^1 = \{A, B\}$, and $A^1 = \{a, b, c, d\}$.

Consider clauses 1) - 3) of the definition of M_1. There are the following value combinations for $f(A)$ and $f(B)$:

$f(A)$	$f(B)$	clauses 1) - 3) yield X^*	whence axiom
2	2	$\{\langle A, c\rangle, \langle B, c\rangle\}$	A1 is satisfied in $\langle X^*, f^1_L, f^1_S, f^1\rangle$
1	1	$\{\langle A, c\rangle, \langle B, c\rangle\}$	A4 is satisfied in $\langle X^*, f^1_L, f^1_S, f^1\rangle$ as well as are axioms MiA6, MiA11 and MiA13
2	0	$\{\langle A, a\rangle\}$	A7 is satisfied in $\langle X^*, f^1_L, f^1_S, f^1\rangle$
1	0	$\{\langle A, a\rangle\}$	A8 is satisfied as well as is MiA15 in $\langle X^*, f^1_L, f^1_S, f^1\rangle$
0	2	$\{\langle B, b\rangle\}$	A10 is satisfied in $\langle X^*, f^1_L, f^1_S, f^1\rangle$
0	1	$\{\langle B, b\rangle\}$	A12 is satisfied as well as MiA14 is in $\langle X^*, f^1_L, f^1_S, f^1\rangle$
0	0	$\{\langle A, d\rangle, \langle B, d\rangle\}$	A16 is satisfied in $\langle X^*, f^1_L, f^1_S, f^1\rangle$
1	2	$\{\langle B, b\rangle\}$	MiA2 is satisfied as well as MiA9 is in $\langle X^*, f^1_L, f^1_S, f^1\rangle$
2	1	$\{\langle A, a\rangle\}$	MiA3 is satisfied as well as MiA5 is in $\langle X^*, f^1_L, f^1_S, f^1\rangle$

Hence, it is shown that theory-element RCT_1 contains exactly the content of Gross', Mason's and McEachern's role conflict theory with mixed orientation and without any orientation. Adding an extra assumption

(15) for any $E_i, i = 1, 2, E_i \in E^1 : f^1_S(E_i) = 0$

to clauses (14a,b) and to defining clauses of M of $GRCT$, yields a theory-element RCT_2 such that it holds for M_2, the set of models of RCT_2, that $M_2 \subseteq M$ and for I_2, the related set of intended applications $I_2 \subseteq I$. Then RCT_2 is a specialization of $GRCT$. Moreover, RCT_2 is adequate for the Gross', Mason's and McEachern's role conflict theory in the sense that M_2 contains precisely the models for axioms A1 - A16 plus MoA2, MoA3, MoA5, MoA6, MoA9, MoA11, MoA13, MoA14 and MoA15. The interested reader may easily verify these claims.

Completely analogously, adding two extra assumptions

(16a) for any $E_i, i = 1, 2, E_i \in E^1 : f_L^1(E_i) = 0$
(16b) for any $E_i, i = 1, 2, E_i \in E^1 : \langle E_i, d\rangle \notin X^*$
to clauses (14a,b) and to defining clauses of M of $GRCT$ yields a theory-element RCT_3 which is a specialization of $GRCT$. Respectively, as in the cases above, M_3 contains precisely the models for axioms A1 - A16 plus EA2, EA3, EA5, EA6, EA9, EA11, EA13, EA14 and EA15. Assumption (16a) is self-explanatory. Assumption (16b) is justified by the basic assumption of role conflict theory for the effects of sanction: if $\neg S(A)$ and $\neg S(B)$ then the action is completely unspecified. These claims are easily checked by the same means as above.

Hence, the relation of sets of models M_1, M_2 and M_3 is presentable as the following figure.

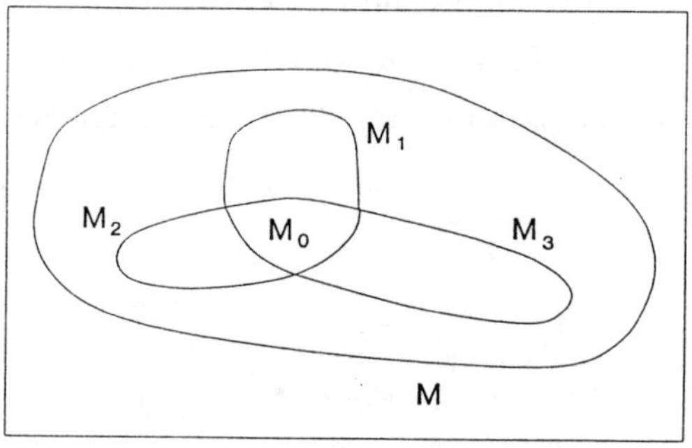

M_0 contains precisely the models for axioms A1, A4, A7, A8, A10, A12 and A16, i.e. M_0 characterizes the mutually compatible content of theory- elements RCT_1, RCT_2 and RCT_3. $M_1 \backslash M_0$, $M_2 \backslash M_0$ and $M_3 \backslash M_0$ characterize the mutually incompatible content of these theory-elements. Finally, recall that M_1, M_2 and M_3 together as well as separately, form a part of the set of models, M for the basic-element $GRCT$ of the related theory-net.

A Generalized Theory-Element of Role Conflict Theory with Different Degrees of Justification

Consider finally one way of enriching the generalized theory-element of role conflicts by introducing a function for the different degrees of justification. Consider $E_i, E_j \in E$. Assume that the justification function f gives the following values for E_i and E_j : $f(E_i) = 0$ and $f(E_j) = 1$. Then we may say that role expectation E_j is justified at least to the same extent as E_i. In general we define: for any $E_i, E_j \in E$: E_i is justified at least to the same extent as E_j only if $f(E_i) \geq f(E_j)$.

Consider now a weak ordering relation $R \subseteq E \times E$, which is defined as follows:

(17) $R = \{\langle E_i, E_j\rangle : f(E_i) \geq 1$ and E_i is justified at least to the same extent as $E_j\}$.

Condition $f(E_i) \geq 1$ derives from the fact that if $f(E_i) = 0$ then expectation E_i is not at all justified. So, the cases of form $\langle E_i, E_j \rangle, f(E_i) = 0, f(E_j) = 0$ are excluded from R, although it can be said rather trivially in such cases that E_i is justified at least to the same extent as E_j. Note that condition "$f(E_i) \geq f(E_j)$" is only a necessary condition for relation R.

Obviously relation R is reflexive and transitive in set E. Clearly it holds: $f(E_i) \geq f(E_i)$ and if $f(E_i) \geq f(E_j)$ and $f(E_j) \geq f(E_{j'})$ then $f(E_i) \geq f(E_{j'})$; which read informally "any role expectation is justified at least to the extent that it is" and "if one role expectation is justified at least to the same extent as another one and that one is justified at least to the same extent as a third one then the first role expectation is justified at least to the same extent as the third one". If the following special conditions are satisfied then relation R is also connected in E. The first condition reads as "there exists at most one $E_i \in E$ such that $f(E_i) = 0$" and the other condition also strengthens condition "$f(E_i) \geq f(E_j)$" to a sufficient condition for relation R. Now let E_i be the only element in E with $f(E_i) = 0$. Then it holds for any $E_j, j \neq i : f(E_j) > f(E_i)$ and consequently $\langle E_j, E_i \rangle \in R$ for all $j, j \neq i$. On the other hand it holds for any $E_j, E_{j'} \in E, j, j' \neq i : f(E_j) \geq 1, f(E_{j'}) \geq 1$ and $f(E_j) \geq f(E_{j'})$ or $f(E_{j'}) \geq f(E_j)$ whence $\langle E_j, E_{j'} \rangle \in R$ or $\langle E_{j'}, E_j \rangle \in R$. This special case is interesting, because then relation R is formally completely analogous to the classical preference-relation.

Now define a function which determines the degree of justification for any $E_i \in E$. Let m_i denote the number of elements in R in which role expectation E_i occurs as the first component. Let the number of elements in E be n. Define a function $J : E \rightarrow \{0, 1, ...n\}$ as follows : for all $E_i \in E$

$$\textbf{(18)} \begin{cases} J(E_i) = 0 & \text{if } f(E_i) = 0; \\ J(E_i) = m_i & \text{if } f(E_i) = 1 \text{ and } \langle E_i, E_j \rangle, j = 1, ...n \\ & \text{occurs in } R\ m_i \text{ times;} \\ J(E_i) = 2m_i & \text{if } f(E_i) = 2 \text{ and } \langle E_i, E_j \rangle, j = 1, ...n \\ & \text{occurs in } R\ m_i \text{ times.} \end{cases}$$

Consider $R^*, R^* \subseteq R, R^* = \{\langle E_i, E_i \rangle : f(E_i) = 1 \text{ or } f(E_i) = 2\}$. That R^* is non-empty is intuitively quite plausible an assumption, given that E contains elements E_i with values $f(E_i) > 0$. Assume now that an arbitrary $\langle E_j, E_j \rangle \notin R^*$. Then $f(E_j) = 0$ which yields $J(E_j) = 0$. Assume then that $\langle E_j, E_j \rangle \in R^*$. Then E_j occurs as the first component in the elements of R^* precisely once, whence $m_j = 1$. Let $f(E_j) = 1$. Then $J(E_j) = 1$. Let $f(E_j) = 2$. Then $J(E_j) = 2$. These considerations show that if an $R^* \subseteq R$ is appropriately selected then a J', $J' \subset J$ is yielded such that $J' = f$.

Choose now $R^* \subseteq R$, $R^* = \{\langle E_1, E_1 \rangle, \langle E_2, E_2 \rangle, ...\langle E_n, E_n \rangle\}$. Then $m_i = 1$ for any $E_i \in E$ and J yields for any $E_i \in E$ precisely the same value as does f. These considerations show that if the relation R is restricted in a suitable way then the general justification function J with degrees reduces to justification function f, defined earlier. In particular, we have shown that

(19) $f \subset J$

and if $R = \emptyset$ then J reduces to $f' = \{\langle E_i, 0 \rangle : E_i \in E\} \subset f$ and if $R = R^*$ then J reduces to $f \backslash f'$.

These results show that there exists a structuralist theory-relation between the generalized theory-element $GRCT$ and the theory-element with different degrees of justification. The procedure we have followed indicates that the theory-relation is a theoretization. However, it is possible to start from the generalized theory-element with different degrees of justification. Then restricting relation R and consequently function J in an appropriate way (as indicated above) yields a structuralist specialization-relation. The interested reader may easily construct in detail the generalized theory-element with degrees of justification and then show that there really exists a specialization-relation or a structuralist theoretization-relation between the related theory-elements.

General Conclusions

The analysis above rather strongly supports the following general claims:

- Role Conflict Theory (in the sense in which it is used by Gross, Mason and McEachern as well as in the sense of two variants of generalized theory) is adequately identifiable as a theory-net, precisely as the structuralists propose.
- The structure of Role Conflict Theory from the micro and macro points of view, i.e. the structures of the related theory-elements as well as theory-relations of the related theory-elements, are adequately presentable in terms of structuralism. By means of the traditional statement-view of theories it is almost impossible or at least much more complicated to present the micro- and macro-structures of Role Conflict Theory.
- The structuralist theory of science may serve as a method for concept and theory formation. Structuralist theory of science is restricted by no means to reconstruction of theories and related metatheoretical considerations. The structuralist theory of science may clearly make a direct contribution to theory construction.

References

Balzer, W., Moulines, C.U., & Sneed, J.D. (1987): *An architectonic for science.* Dordrecht: Reidel.

Biddle, B.J., & Thomas, E.J. (Eds.) (1966): *Role theory, concepts and research.* New York: Wiley.

Gross, N., Mason, W.S., & McEachern, A.W. (1958): *Explorations in role analysis.* New York: Wiley.

Sarbin, T.R., & Allen, V.L. (1968): Role Theory. In G. Lindzey & E. Aronson (Eds.). *Handbook of Social Psychology, Vol.I* (pp. 488 - 567). Reading, Mass.: Addison-Wesley. Sec.ed.

Secord, P.F., & Backman, C.W. (1964): *Social psychology.* New York : McGraw-Hill.

Tuomela, R. (1973): *Theoretical concepts.* New York : Springer.

Chapter 7

The Theory of Behavior Interaction

A Structuralist Construction of a Theory and a Reconstruction of its Theoretical Environment[1]

Hans Westmeyer

Free University of Berlin

Abstract

A structuralist construction of a theory of behavior interaction is described. The theory, which deals with behavior changes in intra-situational dynamic interactions between two or more persons, is constructed as a theory-net comprising a basic and several more specific theory-elements, which are linked to elements and structures of a more general nature common to many other psychological theories. Intended applications of the theory which have already been investigated include behavior interactions in mother-child dyads, in father-mother-child triads, in client-therapist dyads, and in dyads of young adults getting into contact with one another.

Basic Concepts and Assumptions of the Theory

The theory of behavior interaction to be presented in this chapter is a structuralist (cf. Balzer et al., 1987; Stegmüller, 1986) construction of a theory of intrasituational, dynamic behavioral interactions between two or more persons. It can be conceived of as a specialization of the general interactionist behavior theory outlined by Magnusson (1980) in the following four propositions (p. 20f):

> (M1) For each individual there is a certain population of possible behaviors. To some extent this population is different for different individuals. ... Initially, no probability is attached to a certain behavior act.
> (M2) The probability of a certain actual behavior is conditional and determined by the situational context: (a) by the situational frame of reference ..., and (b) by the continuously changing situational conditions functioning as sources of each specific behavioral act .... The key factor determining the probability of each specific behavioral act is the individual's own interpretation of the total situation and of the situational cues.
> The factors working under (a) have been designated *between situation* factors, and those working under (b) *within situation* factors.
> (M3) As soon as a person occurs in a certain situation, ... two things happen, which have implications for studying behavior across different situations.: (a) a restricted sample of possible and probable behaviors is defined, the samples apparently differing between the situations ..., and (b) a probability of single acts of behavior is determined to some degree ....
> (M4) Within the frame of reference given by a certain situation, the probabilities for a certain behavior change with changes in the flow of situational cues, as a result of changes in the physical

[1] I would like to thank C.U.Moulines for his most valuable comments on a former draft of this paper.

situation, as a result of other persons' behavior, as a result of one's own actions, or as a result of a combination of two or three of these factors.

Viewed from the structuralist perspective, these propositions, far from constituting a fully explicated theory, would be regarded as being but the core assumptions of the basic element of a global structure of interactionist theories, which comprises all those theories of interaction which share the assumptions expressed by M1 to M4.

To give a first impression of the theory of behavior interaction presented in this chapter and its relation to the general interactionist view of behavior, corresponding concepts of both theories are listed in Table 1.

Table 1: *The theory of behavior interaction as a variant of the general interactionist view of behavior*

Interactionist view of behavior	*Theory of behavior interaction*
Basic Concepts	
actual behavior of a person	behavior category of a person
restricted sample of possible and probable behaviors	set of behavior categories
probability of a behavior	absolute/relative frequency of a behavior category
change in the probability of a behavior	frequency course of a behavior category
determined behavior	controlled behavior category
(determining) within situation factors	controlling behavior categories
• physical situation	• no specific equivalent
• behaviors of a person	• controlling behavior categories of a person
• other persons' behaviors	• controlling behavior categories of the interaction partners
change in a within situation factor	frequency course of a controlling behavior category
Fundamental law	
Changes in the probabilities of actual behaviors in a certain situation are a function of changes in factors within this situation.	Frequency courses of controlled behavior categories are a function of frequency courses of controlling behavior categories.

As indicated in Table 1, the behavior of interacting persons is described by behavior categories; the (relative) frequency of these behavior categories is the central parameter chosen to characterize interactional episodes; and changes in these frequencies (referred to as *frequency courses* of behavior categories) make up the events which are analyzed and explained by the theory. The basic assumption of the theory is that the frequency course of controlled behavior categories is determined by two kinds of within-situation factors: (a) controlling behavior categories of the person; (b) controlling behavior categories of the interaction partners of the person.

The totality of the relations between controlling and controlled behavior categories constitute an *interaction structure*. Within any given interaction structure, the *frequency dynamics*, i.e. the frequency courses of the involved behavior categories, is of primary concern. The theory of behavior interaction imposes certain restrictions on this frequency dynamics such that only certain frequency courses of controlled behavior categories are admissible, given a particular interaction structure and specific frequency courses of the controlling behavior categories. Other conceivable frequency courses of controlled behavior categories are excluded as being not in accord with the theory.

Which frequency courses of controlled categories confirm or disconfirm the theory under which boundary conditions is not decided at the basic level of the theory, but is specified in the course of further elaboration of the theory-net (for an intuitive structuralist outline of a previous version of the theory-net, see Westmeyer & Nell, 1987).

As the core assumption of the theory of behavior interaction reveals (cf. Table 1), the theory departs in one important respect from Magnusson's interactionist view of behavior. Other than the interactionist theory, the theory of behavior interaction does not assume that the key factor determining the probability of each specific behavior is the individual's subjective interpretation of the total situation and of the situational cues (cf. postulate M2 above). On the contrary, the theory of behavior interaction definitely dispenses with such cognitive factors and consistently adheres to a behavioral level of analysis. Whether this restriction has unpleasant consequences regarding the corroboration of the theory, is an empirical question.

In fact, the theory has already been tested and found confirmed in several empirical studies dealing with the following elements of its domain of intended applications: behavior interactions between mother and child in the natural setting of their home (cf. Westmeyer et al., 1984, 1988); behavior interactions in dyadic face-to-face encounters between persons which never met before (Nell, 1982; Westmeyer, 1987, 1989); and behavior interactions in father-mother-child triads within a specific social setting (Nell et al., 1988; Westmeyer et al., 1987). A further investigation of behavior interactions between clients and therapists in a client-centered therapeutic setting is currently in the making. However, the central issue of this chapter is not the empirical foundation of the theory, but its logical structure.

The Conceptual Apparatus of the Theory of Behavior Interaction

As the first step in unfolding the structuralist construction of the theory of behavior interaction, its basic concepts and assumptions will now be introduced in a systematic manner. Three basic sets (S, CS, and P) and four basic functions and relations (AF, $\leq_p$, FRC, and CR) are required:

S is a set of subjects comprising only those persons whose behavior interactions are the subject matter of the theory. $\mid S \mid$ is the number of elements of S. Thus, $\mid S \mid = 2$ in the case of dyads, $\mid S \mid = 3$ in the case of triads, etc.

CS is a set of behavior categories used to describe the behavior of the interacting persons. Examples of CS are concrete category systems as used in systematic behavior observation (cf. Bakeman & Gottman, 1986; Manns et al., 1987).

P is a set of time periods. A time period is the most extensive time unit considered within the theory. Other kinds of time units , e.g. time segments, time intervals, and instants of time, will be introduced later. In an empirical investigation of the theory, a time period might consist of a week, a time segment of a day, and a time interval of a few seconds.

AF is an assignment function, defined on CS, the set of behavior categories. In most cases, CS is a set system composed of subsets which are specific to the several elements of S. The purpose of AF is to decompose CS and assign the proper subset CS to each element s of S. Because of AF, we know for each category c to which person it refers.

$\leq_p$ is a total ordering of the set P of time periods, i.e., $\leq_p$ is reflexive, antisymmetric, transitive, and connected in P.

FRC is a frequency course function. It indicates the course which the relative frequency of a behavior category takes over two (usually different) periods of time, and it can be conceived of as either a quantitative or a categorical concept (both options are realized within the theory). On the most general level, the range of FRC is the set of real numbers $\mathbb{R}$. Through further specialization, the range of FRC is restricted to a subset of $\mathbb{R}$ consisting of only three values, which represent the following kinds of frequency courses: the relative frequency of a behavior category c *increases* in time period p_3 relative to time period p_2 ; the relative frequency of c *decreases* in p_3 relative to p_2 ; and the relative frequency of c *remains constant* in p_3 relative to p_2. This could be expressed by $FRC(c, p_3, p_2) = 1$, $FRC(c, p_3, p_2) = -1$, and $FRC(c, p_3, p_2) = 0$, respectively.

Finally, CR is a category relation function. As in the case of FRC, on the most general level of the theory CR is introduced as a quantitative concept, with $\mathbb{R}$ as its range. By means of specialization, the quantitative concept is transformed into a categorical one which assigns certain kinds of category relations to pairs of categories for a period of time. Similarly to FRC, the range of CR is restricted to a set of three values referring to the following category relations: a *facilitating* category relation between behavior categories c_j and c during time period p_1 ; an *inhibiting* category relation between c_j and c during p_1 ; and a *neutral* category relation between c_j and c during p_1. This will for convenience be symbolized by $CR(c_j, c, p_1) = 1$, $CR(c_j, c, p_1) = -1$, and $CR(c_j, c, p_1) = 0$, respectively.

There is a close resemblance between the concepts of facilitating and inhibiting category relations on the one hand, and the concepts of facilitating and inhibiting stimuli to be found in the performance theory of Patterson (1979), on the other. Patterson gives the following definitions of his concepts (p. 124): "A facilitating stimulus is an antecedent event associated with a significant increase in the probability of a response following the event on the time line. An inhibiting stimulus is an antecedent event associated with a significant decrease in the probability of a response following the event on the time line." In the case of facilitating and inhibiting category relations, the antecedent stimuli and succedent responses are themselves behavior categories, but otherwise, Patterson's basic ideas are retained.

Important Defined Concepts of the Theory

The concepts of facilitating and inhibiting category relations are fundamental to most elements of the theory of behavior interaction. As the following list of definitions or meaning postulates reveals, many important concepts of the theory can be defined by these two notions:

D1 c_j is a *facilitating category for c during p* iff there is a facilitating category relation between c_j and c during p.

D2 c_j is a *facilitating category during p* iff there exists a c such that c_j is a facilitating category for c during p.

D3 c is a category *facilitated by c_j during p* iff c_j is a facilitating category for c during p.

D4 c is a *facilitated category during p* iff there exists a c_j such that c is a category facilitated by c_j during p.

D5 c_j is an *inhibiting category* for c during p iff there is an inhibiting category relation between c_j and c during p.

D6 c_j is an *inhibiting category during p* iff there exists a c such that c_j is an inhibiting category for c during p.

D7 c is a *category inhibited by c_j during p* iff c_j is an inhibiting category for c during p.

D8 c is an *inhibited category during p* iff there exists a c_j such that c is a category inhibited by c_j during p.

D9 c_j is a *controlling category for c during p* iff c_j is a facilitating category for c during p or c_j is an inhibiting category for c during p.

D10 c_j is a *controlling category during p* iff there exists a c such that c_j is a controlling category for c during p.

D11 c is a *category controlled by c_j* during p iff c_j is a controlling category for c during p.

D12 c is a *controlled category during p* iff there exists a c_j such that c is a category controlled by c_j during p.

D13 There is a *controlling category relation between c_j and c during p* iff c_j is a controlling category for c during p.

D14 There is a *neutral category relation between c_j and c during p* iff there is no controlling category relation between c_j and c during p.

D15 c_j is a *neutral category for c during p* iff there is a neutral category relation between c_j and c during p.

D16 c_j is a *neutral category during p* iff there exists no category c such that c_j is a controlling category for c during p.

D17 c is an *uncontrolled category during p* iff there exists no category c_j such that c_j is a controlling category for c during p.

As mentioned before, the basic assumption of the theory imposes restrictions on the frequency dynamics within a given interaction structure. On the basis of the already introduced terms, the two central concepts occuring in this fundamental postulate - interaction structure and frequency dynamics - can now be precisely defined.

D18 $IntStr(s_1, p)$ is the *interaction structure within* person s_1 *during* time period p iff there exists CS_1 such that:
1. CS_1 is the set of categories for person s;

2. $IntStr(s_1, p)$ is the set of controlling category relations between the elements of CS_1 during p.

D19 $IntStr(s_1, s_2, p)$ is the *interaction structure between* person s_1 *and* person s_2 *during* time period p iff there exist CS_1, CS_2, CR_1, CR_2 such that:
1. CS_1 is the set of categories for person s_1;
2. CS_2 is the set of categories for person s_2;
3. CR_1 is the set of controlling category relations between elements of CS_1 and elements of CS_2 during p;
4. CR_2 is the set of controlling category relations between elements of CS_2 and elements of CS_1 during p;
5. $IntStr(s_1, s_2, p)$ is the union of CR_1 and CR_2.

D20 $IntStr_1(s_1, p)$ is a *monadic interaction structure during* p iff there exists S such that:
1. S forms a monad;
2. $S = \{s_1\}$;
3. $IntStr_1(s_1, p)$ is the interaction structure within s_1 during p.

D21 $IntStr_2(s_1, s_2, p)$ is a *dyadic interaction structure during* p iff there exists S such that:
1. S forms a dyad;
2. $S = \{s_1, s_2\}$;
3. $IntStr_2(s_1, s_2, p)$ is the interaction structure between s_1 and s_2 during p.

D22 $IntStr_3(s_1, s_2, s_3, p)$ is a *triadic interaction structure during* p iff there exist S, $IntStr(s_1, s_2, p)$, $IntStr(s_1, s_3, p)$, $IntStr(s_2, s_3, p)$ such that:
1. S forms a triad;
2. $S = \{s_1, s_2, s_3\}$;
3. $IntStr(s_1, s_2, p)$ is the interaction structure between s_1 and s_2 during p;
4. $IntStr(s_1, s_3, p)$ is the interaction structure between s_1 and s_3 during p;
5. $IntStr(s_2, s_3, p)$ is the interaction structure between s_2 and s_3 during p;
6. $IntStr_3(s_1, s_2, s_3, p)$ is the union of $IntStr(s_1, s_2, p)$, $IntStr(s_1, s_3, p)$, and $IntStr(s_2, s_3, p)$.

D23 $IntStr_4(s_1, s_2, s_3, s_4, p)$ is a *tetradic interaction structure during* p iff there exist S, $IntStr(s_1, s_2, p)$, $IntStr(s_1, s_3, p)$, $IntStr(s_1, s_4, p)$, $IntStr(s_2, s_3, p)$, $IntStr(s_2, s_4, p)$, $IntStr(s_3, s_4, p)$ such that:
1. S forms a tetrad;
2. $S = \{s_1, s_2, s_3, s_4\}$;
3. $IntStr(s_1, s_2, p)$ is the interaction structure between s_1 and s_2 during p;
4. $IntStr(s_1, s_3, p)$ is the interaction structure between s_1 and s_3 during p;
5. $IntStr(s_1, s_4, p)$ is the interaction structure between s_1 and s_4 during p;
6. $IntStr(s_2, s_3, p)$ is the interaction structure between s_2 and s_3 during p;
7. $IntStr(s_2, s_4, p)$ is the interaction structure between s_2 and s_4 during p;
8. $IntStr(s_3, s_4, p)$ is the interaction structure between s_3 and s_4 during p;
9. $IntStr_4(s_1, s_2, s_3, s_4, p)$ is the union of $IntStr(s_1, s_2, p)$, $IntStr(s_1, s_3, p)$, $IntStr(s_1, s_4, p)$, $IntStr(s_2, s_3, p)$, $IntStr(s_2, s_4, p)$ and $IntStr(s_3, s_4, p)$.

D24 $FreDyn_1(s_1, p_2, p_1)$ is the *frequency dynamics for* person s_1 *in* time period p_2 *relative to* time period p_1 iff there exist CS_1, FRC_1 such that:

1. CS_1 is the set of categories for person s;
2. p_1 is a time period prior to p_2;
3. $FreDyn_1(s_1, p_2, p_1)$ is the set of frequency courses which the elements of CS_1 take in p_2 relative to p_1.

D25 $FreDyn_n(S, p_2, p_1)$ is the *frequency dynamics for a set* of persons S *in* p_2 *relative to* p_1 iff there exist $FreDyn_1(s_1, p_2, p_1)$, ..., $FreDyn_1(s_n, p_2, p_1)$ such that:
1. n is the number of elements in S;
2. for all $1 \leq i \leq n$: $FreDyn_1(s_i, p_2, p_1)$ is the frequency dynamics for person s_i in p_2 relative to p_1;
3. $FreDyn_n(S, p_2, p_1)$ is the union (over i) of all $FreDyn_1(s_i, p_2, p_1)$.

It is easy to see that an interaction structure is a subset of CR, and a frequency dynamics a subset of FRC. Interaction structures in groups of more than two persons are simply composed of the interaction structures for all pairs of members of the group.

Additional Concepts

To further analyze the restrictions imposed by the theory on the frequency dynamics of interactions, it is necessary to introduce two additional concepts and to define a third one.

First, DI is a *direct* influence function. It captures the idea that the frequency course of a behavior category c_j in time period p_3 relative to time period p_2 — with c_j standing in a certain category relation to a behavior category c during time period p_1 — has a direct influence on category c in time period p_4 . Direct influences are designated by real numbers. Which ones are assigned in which cases is determined by the special laws of the respective theory-elements.

Second, IDI is an indirect influence function. If the relative frequency of a behavior category c_j controlling a category c during time period p_1 does not change in p_3 relative to p_2, then it is reasonable to assume that no direct influence is exerted on c by c_j in time period p_4 . However, if c_j is itself controlled by a behavior category c_k during p_1, and the frequency of c_k changes in p_3 relative to p_2, then there is an indirect influence of c_k on c in p_4 which is mediated by c_j. Of special interest are those cases in which c_k and c are (possibly even identical) behavior categories of the same person, whereas c_j is a category of an interaction partner. Under these circumstances, the indirect influence function expresses a particular kind of behavioral self-control, namely, self-control mediated by another person's behavior. On the most abstract level of the theory, the theoretical assumptions are formulated so generally that all other possible constellations of category relations and frequency courses are also dealt with. As in the case of direct influences, indirect influences are designated by real numbers, and again, which ones are assigned in which cases is determined by the special laws of the respective theory-elements.

Finally, $SUMI$ is a sum-of-influence function. For a given behavior category c, there may and, in most cases, will be several direct and/or indirect influences impinging on c. $SUMI$ yields a simple additive combination of these influences per category and for a certain time period.

We are now ready to formulate the various theory-elements of the theory of behavior interaction. This will be done in the usual way by defining the respective theory-elements and all their components within a set-theoretical framework (cf. Balzer et al., 1987; Stegmüller, 1986; see also Chapter 1 of this book). If necessary, the definitions will be commented upon.

Theory-Element "Behavior Interaction"

Def-TE(BI)

$TE(BI)$ is the theory-element "behavior interaction" iff there exist $K(BI)$ and $I(BI)$ such that

(1) $TE(BI) = \langle K(BI), I(BI)\rangle$;
(2) $K(BI) = \langle M_p(BI), M(BI), M_{pp}(BI), C(BI), L(BI)\rangle$ is the core of $TE(BI)$;
(3) $I(BI)$ is the domain of intended applications of $K(BI)$.

Def-Mp(BI)

$M_p(BI) = \{x : x$ is a *potential model* of the theory-element $BI\}$
x is a potential model of the theory-element BI iff there exist S, CS, AF, P, $\leq_p$, FRC, CR, DI, IDI such that

(1) $x = \langle S, CS, AF, P, \leq_p, FRC, CR, DI, IDI\rangle$;
(2) S and CS are non-empty, finite sets;
(3) $AF : S \Rightarrow Po(CS)$;
if $CS_i := AF(s_i)$ with $i = 1, ..., n$ and $n = |S|$, then $\{CS_1, ..., CS_n\}$ is a decomposition[2] of CS;
(4) P is a non-empty, finite set ordered by $\leq_p$;
(5) $FRC : CS \times P \times P \Longrightarrow \mathbb{R}$;
(6) $CR : CS \times CS \times P \Longrightarrow \mathbb{R}$;
(7) $DI : CS \times CS \times P \Longrightarrow \mathbb{R}$;
(8) $IDI : CS \times CS \times CS \times P \Longrightarrow \mathbb{R}$.

Def-M(BI)

$M(BI) := \{$x : x is a *model* of the theory-element BI $\}$;
x is a model of the theory-element BI iff

(1) $x \in M_p(BI)$;
(2) $\forall c_k, c_j, c \in CS\ \forall p \in P : SUMI(c,p) := \sum_j DI(c_j, c, p) + \sum_k \sum_j IDI(c_k, c_j, c, p)$;
(3) $\exists p_1, ..., p_6 \in P$ with $\{\langle p_1,p_3\rangle, \langle p_2,p_3\rangle, \langle p_2,p_5\rangle, \langle p_3,p_4\rangle, \langle p_4,p_6\rangle, \langle p_5,p_6\rangle\} \subseteq \leq_p$
$\forall c_k, c_j, c \in CS\ \forall w, w_1, w_2, v \in \mathbb{R}\ \exists f, f_1, f_2$ with $f : \mathbb{R} \Longrightarrow \mathbb{R}$, $f_1 : \mathbb{R}^2 \Longrightarrow \mathbb{R}$ and $f_2 : \mathbb{R}^3 \Longrightarrow \mathbb{R}$:
   (a) $CR(c_j, c, p_1) = w_1 \wedge FRC(c_j, p_3, p_2) = v \longrightarrow DI(c_j, c, p_4) = f_1(w_1, v)$,
   (b) $CR(c_k, c_j, p_1) = w_1 \wedge CR(c_j, c, p_1) = w \wedge FRC(c_k, p_3, p_2) = v \wedge$
   $FRC(c_j, p_3, p_2) = 0 \longrightarrow \exists a \in \mathbb{R}^+ (IDI(c_k, c_j, c, p_4) = a \cdot f_2(w_1, w_2, v))$,
   (c) $SUMI(c, p_4) = w \longrightarrow FRC(c, p_6, p_5) = f(w)$.

Def-M_{pp}(BI)

$M_{pp}(BI) = \{\langle S, CS, AF, P, \leq_p, FRC, CR\rangle$: there exist DI, IDI such that

[2]The definition of AF implies, that there is a specific set of behavior categories for each person in S. This requirement can easily be met even in those cases in which the original category system contains only a single set of categories for the description of the behavior of the persons in S. In these cases, it is customary to add a specific sign designating the observed person to the category names.

$\langle S, CS, AF, P, \leq_p, FRC, CR, DI, IDI\rangle \in M_p(BI)\}$.

Def-C(BI)

$C(BI) = \{X : X$ satisfies the *constraint* of the theory-element $BI\}$

X satisfies the constraint of the theory-element BI iff

(1) $X \subseteq M_p(BI)$;

(2) $X \neq \emptyset$;

(3) $\forall x_1, x_2 \in X : pr_2(x_1) = pr_2(x_2)$.

Def-L(BI)

$L(BI) \subseteq M_p(BI)$.

Def-I(BI)

The elements of $I(BI)$ are the behavior interactions in *monads and polyads*, i.e., the frequency dynamics within monadic and polyadic interaction structures, as described by the non-theoretical concepts of the theory, and $I(BI) \subseteq M_{pp}(BI)$.

Comments

$TE(BI)$ is the most general theory-element of the theory of behavior interaction. As all concepts used to define the set of potential models have already been introduced, only the definitions of $M(BI)$, $M_{pp}(BI)$, and $C(BI)$ are in need of some elucidation.

Stipulation (2) of Def-$M(BI)$ is the definition of the sum-of-influence function $SUMI$. Stipulation (3) expresses the idea that, given certain time periods which are ordered in a certain way, (a) the direct influence exerted on category c by category c_j is a function f_1 of the category relation between c_j and c and of the frequency course of c_j; (b) if the frequency course of c_j is 0, then the indirect influence exerted on c by c_k, i.e., the influence mediated by c_j, is a function f_2 of the category relation between c_k and c_j, of the category relation between c_j and c, and of the frequency course of c_k; (c) the frequency course of c is a function of the sum of influences, direct or indirect, which are exerted on c. For each combination of category relations and frequency courses, there is a, not necessarily different, positive real number to weigh the value of f_2.

It should be noted that these assumptions have been deliberately formulated in very general terms, that is, they leave many details open for further specification. Table 2 makes this very clear. The specification of these details, without which the theory is not testable by empirical investigations, have however been relegated to other theory-elements.

Table 2 *Values of the direct and indirect influence functions as fixed by $M(BI)$*

$CR(c_k, c_j)$	$FRC(c_k)$	$CR(c_j, c)$	$FRC(c_j)$	$DI(c_j, c)$	$IDI(c_k, c_j, c)$
		w_1	v	$f_1(w_1, v)$	
w_1	v	w_2	0		$a \cdot f_2(w_1, w_2, v)$

Note: w_1, w_2, v are elements of $\mathbb{R}$; a is an element of $\mathbb{R}^+$.

As indicated by the comparison of $Def\text{-}M_{pp}(BI)$ with $Def\text{-}M_p(BI)$, the direct and indirect influence functions are taken to be the theoretical concepts of the theory of behavior interaction. That is, it is impossible to determine the values of these functions for the elements of their domains without applying the theory, and this can be effected only by an application of the assumptions formulated in $Def\text{-}M(BI)$. DI and IDI are also the only concepts of the theory of behavior interaction specific to this theory. All other concepts used in $Def\text{-}M_p(BI)$ are either interpretable by concepts occurring in other theories ($FRC, CR, P, \leq_p$), or else they are base sets (S, CS) and functions (AF) which may occur in many different theories.

The constraint $C(BI)$ postulates the existence of a non-empty set of potential models sharing *the same category system* for the description of behavior interactions. This is a rather weak assumption, but it is not completely trivial because it is at least theoretically conceivable that a separate category system CS is required for each distinct set of persons S. This might perhaps indeed be claimed by a devoted adherent of a qualitative approach. Usually, however, the developer of a category system presupposes the applicability of the system to many different sets of persons. The term "pr_2" used in $C(BI)$ refers to the projection function which yields, for every tuple, its second element. In the same way, pr_1 yields the first, pr_3 the third, ... pr_n the n-th element of a tuple.

The link $L(BI)$ is introduced at this point only to give a complete definition of $TE(BI)$. Precise definitions of the more important links which exist between certain theory-elements of the theory of behavior interaction and theory-elements of different theory-nets will be presented later.

It should be noted that the domain of intended applications of the theory of behavior interaction includes the frequency courses of the behaviors of single persons. That is, the theory can in principle be applied to the analysis of frequency dynamics in monadic interaction structures. However, no empirical studies of monadic interaction structures have been conducted so far.

$TE(BI)$ may be specialized in various ways. There are many options for specifying the functions f_1, f_2, and f, and the weighting factor a. One specialization of $TE(BI)$ is the following theory-element.

Specialization 1 of the Theory-Element "Behavior Interaction"

Def-TE(BI$_1$)

$TE(BI_1)$ is specialization 1 of the theory-element "behavior interaction" iff there exist $K(BI_1)$ and $I(BI_1)$ such that

(1) $TE(BI_1) = \langle K(BI_1), I(BI_1)\rangle$;
(2) $K(BI_1) = \langle M_p(BI_1), M(BI_1), M_{pp}(BI_1), C(BI_1), L(BI_1)\rangle$ is the core of $TE(BI_1)$;
(3) $I(BI_1)$ is the domain of intended applications of $K(BI_1)$.

Def-M$_p$(BI$_1$)
$M_p(BI_1) = M_p(BI)$.

Def-M(BI$_1$)[3]
$M(BI_1) := \{x : x \text{ is a } \textit{model} \text{ of the theory-element } BI_1\}$
x is a model of the theory-element BI_1 iff

(1) $x \in M_p(BI_1)$;
(2) $x \in M(BI)$;
(3) $ran(CR) = \{-a_1, 0, a\} \subset \mathbb{R}$ with $a_1 \neq 0$;
(4) $ran(FRC) = \{-a_2, 0, a_2\} \subset \mathbb{R}$ with $a_2 \neq 0$;
(5) $\forall w_1, w_2 \in ran(CR)\ \forall v \in ran(FRC)$:
  (a) $w_1 = 0 \vee v = 0 \longrightarrow f_1(w_1, v) = 0$,
  (b) $w_1 = 0 \vee w_2 = 0 \vee v = 0 \longrightarrow f_2(w_1, w_2, v) = 0$;
(6) $\exists\, p_4, p_5, p_6 \in P$ with $\{\langle p_4, p_6\rangle, \langle p_5, p_6\rangle\} \subseteq \leq_p\ \forall c \in CS$: $(SUMI(c, p_4) > 0 \longrightarrow FRC(c, p_6, p_5) \neq -a_2) \wedge (SUMI(c, p_4) < 0 \longrightarrow FRC(c, p_6, p_5) \neq a_2)$.

Def-M$_{pp}$(BI$_1$)
$M_{pp}(BI_1) = M_{pp}(BI)$.

Def-C(BI$_1$)
$C(BI_1) \subseteq C(BI)$.

Def-L(BI$_1$)
$L(BI_1) \subseteq L(BI)$.

Def-I(BI$_1$)
$I(BI_1) \subseteq I(BI)$.

Comments

In this theory-element, restrictions are imposed on the category relation and frequency course functions, as well as on the direct and indirect influence functions. The ranges of both CR and FCR are confined to three values one of which is fixed at 0 for both functions (cf. [3],[4]). If at least one argument of f_1 or f_2 is 0, f_1 and f_2 yield the value 0 (cf. [5]). As shown in Table 3, these additional specifications result in a far more informative picture of the functions f_1 and f_2 than the original, weaker requirements (cf. Table 2).

The function f of *Def-M*(BI) is completely specified in *Def-M*(BI_1) as being a comparative relation between $SUMI$ and FRC (cf.[6]): If the sum of influences on a category c is greater than 0, the frequency course of c will be different from $-a_2$, i.e., it will be a_2 or 0;

[3] In *Def-M*(BI), p_1,..., p_6, f, f_1, and f_2 are introduced as variables. To simplify the definitions of those theory-elements which are specializations of $TE(BI)$, only the additional requirements which these specializations must meet, are mentioned explicitely. Therefore, "f_1" in stipulation (5a) of *Def-M*(BI_1) refers to the function variable f_1, as introduced in stipulation (3a) of *Def-M*(BI);"f_2" relates to the function variable "f_2", as introduced in stipulation (3b) of *Def-M*(BI); etc.

Table 3 *Values of the direct and indirect influence functions as fixed by $M(BI_1)$*

$CR(c_k, c_j)$	$FRC(c_k)$	$CR(c_j, c)$	$FRC(c_j)$	$DI(c_j, c)$	$IDI(c_k, c_j, c)$
		a_1	a_2	$f_1(a_1, a_2)$	
		a_1	0	0	
		a_1	$-a_2$	$f_1(a_1, -a_2)$	
		0	a_2	0	
		0	0	0	
		0	$-a_2$	0	
		$-a_1$	a_2	$f_1(-a_1, a_2)$	
		$-a_1$	0	0	
		$-a_1$	$-a_2$	$f_1(-a_1, -a_2)$	
a_1	a_2	a_1	0		$g_1 \cdot f_2(a_1, a_1, a_2)$
a_1	a_2	0	0		0
a_1	a_2	$-a_1$	0		$g_2 \cdot f_2(a_1, -a_1, a_2)$
a_1	0	a_1	0		0
a_1	0	0	0		0
a_1	0	$-a_1$	0		0
a_1	$-a_2$	a_1	0		$g_3 \cdot f_2(a_1, a_1, -a_2)$
a_1	$-a_2$	0	0		0
a_1	$-a_2$	$-a_1$	0		$g_4 \cdot f_2(a_1, -a_1, -a_2)$
0	a_2	a_1	0		0
0	a_2	0	0		0
0	a_2	$-a_1$	0		0
0	0	a_1	0		0
0	0	0	0		0
0	0	$-a_1$	0		0
0	$-a_2$	a_1	0		0
0	$-a_2$	0	0		0
0	$-a_2$	$-a_1$	0		0
$-a_1$	a_2	a_1	0		$g_5 \cdot f_2(-a_1, a_1, a_2)$
$-a_1$	a_2	0	0		0
$-a_1$	a_2	$-a_1$	0		$g_6 \cdot f_2(-a_1, -a_1, a_2)$
$-a_1$	0	a_1	0		0
$-a_1$	0	0	0		0
$-a_1$	0	$-a_1$	0		0
$-a_1$	$-a_2$	a_1	0		$g_7 \cdot f_2(-a_1, a_1, -a_2)$
$-a_1$	$-a_2$	0	0		0
$-a_1$	$-a_2$	$-a_1$	0		$g_8 \cdot f_2(-a_1, -a_1, -a_2)$

Note: a_1, a_2 and $g_1, \ldots, g_8$ are (not necessarily different) elements of $\mathbb{R}^+$.

if the sum of influences on c is smaller than 0, the frequency course of c will be different from a, i.e., it will be $-a_2$ or 0.

By means of a further specialization, the behavior interaction in monads is excluded from the field of intended applications.

Theory-Element "Behavior Interaction in Small Groups"

Def-TE(BISG)

$TE(BISG)$ is the theory-element "behavior interaction in small groups" iff there exist $K(BISG)$ and $I(BISG)$ such that

(1) $TE(BISG) = \langle K(BISG), I(BISG)\rangle$;

(2) $K(BISG) = \langle M_p(BISG), M(BISG), M_{pp}(BISG), C(BISG), L(BISG)\rangle$ is the core of $TE(BISG)$;

(3) $I(BISG)$ is the domain of intended applications of $K(BISG)$.

Def-M$_p$(BISG)

$M_p(BISG) = M_p(BI_1)$.

Def-M(BISG)

$M(BISG) := \{x : x \text{ is a } \textit{model} \text{ of the theory-element } BISG\}$

x is a model of the theory-element $BISG$ iff

(1) $x \in M_p(BISG)$

(2) $x \in M(BI_1)$;

(3) $|S| > 1$;

(4) $\forall c_j, c \in CS \;\; \forall i_1, i_2 \in \{1, ..., n\} \;\; \forall p \in P$:
$c_j \in AF(s_{i1}) \land c \in AF(s_{i1}) \longrightarrow \langle c_j, c, p\rangle \notin dom(CR)$.

Def-M$_{pp}$(BISG)

$M_{pp}(BISG) = M_{pp}(BI_1)$.

Def-C(BISG)

$C(BISG) \subseteq C(BI_1)$.

Def-L(BISG)

$L(BISG) \subseteq L(BI_1)$.

Def-I(BISG)

The elements of $I(BISG)$ are the behavior interactions in *polyads*, i.e., the frequency dynamics within polyadic interaction structures, as described by the non-theoretical concepts of the theory; and $I(BISG) \subseteq M_{pp}(BISG)$ and $I(BISG) \subset I(BI)$.

Comments

This further specialization of specialization 1 of the theory-element "behavior interaction" restricts the field of intended applications of the theory to sets of persons containing more than one element. In accord with this restriction, it confines the domains of CR, and, as a consequence, those of DI, and IDI. By stipulation (4) in $Def\text{-}M(BISG)$, category relations between categories of one and the same person are excluded from further consideration.

This entails that

$\forall c_k, c_j, c \in CS \; \forall i_1, i_2, i_3 \in \{1, ..., n\} \; \forall p \in P$:
$(c_j \in AF(s_{i1}) \land c \in AF(s_{i1}) \longrightarrow \langle c_j, c, p\rangle \notin dom(DI)) \land$
$(c_k \in AF(s_{i1}) \land c_j \in AF(s_{i2}) \land c \in AF(s_{i3}) \land (i_1 = i_2 \lor i_2 = i_3) \longrightarrow \langle c_k, c_j, c, p\rangle \notin dom(IDI))$.

Hence, direct influences on a behavior category can only be exerted by behavior categories of other persons, and indirect influences on a behavior category can only be mediated by behavior categories of other persons.

As is the case for $TE(BI)$, there are many options to specialize $TE(BISG)$. Only one will be presented here.

Specialization 1 of the Theory-Element "Behavior Interaction in Small Groups"

Def-TE(BISG$_1$)
$TE(BISG_1)$ is specialization 1 of the theory-element "behavior interaction in small groups" iff there exist $K(BISG_1)$ and $I(BISG_1)$ such that

(1) $TE(BISG_1) = \langle K(BISG_1), I(BISG_1)\rangle$;
(2) $K(BISG_1) = \langle M_p(BISG_1), M(BISG_1), M_{pp}(BISG_1), C(BISG_1), L(BISG_1)\rangle$ is the core of $TE(BISG_1)$;
(3) $I(BISG_1)$ is the domain of intended applications of $K(BISG_1)$.

Def-M$_p$(BISG$_1$)
$M_p(BISG_1) = M_p(BISG)$.

Def-M(BISG$_1$)
$M(BISG_1) := \{x : x \text{ is a } model \text{ of the theory-element } BISG_1\}$
x is a model of the theory-element BISG$_1$ iff

(1) $x \in M_p(BISG_1)$;
(2) $x \in M(BISG)$;
(3) $ran(CR) = ran(FRC) = \{-1, 0, 1\}$;
(4) $\forall c_j, c \in CS\ \forall p \in P\ \forall w_1, w_2 \in \{-1, 1\}$:
$CR(c, c_j, p) = w_1 \wedge CR(c_j, c, p) = w_2 \longrightarrow w_1 = w_2$.
(5) $\exists\ p_1, ..., p_6 \in P$ with $\{\langle p_1, p_3\rangle, \langle p_2, p_3\rangle, \langle p_2, p_5\rangle, \langle p_3, p_4\rangle, \langle p_4, p_6\rangle, \langle p_5, p_6\rangle\} \subseteq \leq_p$
$\forall c_k, c_j, c \in CS\ \forall w_1, w_2, v \in \{-1, 0, 1\}$:

(a) $CR(c_j, c, p_1) = w_1 \wedge FRC(c_j, p_3, p_2) = v \longrightarrow DI(c_j, c, p_4) = w_1 \cdot v$,
(b) $CR(c_k, c_j, p_1) = w_1 \wedge CR(c_j, c, p_1) = w_2 \wedge$
$FRC(c_k, p_3, p_2) = v \wedge FRC(c_j, p_3, p_2) = 0 \longrightarrow$
$(c_k = c \longrightarrow IDI(c_k, c_j, c, p_4) = 2 \cdot w_1 \cdot w_2 \cdot v) \wedge$
$(c_k \neq c \longrightarrow IDI(c_k, c_j, c, p_4) = w_1 \cdot w_2 \cdot v)$,
(c) $(SUMI(c, p_4) > 0 \longrightarrow FRC(c, p_6, p_5) \neq -1) \wedge (SUMI(c, p_4) < 0 \longrightarrow$
$FRC(c, p_6, p_5) \neq 1)$.

Def-M$_{pp}$(BISG$_1$)
$M_{pp}(BISG_1) = M_{pp}(BISG)$.

Def-C(BISG$_1$)
$C(BISG_1) \subseteq C(BISG)$.

Def-L(BISG$_1$)
$L(BISG_1) \subseteq L(BISG)$.

Def-I(BISG$_1$)
$I(BISG_1) \subseteq I(BISG)$.

Table 4: *Values of the direct and indirect influence functions as fixed by* $M(BISG_1)$

$CR(c_k, c_j)$	$FRC(c_k)$	$CR(c_j, c)$	$FRC(c_j)$	$DI(c_j, c)$	$IDI(c_k, c_j, c)$	
					$c_k = c$	$c_k \neq c$
		1	1	1		
		1	0	0		
		1	-1	-1		
		0	1	0		
		0	0	0		
		0	-1	0		
		-1	1	-1		
		-1	0	0		
		-1	-1	1		
1	1	1	0		2	1
1	1	0	0		0	0
1	1	-1	0		*	-1
1	0	1	0		0	0
1	0	0	0		0	0
1	0	-1	0		0	0
1	-1	1	0		-2	-1
1	-1	0	0		0	0
1	-1	-1	0		*	1
0	1	1	0		0	0
0	1	0	0		0	0
0	1	-1	0		0	0
0	0	1	0		0	0
0	0	0	0		0	0
0	0	-1	0		0	0
0	-1	1	0		0	0
0	-1	0	0		0	0
0	-1	-1	0		0	0
-1	1	1	0		*	-1
-1	1	0	0		0	0
-1	1	-1	0		2	1
-1	0	1	0		0	0
-1	0	0	0		0	0
-1	0	-1	0		0	0
-1	-1	1	0		*	1
-1	-1	0	0		0	0
-1	-1	-1	0		-2	-1

Comments

By this specialization, a far-reaching fixation of the functions f_1 and f_2 is effected. After restricting the ranges of CR and FCR in $Def\text{-}M(BISG_1)$ to $\{-1, 0, 1\}$, f_1 and f_2 are specified as simple multiplicative combinations of their arguments. The weighting factor a is set at 1, if the behavior category c_k exerting an indirect influence on a category c is different from c; it is set at 2, if c_k and c are the same category. Table 4 provides a listing of values of DI and IDI for all possible combinations of arguments.

As can be seen from Table 4, indirect influences are left unspecified for four arguments (marked by a star), for all of which c_k and c are one and the same category. The reason is that the theory assumes (cf. [4] in $Def\text{-}M[BISG_1]$) that no such combinations occur in reality. If there are category relations between c_j and c, and between c and c_j, they have to be of the same kind. It is a matter of reality whether this assumption is valid, and it is easy to test. The theory could, of course, do without this hypothesis and postulate, for example, a value of 0 for f_2 in these cases; however, the assumption increases the empirical content of the theory.

Further specializations are possible by restricting the number of elements of S.

Theory-Element "Behavior Interaction in Dyads"

Def-TE(BID)
$TE(BID)$ is the theory-element "behavior interaction in dyads" iff there exist $K(BID)$ and $I(BID)$ such that
(1) $TE(BID) = \langle K(BID), I(BID)\rangle$;
(2) $K(BID) = \langle M_p(BID), M(BID), M_{pp}(BID), C(BID), L(BID)\rangle$ is the core of $TE(BID)$;
(3) $I(BID)$ is the class of intended applications of $K(BID)$.

Def-M_p(BID)
$M_p(BID) = M_p(BISG_1)$.

Def-M(BID)
$M(BID) := \{x : x \text{ is a } \mathit{model} \text{ of the theory-element } BID\}$
x is a model of the theory-element BID iff
(1) $x \in M_p(BID)$;
(2) $x \in M(BISG_1)$;
(3) $|S| = 2$.

Def-M_{pp}(BID)
$M_{pp}(BID) = M_{pp}(BISG_1)$.

Def-C(BID)
$C(BID) \subset C(BISG_1)$.

Def-L(BID)
$L(BID) \subseteq L(BISG_1)$.

Def-I(BID)
The elements of $I(BID)$ are the behavior interactions in *dyads*, i.e., the frequency dynamics within dyadic interaction structures, as described by the non-theoretical concepts of the theory; and $I(BID) \subseteq M_{pp}(BID)$, and $I(BID) \subset I(BISG_1)$.

Comments

As this theory-element refers only to the behavior interaction in dyads, the number of elements of S is confined to 2. Most of the empirical studies which have so far been conducted to test the theory of behavior interaction dealt with this theory-element and its specializations (cf. Nell 1982; Westmeyer, 1987, 1989; Westmeyer et al., 1984, 1988).

Table 5

Previous formulation of the special laws of the theory-element "behavior interaction in dyads"

c and c_k are different behavior category variables for one person, c_j is a behavior category variable for the interaction partner. "a ... influence" in SLD 1-6 means "exactly one ... influence".

(SLD 1) Let c_j be a facilitating category for c.
Then:
(a) If the frequency of c_j increases, this has a positive influence on c.
(b) If the frequency of c_j decreases, this has a negative influence on c.

(SLD 2) Let c_j be an inhibiting category for c.
Then:
(a) If the frequency of c_j increases, this has a negative influence on c.
(b) If the frequency of c_j decreases, this has a positive influence on c.

(SLD 3.1) Let c be a facilitating category for c_j and c_j a facilitating category for c.
Then:
(a) If the frequency of c increases and the frequency of c_j remains the same, this has a doubly positive influence on c. (b) If the frequency of c decreases and the frequency of c_j remains the same, this has a doubly negative influence on c.

(SLD 3.2) Let c_k be a facilitating category for c_j and c_j a facilitating category for c.
Then:
(a) If the frequency of c_k increases and the frequency of c_j remains the same, this has a positive influence on c.
(b) If the frequency of c_k decreases and the frequency of c_j remains the same, this has a negative influence on c.

(SLD 4) Let c_k be a facilitating category for c_j and c_j an inhibiting category for c.
Then:
(a) If the frequency of c_k increases and the frequency of c_j remains the same, this has a negative influence on c.
(b) If the frequency of c_k decreases and the frequency of c_j remains the same, this has a positive influence on c.

(SLD 5) Let c_k be an inhibiting category for c_j and c_j a facilitating category for c.
Then:
(a) If the frequency of c_k increases and the frequency of c_j remains the same, this has a negative influence on c.
(b) If the frequency of c_k decreases and the frequency of c_j remains the same, this has a positive influence on c.

(SLD 6.1) Let c be an inhibiting category for c_j and c_j an inhibiting category for c.
Then:
(a) If the frequency of c increases and the frequency of c_j remains the same, this has a doubly positive influence on c.
(b) If the frequency of c decreases and the frequency of c_j remains the same, this has a doubly negative influence on c.

(SLD 6.2) Let c_k be an inhibiting category for c_j and c_j an inhibiting category for c.
Then:
(a) If the frequency of c_k increases and the frequency of c_j remains the same, this has a positive influence on c.
(b) If the frequency of c_k decreases and the frequency of c_j remains the same, this has a negative influence on c.

(SLD 7) Let SI_c be the set of all positive and/or negative influences which the frequency changes of controlling categories exert upon a (directly and/or indirectly) controlled category c.
Then:
(a) If the number of positive infuences in SI_c is greater than the number of negative influences in SI_c, the frequency of c will increase or remain the same.
(b) If the number of positive influences in SI_c is smaller than the number of negative influences in SI_c, the frequency of c will decrease or remain the same.

To those readers familiar with previous versions of the theory of behavior interaction, it may be of interest to get some cues on how to transform these earlier versions into the new one presented here. Table 5 summarizes the previous formulation of the special laws of the theory-element behavior interaction in dyads", disregarding the time periods and their relations.

Given certain interpretations of the elements of the ranges of CR, FCR, DI, and IDI, $SLD1$ and $SLD2$ are instances of stipulation (5a), $SLD3$ to $SLD6$ are instances of (5b), and $SLD7$ is an instance of (5c) of $Def\text{-}M(BISG_1)$. The values of DI and IDI, as determined by $SLD1$ to $SLD6$ are shown in Table 6.

Table 6: *Direct and indirect influences contingent upon category relations and frequency courses*

$CR(c_k, c_j)$	$FRC(c_k)$	$CR(c_j, c)$	$FRC(c_j)$	$DI(c_j, c)$	$IDI(c_k, c_j, c)$ $c_k = c$	$IDI(c_k, c_j, c)$ $c_k \neq c$
		F	⇑	pos		
		F	⇓	neg		
		I	⇑	neg		
		I	⇓	pos		
F	⇑	F	=		dpos	pos
F	⇑	I	=			neg
F	⇓	F	=		dneg	neg
F	⇓	I	=			pos
I	⇑	F	=			neg
I	⇑	I	=		dpos	pos
I	⇓	F	=			pos
I	⇓	I	=		dneg	neg

Note: "F", "N", "I" stand for "facilitating", "neutral", "inhibiting"; "⇑", "=", "⇓" stand for "increases", "remains the same", "decreases"; "pos", "neg", "noin", "dpos", "dneg" stand for "positive", "negative", "no influence", "doubly positive", "doubly negative".

In Table 6, only those combinations of category relations and frequency courses are listed which have a positive or negative influence on a category c. If all other possible combinations associated with no influence on the category c are added, we get Table 7.

It it easy to transform Table 7, which refers to the previous version of the theory of behavior interaction, into Table 4, which refers to its most recent formulation, by performing the following substitutions of the values of DI and IDI: "no influence" has to be substituted by "0", "a positive influence" by "1", "a negative influence" by "-1", "a doubly positive influence" by "2", and "a doubly negative influence" by "-2" (cf. the interpretation of the three values -1, 0, 1 of CR and FCR described before).

Another specialization of TE($BISG_1$) leads to the next theory-element.

Theory-Element "Behavior Interaction in Triads"

Def-TE(BIT)

$TE(BIT)$ is the theory-element "behavior interaction in triads" iff there exist $K(BIT)$ and $I(BIT)$ such that

(1) $TE(BIT) = \langle K(BIT), I(BIT) \rangle$;

(2) $K(BIT) = \langle M_p(BIT), M(BIT), M_{pp}(BIT), C(BIT), L(BIT) \rangle$ is the core of $TE(BIT)$;

Table 7 *Direct and indirect influences contingent upon category relations and frequency courses*

$CR(c_k, c_j)$	$FRC(c_k)$	$CR(c_j, c)$	$FRC(c_j)$	$DI(c_j, c)$	$IDI(c_k, c_j, c)$ $c_k = c$	$c_k \neq c$
		F	$\Uparrow$	pos		
		F	=	noin		
		F	$\Downarrow$	neg		
		N	$\Uparrow$	noin		
		N	=	noin		
		N	$\Downarrow$	noin		
		I	$\Uparrow$	neg		
		I	=	noin		
		I	$\Downarrow$	pos		
F	$\Uparrow$	F	=		dpos	pos
F	$\Uparrow$	N	=		noin	noin
F	$\Uparrow$	I	=			neg
F	=	F	=		noin	noin
F	=	N	=		noin	noin
F	=	I	=		noin	noin
F	$\Downarrow$	F	=		dneg	neg
F	$\Downarrow$	N	=		noin	noin
F	$\Downarrow$	I	=			pos
N	$\Uparrow$	F	=		noin	noin
N	$\Uparrow$	N	=		noin	noin
N	$\Uparrow$	I	=		noin	noin
N	=	F	=		noin	noin
N	=	N	=		noin	noin
N	=	I	=		noin	noin
N	$\Downarrow$	F	=		noin	noin
N	$\Downarrow$	N	=		noin	noin
N	$\Downarrow$	I	=		noin	noin
I	$\Uparrow$	F	=			neg
I	$\Uparrow$	N	=		noin	noin
I	$\Uparrow$	I	=		dpos	pos
I	=	F	=		noin	noin
I	=	N	=		noin	noin
I	=	I	=		noin	noin
I	$\Downarrow$	F	=			pos
I	$\Downarrow$	N	=		noin	noin
I	$\Downarrow$	I	=		dneg	neg

Note: "F", "N", and "I" stand for "facilitating", "neutral", and "inhibiting"; "$\Uparrow$", "=", and "$\Downarrow$" stand for "increases", "remains the same", and "decreases"; "pos", "neg", "noin", "dpos", and "dneg" stand for "positive", "negative", "no influence", "doubly positive", and "doubly negative", respectively.

(3) $I(BIT)$ is the domain of intended applications of $K(BIT)$.

Def-M$_p$(BIT)
$M_p(BIT) = M_p(BISG_1)$.

Def-M(BIT)
$M(BIT) := \{x : x$ is a *model* of the theory-element $BIT\}$
x is a model of the theory-element BIT iff

(1) $x \in M_p(BIT)$;
(2) $x \in M(BISG_1)$;
(3) $|S| = 3$.

Def-M$_{pp}$(BIT)
$M_{pp}(BIT) = M_{pp}(BISG_1)$.

Def-C(BIT)
$C(BIT) \subseteq C(BISG_1)$.

Def-L(BIT)
$L(BIT) \subseteq L(BISG_1)$.

Def-I(BIT)
The elements of $I(BIT)$ are the behavior interactions in ***triads***, i.e., the frequency dynamics within triadic interaction structures, as described by the non-theoretical concepts of the theory; and $I(BIT) \subseteq M_{pp}(BIT)$, and $I(BIT) \subset I(BISG_1)$.

Comments

This theory-element refers explicitly to the behavior interaction in triads, and has already been tested by empirical investigations (cf. Nell et al., 1988; Westmeyer et al., 1987). As in the case of $TE(BID)$, it is easy to transform the previous formulation of the special laws of $TE(BIT)$ into the current version. As compared with the theory-element for dyads, the possibility now exists that a controlling category of one person exerts an indirect influence on a controlled category of another person which is mediated by a - simultaneously controlling and controlled - category of a third person. However, this interactional constellation poses no special problems and is covered by stipulation (5b) of $Def\text{-}M(BISG_1)$. Therefore, there is no need for additional special laws to cope with this situation.

$TE(BID)$ and $TE(BIT)$ do not say very much about time periods and the relations which exist between them. As in the case of $TE(BI)$, six time periods are distinguished: the category relation function refers to p_1 ; the frequency course function refers, in the case of controlling categories, to p_3 relative to p_2; the direct and indirect influence functions refer to p_4; and the frequency course function refers, in the case of controlled categories, to p_6 relative to p_5. Only some of the relations between these time periods are fixed by the special laws. Moreover, not all of the six time periods have to be different. As a consequence, various more restrictive specializations of the theory-elements can be defined. Four of these specializations of $TE(BID)$ will be introduced. Corresponding formulations are possible for $TE(BIT)$, but these will be omitted here.

Specialization 1 of the Theory-Element "Behavior Interaction in Dyads"

Def-TE(BID$_1$)
$TE(BID_1)$ is specialization 1 of the theory-element BID iff there exist $K(BID_1)$ and $I(BID_1)$ such that
(1) $TE(BID_1) = \langle K(BID_1), I(BID_1)\rangle$;

(2) $K(BID_1) = \langle M_p(BID_1), M(BID_1), M_{pp}(BID_1), C(BID_1), L(BID_1)\rangle$ is the core of $TE(BID_1)$;
(3) $I(BID_1)$ is the domain of intended applications of $K(BID_1)$.

Def-M$_p$(BID$_1$)
$M_p(BID_1) = M_p(BID)$.

Def-M(BID$_1$)
$M(BID_1) := \{x : x$ is a *model* of the theory-element $BID_1\}$
x is a model of the theory-element BID_1 iff
(1) $x \in M_p(BID_1)$;
(2) $x \in M(BID)$;
(3) $\exists\, p_1, p_2 \in P$ with $\langle p_1, p_2\rangle \in \leq_p$ and $p_1 \neq p_2$ $\forall c_k, c_j, c \in CS$ $\forall w_1, w_2, v \in \{-1, 0, 1\}$:
  (a) $CR(c_j, c, p_1) = w_1 \wedge FRC(c_j, p_2, p_1) = v \longrightarrow DI(c_j, c, p_2) = w_1 \cdot v$,
  (b) $CR(c_k, c_j, p_1) = w_1 \wedge CR(c_j, c, p_1) = w_2 \wedge FRC(c_k, p_2, p_1) = v \wedge$ $FRC(c_j, p_2, p_1) = 0 \longrightarrow$
  $(c_k = c \longrightarrow IDI(c_k, c_j, c, p_2) = 2 \cdot w_1 \cdot w_2 \cdot v) \wedge$
  $(c_k \neq c \longrightarrow IDI(c_k, c_j, c, p_2) = w_1 \cdot w_2 \cdot v)$,
  (c) $(SUMI(c, p_2) > 0 \longrightarrow FRC(c, p_2, p_1) \neq -1) \wedge (SUMI(c, p_2) < 0 \longrightarrow$ $FRC(c, p_2, p_1) \neq 1)$.

Def-M$_{pp}$(BID$_1$)
$M_{pp}(BID_1) = M_{pp}(BID)$.

Def-C(BID$_1$)
$C(BID_1) \subseteq C(BID)$.

Def-I(BID$_1$)
$I(BID_1) \subseteq I(BID)$.

Comments

In this case, the existence of only two different time periods is assumed. p_1 is the phase used for the identification of the dyadic interaction structure; in addition, it is also the reference phase for the determination of the frequency courses of the behavior categories. p_2 is a later time period in which the frequency courses of both controlling and controlled behavior categories are considered, and in which the controlling categories exert their (direct and indirect) influences on the controlled ones.

Further specializations of $TE(BID)$ lead to $TE(BID_2) - TE(BID_4)$. It should be noted that different specializations may be associated with different extents of empirical confirmation of the resulting theory-elements (cf. Westmeyer, 1987).

Specialization 2 of the Theory-Element "Behavior Interaction in Dyads"

Def-TE(BID$_2$)
$TE(BID_2)$ is specialization 2 of the theory-element BID iff there exist $K(BID_2)$ and $I(BID_2)$ such that

(1) $TE(BID_2) = \langle K(BID_2), I(BID_2)\rangle$;
(2) $K(BID_2) = \langle M_p(BID_2), M(BID_2), M_{pp}(BID_2), C(BID_2), L(BID_2)\rangle$ is the core of $TE(BID_2)$;
(3) $I(BID_2)$ is the domain of intended applications of $K(BID_2)$.

Def-M$_p$(BID$_2$)
$M_p(BID_2) = M_p(BID)$.

Def-M(BID$_2$)
$M(BID_2) := \{x : x \text{ is a } \textit{model} \text{ of the theory-element } BID_2\}$
x is a model of the theory-element BID_2 iff
(1) $x \in M_p(BID_2)$;
(2) $x \in M(BID)$;
(3) $\exists\, p_1, p_2, p_3, p \in P$ with $\langle p_1, p_2\rangle, \langle p_2, p_3\rangle \in \leq_p$ and $p_1 \neq p_2 \neq p_3$ and $p = p_1 \cup p_2$
$\forall c_k, c_j, c \in CS$
$\forall w_1, w_2, v \in \{-1, 0, 1\}$:
(a) $CR(c_j, c, p_2) = w_1 \wedge FRC(c_j, p_3, p) = v \longrightarrow DI(c_j, c, p_3) = w_1 \cdot v$,
(b) $CR(c_k, c_j, p_2) = w_1 \wedge CR(c_j, c, p_2) = w_2 \wedge FRC(c_k, p_3, p) = v \wedge FRC(c_j, p_3, p) = 0 \longrightarrow$
$(c_k = c \longrightarrow IDI(c_k, c_j, c, p_3) = 2 \cdot w_1 \cdot w_2 \cdot v) \wedge$
$(c_k \neq c \longrightarrow IDI(c_k, c_j, c, p_3) = w_1 \cdot w_2 \cdot v)$,
(c) $(SUMI(c, p_3) > 0 \longrightarrow FRC(c, p_3, p) \neq -1) \wedge (SUMI(c, p_3) < 0 \longrightarrow FRC(c, p_3, p) \neq 1)$.

Def-M$_{pp}$(BID$_2$)
$M_{pp}(BID_2) = M_{pp}(BID)$.

Def-C(BID$_2$)
$C(BID_2) \subseteq C(BID)$.

Def-I(BID$_2$)
$I(BID_2) \subseteq I(BID)$.

Specialization 3 of the Theory-Element "Behavior Interaction in Dyads"

Def-TE(BID$_3$)
$TE(BID_3)$ is specialization 3 of the theory-element BID iff there exist $K(BID_3)$ and $I(BID_3)$ such that
(1) $TE(BID_3) = \langle K(BID_3), I(BID_3)\rangle$;
(2) $K(BID_3) = \langle M_p(BID_3), M(BID_3), M_{pp}(BID_3), C(BID_3), L(BID_3)\rangle$ is the core of $TE(BID_3)$;
(3) $I(BID_3)$ is the domain of intended applications of $K(BID_3)$.

Def-M$_p$(BID$_3$)
$M_p(BID_3) = M_p(BID)$.

Def-M(BID$_3$)
$M(BID_3) := \{x : x \text{ is a } \textit{model} \text{ of the theory-element } BID_3\}$
x is a model of the theory-element BID_3 iff

(1) $x \in M_p(BID_3)$;
(2) $x \in M(BID)$;
(3) $\exists\, p_1, p_2, p_3 \in P$ with $\langle p_1, p_2\rangle, \langle p_2, p_3\rangle \in \leq_p$ and $p_1 \neq p_2 \neq p_3$ $\forall c_k, c_j, c \in CS$ $\forall w_1, w_2, v \in \{-1, 0, 1\}$:

(a) $CR(c_j, c, p_2) = w_1 \wedge FRC(c_j, p_3, p_1) = v \longrightarrow DI(c_j, c, p_3) = w_1 \cdot v$,
(b) $CR(c_k, c_j, p_2) = w_1 \wedge CR(c_j, c, p_2) = w_2 \wedge FRC(c_k, p_3, p_1) = v \wedge$ $FRC(c_j, p_3, p_1) = 0 \longrightarrow$ $(c_k = c \longrightarrow IDI(c_k, c_j, c, p_3) = 2 \cdot w_1 \cdot w_2 \cdot v) \wedge$ $(c_k \neq c \longrightarrow IDI(c_k, c_j, c, p_3) = w_1 \cdot w_2 \cdot v)$,
(c) $(SUMI(c, p_3) > 0 \longrightarrow FRC(c, p_3, p_1) \neq -1) \wedge (SUMI(c, p_3) < 0 \longrightarrow$ $FRC(c, p_3, p_1) \neq 1)$.

Def-M$_{pp}$(BID$_3$)
$M_{pp}(BID_3) = M_{pp}(BID)$.

Def-C(BID$_3$)
$C(BID_3) \subseteq C(BID)$.

Def-I(BID$_3$)
$I(BID_3) \subseteq I(BID)$.

Specialization 4 of the Theory-Element "Behavior Interaction in Dyads"

Def-TE(BID$_4$)
$TE(BID_4)$ is specialization 4 of the theory-element BID iff there exist $K(BID_4)$ and $I(BID_4)$ such that

(1) $TE(BID_4) = \langle K(BID_4), I(BID_4)\rangle$;
(2) $K(BID_4) = \langle M_p(BID_4), M(BID_4), M_{pp}(BID_4), C(BID_4), L(BID_4)\rangle$ is the core of $TE(BID_4)$;
(3) $I(BID_4)$ is the domain of intended applications of $K(BID_4)$.

Def-M$_p$(BID$_4$)
$M_p(BID_4) = M_p(BID)$.

Def-M(BID$_4$)
$M(BID_4) := \{x : x \text{ is a } \textit{model} \text{ of the theory-element } BID_4\}$
x is a model of the theory-element BID_4 iff

(1) $x \in M_p(BID_4)$;
(2) $x \in M(BID)$;
(3) $\exists\, p_1, p_2 \in P$ with $\langle p_1, p_2\rangle \in \leq_p$ and $p_1 \neq p_2$ $\forall c_k, c_j, c \in CS$ $\forall w_1, w_2, v \in \{-1, 0, 1\}$:

(a) $CR(c_j, c, p_1) = w_1 \wedge FRC(c_j, p_2, p_1) = v \longrightarrow DI(c_j, c, p_2) = w_1 \cdot v$,
(b) $CR(c_k, c_j, p_1) = w_1 \wedge CR(c_j, c, p_1) = w_2 \wedge FRC(c_k, p_2, p_1) = v \wedge$ $FRC(c_j, p_2, p_1) = 0 \longrightarrow$ $(c_k = c \longrightarrow IDI(c_k, c_j, c, p_2) = 2 \cdot w_1 \cdot w_2 \cdot v) \wedge$ $(c_k \neq c \longrightarrow IDI(c_k, c_j, c, p_2) = w_1 \cdot w_2 \cdot v)$,

(c) $(SUMI(c,p_2) > 0 \longrightarrow FRC(c,p_2,p_1) \neq -1) \wedge (SUMI(c,p_2) < 0 \longrightarrow FRC(c,p_2,p_1) \neq 1)$.

Def-$\mathbf{M}_{pp}$(BID$_4$)
$M_{pp}(BID_4) = M_{pp}(BID)$.

Def-C(BID$_4$)
$C(BID_4) \subseteq C(BID)$.

Def-I(BID$_4$)
$I(BID_4) \subseteq I(BID)$.

Comments

$TE(BID_4)$ is a special variant of BID which is used as a lower reference point for judgments about the empirical adequacy of the other specializations of $TE(BID)$. In $TE(BID_4)$, the dyadic interaction structure is determined for the same time period as are the frequency courses of the categories and the direct and indirect influences impinging on them. Only the reference phase for the frequency courses is a prior time period. Hence, this variant lacks any prognostic content. However, it is assumed that most interaction structures are more adequately described by the other specializations of $TE(BID)$. This seems indeed to be the case (see in Westmeyer, 1987, for more detail).

Links to the Theory of Behavior Interaction

The theory of behavior interaction, conceived of as a theory-net, can be linked to other theory-nets of a more elementary nature. Through the use of interpreting links (cf. Balzer et al., 1987; Stegmüller, 1986), the concepts of category relation and frequency course are interpreted by concepts characteristic of theory-elements of other theory-nets. One theory-net which can be referred to for the interpretation of the concept of frequency course deals with indifference structures (IS); another one, which can be used for the interpretation of the concept of category relation, deals with certain probability structures (PS).

To give a precise definition of these intertheoretical links, it is necessary to introduce several new concepts, namely, Q, $\leq_q$, FR, IR, and $PROB$, which are components of these structures.

Q is a set of time segments. It is assumed that every time period can be decomposed into a set of time segments. A time segment is therefore a subset of a time period and is itself a set.

$\leq_q$ is a total ordering of the set Q, i.e., $\leq_q$ is reflexive, antisymmetric, transitive, and connected in Q.

FR is a relative frequency function. It assigns a real number out of the interval $[0,1]$ to a behavior category for a time period or time segment.

IR is an indifference range function. The indifference range of a category for a certain period of time is a compact subset of the range of the relative frequency function.

$PROB$ is a probability function.

The set of potential models of the theory-element "indifference structure" can now be defined as follows:

Def-M_p(IS)
$M_p(IS) = \{y_1 : y_1$ is a *potential model* of the theory-element $IS\}$
y_1 is a potential model of the theory-element IS iff there exist S, CS, AF, P, $\leq_p$, Q, $\leq_q$, FR, IR such that

(1) $y_1 = \langle S, CS, AF, P, \leq_p, Q, \leq_q, FR, IR\rangle$;
(2) S and CS are non-empty, finite sets;
(3) $AF : S \Longrightarrow Po(CS)$;
if $CS_i := AF(s_i)$ with $i = 1, ..., n$ and $n = |S|$, then $\{CS_1, ..., CS_n\}$ is a decomposition of CS;
(4) P and Q are non-empty, finite sets ordered by $\leq_p$ and $\leq_q$ resp., and $\exists X(Q \subseteq Po(X))$;
(5) $FR : CS \times P \cup Q \Longrightarrow [0,1] \subset \mathbb{R}$;
(6) $IR : CS \times P \Longrightarrow Po([0,1])$.

A corresponding definition of the set of potential models of the theory-element "probability structure" will be given elsewhere.

The interpreting links to the elements of the theory-net of behavior interaction can now be defined in the following way:

Def-L(BID_1)
$x \in L(BID_1)$ iff there exist y_1 and y_2 such that $\langle y_1, x\rangle \in L_1(BID_1)$ and $\langle y_2, x\rangle \in L_2(BID_1)$.

Def-L_1(BID_1)
$L_1(BID_1)$ is a *link from* $M_p(IS)$ *to* $M_p(BID_1)$ iff
$L_1(BID_1) \subseteq M_p(IS) \times M_p(BID_1)$.
$\langle y_1, x\rangle \in L_1(BID_1)$ iff

(1) $x = \langle S, CS, AF, P, \leq_p, FRC, CR, DI, IDI\rangle$;
(2) $y_1 = \langle S, CS, AF, P, \leq_p, Q, \leq_q, FR, IR\rangle$;
(3) $\forall c \in CS \ \forall p_1, p_2 \in P$ with $\langle p_1, p_2\rangle$:

(a) $FRC(c, p_2, p_1) = 1$ iff $FR(c, p_2) > sup(IR(c, p_1))$,
(b) $FRC(c, p_2, p_1) = 0$ iff $FR(c, p_2) \in IR(c, p_1)$,
(c) $FRC(c, p_2, p_1) = -1$ iff $FR(c, p_2) < inf(IR(c, p_1))$.

Def-L_2(BID_1)
$L_2(BID_1)$ is a *link from* $M_p(PS_1)$ *to* $M_p(BID_1)$ iff
$L_2(BID_1) \subseteq M_p(PS_1) \times Mp(BID_1)$.
$\langle y_2, x\rangle \in L_2(BID_1)$ iff

(1) $x \in M_p(BID_1)$;
(2) $y_1 \in M_p(PS_1)$;
(3) $\forall c_j \in AF(s_{i1})$, $c \in AF(s_{i2})$ with $i_1, i_2 = 1, 2$ and $i_1 \neq i_2$ $\forall p \in P$:

(a) $CR(c_j, c, p) = 1$ iff $PROB(c|c_j, p) > PROB(c, p)$,
(b) $CR(c_j, c, p) = 0$ iff $PROB(c|c_j, p) = PROB(c, p)$,
(c) $CR(c_j, c, p) = -1$ iff $PROB(c|c_j, p) < PROB(c, p)$.

Def-L(BID$_2$)-L(BID$_4$)
$L(BID_2) = L(BID_3) = L(BID_4) = L(BID_1)$.

Comments

Assumption (3) of $Def\text{-}L_1(BID_1)$ states that the concept of frequency course can be interpreted by the concepts of relative frequency and indifference range. The frequency course of c in p_2 relative to p_1 is equal to 1, i.e., the frequency of c increases in p_2 relative to p_1 , if and only if the relative frequency of a behavior category c in time period p_2 is greater than the supremum of the indifference range of c in time period p_1 ; the frequency course of c in p_2 relative to p_1 is equal to -1, i.e., the frequency of c decreases in p_2 relative to p_1, if and only if the relative frequency of c in p_2 is smaller than the infimum of the indifference range of c in p_1; and the frequency course of c in p_2 relative to p_1 is equal to 0, i.e., the frequency of c remains constant in p_2 relative to p_1, if and only if the relative frequency of c in p_2 stays within the limits of the indifference range of c in p_1. FR and IR are concepts of a simple theory-net dealing with indifference structures for behavior categories.

Stipulation (4) of $Def\text{-}L_2(BID_1)$ interprets the concept of category relation by the concepts of absolute and conditional probability. There is a facilitating category relation between c_j and c during p, if and only if the conditional probability of a behavior category c, given a category c_j, in time period p is greater than the absolute probability of c in p; there is an inhibiting category relation between c_j and c, if and only if the conditional probability is smaller than the absolute one; and there is a neutral category relation between c_j and c, if and only if the two probabilities are the same.

The concepts of absolute and conditional probability are part of a theory-element $TE(PS_1)$ concerned with probability structures of a certain kind. This theory-element and all other ones which together constitute a separate theory-net are not elaborated in this chapter. It may be noted, however, that the comparison of absolute and conditional probabilities required in $Def\text{-}L_2(BID_1)$ poses difficult problems, which are the subject-matter of the theory of stochastic processes (cf. Suen & Ary, 1989). To cope with these problems, in the existing empirical investigations of the theory of behavior interaction a special procedure, called INSEDA, has been used for the sequential analysis of categorical interaction data. This procedure takes into account the autodependencies of the behavior of the observed subjects, i.e., the interaction structures within each person (cf. Holling & Schultze, 1985).

An elaboration of the theory-net dealing with indifference structures can now be formulated as follows.

Theory-Element "Indifference Structure"

Def-TE(IS)
$TE(IS)$ is the theory-element IS iff there exist $K(IS)$ and $I(IS)$ such that
(1) $TE(IS) = \langle K(IS), I(IS) \langle$;
(2) $K(IS) = \langle M_p(IS), M(IS), M_{pp}(IS), C(IS), L(IS) \rangle$ is the core of $TE(IS)$;
(3) $I(IS)$ is the domain of intended applications of $K(IS)$.

Def-M_p(IS)
has already been introduced.

Def-M(IS)
$M(IS) := \{y_1 : y_1$ is a *model* of the theory-element $IS\}$
y_1 is a model of the theory-element IS iff
(1) $y_1 \in M_p(IS)$;
(2) $\forall p \in P \ \exists q_1, ..., q_{n1} \in Q \ \forall j1, j2 \in \{1, ..., n1\}$:

(a) $\{q_1, ..., q_{n1}\}$ is a decomposition of p,
(b) if $j2 > j1$, then $\langle q_{j1}, q_{j2} \rangle$,
(c) $|q_{j1}| \cong |q_{j2}|$,
(d) $\exists f_3, f_4$ with $f_3, f_4 : [0,1]^{n1} \Longrightarrow [0,1] : \forall c \in CS \ \forall v_1, ..., v_{n1} \in [0,1]$:
$FR(c, q_1) = v_1 \wedge ... \wedge FR(c, q_{n1}) = v_{n1} \longrightarrow sup\,(IR(c,p)) = f_3(v_1, ..., v_{n1})$
$\wedge \ inf(IR(c,p)) = f_4(v_1, ..., v_{n1})$.

Def-M_{pp}(IS)
$M_{pp}(IS) = \{\langle S, CS, AF, P, \leq_p, Q, \leq_q, FR \rangle$: there exists IR such that
$\langle S, CS, AF, P, \leq_p, Q, \leq_q, FR, IR \rangle \in M_p(IS)\}$.

Def-C(IS)
$C(IS) = \{Y_1 : Y_1$ satisfies the *constraint* of the theory-element $IS\}$
Y_1 satisfies the constraint of the theory-element IS iff
(1) $Y_1 \subseteq M_p(IS)$;
(2) $Y_1 \neq \emptyset$;
(3) $\forall y_{11}, y \in Y \ : \ pr_2(y_1) = pr_2(y_2)$.

Def-I(IS)
The elements of $I(IS)$ are the relative frequencies of behavior categories within time periods and time segments, as described by the non-theoretical concepts of IS; and $I(IS) \subseteq M_{pp}(IS)$.

Comments

All components of the potential models of $TE(IS)$ have already been introduced. In *Def-M(IS)*, the existence of a decomposition of a time period p into a set of $n1$ succedent time segments (cf. [2a],[2b]) of approximately equal length (cf. [2c]) is assumed. The supremum of the indifference range of a category c within time period p is a function f_3 of the relative frequencies of c within the $n1$ time segments, and the infimum of the indifference range is a function f_4 of the same relative frequency values.

As *Def-M_{pp}(IS)* indicates, IR is taken to be a theoretical concept of the theory-element IS. The constraint $C(IS)$ postulates the existence of a non-empty set of potential models of $TE(IS)$ which use the same category system for the description of behavior, and $I(IS)$ describes the subject matter of this theory-net.

In *Def-M(IS)*, the functions f_3 and f_4 are left largely unspecified. There are many options for the fixing of f_3 and f_4, and four of them are suggested in the following specializations of $TE(IS)$. Each of these specializations has been used in empirical investigations of the theory of behavior interaction, and it was found that the extent of empirical confirmation of the theory depends on the formula chosen for the computation of indifference ranges (cf. Westmeyer, 1987).

Specialization 1 of the Theory-Element "Indifference Structure"

Def-TE(IS$_1$)
$TE(IS_1)$ is the theory-element IS_1 iff there exist $K(IS_1)$ and $I(IS_1)$ such that
(1) $TE(IS_1) = \langle K(IS_1), I(IS_1)\rangle$;
(2) $K(IS_1) = \langle M_p(IS_1), M(IS_1), M_{pp}(IS_1), C(IS_1), L(IS_1)\rangle$ is the core of $TE(IS_1)$;
(3) $I(IS_1)$ is the domain of intended applications of $K(IS_1)$.

Def-M$_p$(IS$_1$)
$M_p(IS_1) = M_p(IS)$.

Def-M(IS$_1$)[4]
$M(IS_1) := \{y_1 : y_1$ is a *model* of the theory-element $IS_1\}$
y_1 is a model of the theory-element IS_1 iff
(1) $y_1 \in M_p(IS_1)$;
(2) $y_1 \in M(IS)$;
(3) $n1 = 2$;
(4) $\forall v_1, v_2 \in [0,1] \ : \ f_3(v_1, v_2) = m(v_1, v_2) + abs(v_1 - v_2) \wedge$
$f_4(v_1, v_2) = m(v_1, v_2) - abs(v_1 - v_2)$ with $m(v_1, v_2) = (v_1 + v_2)/2$.

Def-M$_{pp}$(IS$_1$)
$M_{pp}(IS_1) = M_{pp}(IS)$.

Def-C(IS$_1$)
$C(IS_1) \subseteq C(IS)$.

Def-I(IS$_1$)
$I(IS_1) \subseteq I(IS)$.

Comments

In this first specialization of $TE(IS)$, a time period p is decomposed into two time segments and, if v_1 and v_2 are the relative frequencies of a category c within these time segments, then the value of f_3 (f_4) for v_1 and v_2 is defined as the average of v_1 and v_2 plus (minus) the absolute value of the difference between v_1 and v_2 .

Specialization 2 of the Theory-Element "Indifference Structure"

Def-TE(IS$_2$)
$TE(IS_2)$ is the theory-element IS_2 iff there exist $K(IS_2)$ and $I(IS_2)$ such that
(1) $TE(IS_2) = \langle K(IS_2), I(IS_2)\rangle$;

[4]In *Def-M(BI)*, f_3, f_4, and n_1 are introduced as variables. To simplify the definitions of those theory-elements which are specializations of TE(IS), only the additional requirements which these specializations must meet are explicitely mentioned. Therefore, "f_3" in stipulation (4) of *Def-M*(IS_1) refers to the function variable f_3, as introduced in stipulation (2d) of *Def-M*(IS); "f_4" refers to the function variable f_4, as introduced in stipulation (2d) of *Def-M*(IS); etc.

(2) $K(IS_2) = \langle M_p(IS_2), M(IS_2), M_{pp}(IS_2), C(IS_2), L(IS_2)\langle$ is the core of $TE(IS_2)$;
(3) $I(IS_2)$ is the domain of intended applications of $K(IS_2)$.

Def-M$_p$(IS$_2$)
$M_p(IS_2) = M_p(IS)$.

Def-M(IS$_2$)
$M(IS_2) := \{y_1 : y_1$ is a *model* of the theory-element $IS_2\}$
y_1 is a model of the theory-element IS_2 iff
(1) $y_1 \in M_p(IS_2)$;
(2) $y_1 \in M(IS)$;
(3) $n1 \geq 4$;
(4) $\forall v_1, ..., v_{n1} \in [0,1] : f_3(v_1, ..., v_{n1}) = m(v_1, ..., v_{n1}) + sd(v_1, ..., v_{n1}1) \wedge$
$f_4(v_1, ..., v_{n1}) = m(v_1, ..., v_{n1}) - sd(v_1, ...v_{n1})$
with $m(v_1, ..., v_{n1}) = (1/n1)\sum_{j1} v_{j1}$ and
$(sd(v_1, ..., v_{n1}))^2 = (1/n1)\sum_{j1}(v_{j1} - m(v_1, ..., v_{n1}))^2$.

Def-M$_{pp}$(IS$_2$)
$M_{pp}(IS_2) = M_{pp}(IS)$.

Def-C(IS$_2$)
$C(IS_2) \subseteq C(IS)$.

Def-I(IS$_2$)
$I(IS_2) \subseteq I(IS)$.

Comments

In the second specialization of $TE(IS)$, a time period p is decomposed into at least four time segments, and the value of f_3 (f_4) for the relative frequencies of a category c within these time segments is defined as the average of the frequencies plus (minus) their standard deviation.

Specialization 3 of the Theory-Element "Indifference Structure"

Def-TE(IS$_3$)
$TE(IS_3)$ is the theory-element IS_3 iff there exist $K(IS_3)$ and $I(IS_3)$ such that
(1) $TE(IS_3) = \langle K(IS_3), I(IS_3)\rangle$;
(2) $K(IS_3) = \langle M_p(IS_3), M(IS_3), M_{pp}(IS_3), C(IS_3), L(IS_3)\rangle$ is the core of $TE(IS_3)$;
(3) $I(IS_3)$ is the domain of intended applications of $K(IS_3)$.

Def-M$_p$(IS$_3$)
$M_p(IS_3) = M_p(IS)$.

Def-M(IS$_3$)
$M(IS_3) := \{y_1 : y_1$ is a *model* of the theory-element $IS_3\}$
y_1 is a model of the theory-element IS_3 iff
(1) $y_1 \in M_p(IS_3)$;
(2) $y_1 \in M(IS)$;
(3) $n1 \geq 4$;

(4) $\forall v_1, ..., v_{n1} \in [0,1] : f_3(v_1, ..., v_{n1}) = max(v_1, ..., v_{n1}) \wedge$
$f_4(v_1, ..., v_{n1}) = min(v_1, ..., v_{n1})$.

Def-M$_{pp}$(IS$_3$)
$M_{pp}(IS_3) = M_{pp}(IS)$.

Def-C(IS$_3$)
$C(IS_3) \subseteq C(IS)$.

Def-I(IS$_3$)
$I(IS_3) \subseteq I(IS)$.

Comments

Here, a time period p is decomposed into at least four time segments, and the value of f_3 (f_4) for the relative frequencies of a category c within these time segments is identical with the maximum (minimum) of these relative frequencies.

Specialization 4 of the Theory-Element "Indifference Structure"

Def-TE(IS$_4$)
$TE(IS_4)$ is the theory-element IS_4 iff there exist $K(IS_4)$ and $I(IS_4)$ such that
(1) $TE(IS_4) = \langle K(IS_4), I(IS_4)\rangle$;
(2) $K(IS_4) = \langle M_p(IS_4), M(IS_4), M_{pp}(IS_4), C(IS_4), L(IS_4)\rangle$ is the core of $TE(IS_4)$;
(3) $I(IS_4)$ is the domain of intended applications of $K(IS_4)$.

Def-M$_p$(IS$_4$)
$M_p(IS_4) = M_p(IS)$.

Def-M(IS$_4$)
$M(IS_4) := \{y_1 : y_1$ is a *model* of the theory-element $IS_4\}$
y_1 is a model of the theory-element IS_4 iff
(1) $y_1 \in M_p(IS_4)$;
(2) $y_1 \in M(IS)$;
(3) $n1 = 2$;
(4) $\forall v_1, v_2 \in [0,1] : f_3(v_1, v_2) = max(v_1, v_2) \wedge f_4(v_1, v_2) = min(v_1, v_2)$.

Def-M$_{pp}$(IS$_4$)
$M_{pp}(IS_4) = M_{pp}(IS)$.

Def-C(IS$_4$)
$C(IS_4) \subseteq C(IS)$.

Def-I(IS$_4$)
$I(IS_4) \subseteq I(IS)$.

Comments

In this final specialization of $TE(IS)$, a time period is decomposed into two time segments, and the value of f_3 (f_4) for v_1 and v_2 is identical with the larger (smaller) one of both.

It should be noted that this formula leads to comparatively narrow indifference ranges. The relative width of the indifference ranges is important because, if the ranges are too narrow, then random fluctuations of relative frequencies over periods of time may be incorrectly interpreted as significant changes of a frequency course; conversely, if the indifference ranges are too wide, real changes of frequency courses may escape notice. Both kinds of errors have important consequences for the testability of the theory (cf. Westmeyer, 1987).

Link to the Theory of Indifference Structures

The theory of indifference structures, conceived of as a simple theory-net, can be linked to yet another theory-net, the theory of coding structures (COS). This theory provides interpretations for six of the nine components of potential models of $TE(IS)$. To achieve this goal, five additional elementary concepts have to be introduced: O, INT, $\leq_{int}$, CO, and CF.

O is a set of observers. Up to this point, we have not dealt with the coding process itself. However, once we ask who applies the behavior categories to the interacting persons, we have to introduce the notion of an observer or coder who assigns categories to the behavior of persons within certain units of time. We assume here that the set of observers contains only one element. Thus, if we consider a second observer, we refer to another coding structure.

INT is a set of time intervals. Time intervals are the second smallest time units used in the theory. A time interval is itself a set.

$\leq_{int}$ is a total ordering of the set INT, i.e., $\leq_{int}$ is reflexive, antisymmetric, transitive, and connected in INT.

CO is a coding function. A coding is defined as the assignment of a category to (the behavior of) a person in a time interval by an observer. Of course, only those categories can be assigned to a person which are elements of the proper subset of CS reserved for the coding of that person's behavior.

CF is a coding frequency function. CF yields a natural number for every category and every subset of INT which expresses the (absolute) frequency with which a category has been coded for a set of time intervals.

The set of potential models of the theory-element "coding structure" can now be defined as follows:

Def-M$_p$(COS)
$M_p(COS) = \{z_1 : z_1$ is a *potential model* of the theory-element $COS\}$
z_1 is a potential model of the theory-element COS iff there exist S, CS, AF, O, INT, $\leq_{int}$, CO, CF such that

(1) $z = \langle S, CS, AF, O, INT, \leq_{int}, CO, CF\rangle$;
(2) S and CS are non-empty, finite sets;
(3) $AF : S \Longrightarrow Po(CS)$;
if $CS_1 := AF(s_1)$ with $i = 1, ..., n$ and $n = |S|$, then $\{CS_1, ..., CS_n\}$ is a decomposition of CS;
(4) O is a set with $|O| = 1$;
(5) INT is a non-empty, finite set ordered by $\leq_{int}$;
(6) $CO : O \times S \times INT \Longrightarrow CS$;
if $CO(o, s, int) = c$, then $c \in AF(s)$;

(7) $CF : CS \times Po(INT) \Longrightarrow \mathbb{N}$.

On the basis of this definition, the interpreting link from the theory of coding structures to the theory of indifference structures can be defined in the following way:

Def-L(IS)

$L(IS)$ is a *link from* $M_p(COS)$ *to* $M_p(IS)$ iff
$L(IS) \subseteq M_p(COS) \times M_p(IS)$.
$\langle z_1, y_1 \rangle \in L(IS)$ iff

(1) $y_1 = \langle S, CS, AF, P, \leq_p, Q, \leq_q, FR, IR \rangle$;
(2) $z_1 = \langle S, CS, AF, O, INT, \leq_{int}, CO, CF \rangle$;
(3) $\exists \phi_1 : P \cup Q \Longrightarrow Po(INT)$;
(4) $\forall p_1, p_2 \in P : \langle p_1, p_2 \rangle \in \leq_p$ iff $\forall int_1 \in \phi_1(p_1),\ int_2 \in \phi_2(p_2) : \langle int_1, int_2 \rangle \in \leq_{int}$;
(5) $\forall q_1, q_2 \in Q : \langle q_1, q_2 \rangle \in \leq_q$ iff $\forall int_1 \in \phi_1(q_1),\ int_2 \in \phi_2(q_2) : \langle int_1, int_2 \rangle \in \leq_{int}$;
(6) $\forall c \in CS\ \forall r \in P \cup Q\ \forall v \in [0,1] :\ FR(c, r) = v$ iff $CF(c, \phi_1(r))/|\phi_1(r)| = v$.

Def-L(IS$_1$)-L(IS$_4$)

$L(IS_1) = L(IS_2) = L(IS_3) = L(IS_4) = L(IS)$.

Comments

The function ϕ_1 assigns an element of the power set of INT to each time period or segment, thereby decomposing the larger time units into smaller components, i.e. into time intervals. Correspondingly, the order relations on the sets of time periods and segments are interpreted by the order relation on the set of intervals. Finally, the relative frequency of a category c in a time period or segment r is reduced to the ratio of the coding frequency of c in r to the number of intervals which make up r.

As the following definition of the theory-element "coding structure" reveals, the relation between the functions CO and CF is of a very simple nature, but the formulation of the constraint requires rather complex conceptual constructions.

Theory-Element "Coding Structure"

Def-TE(COS)

$TE(COS)$ is the theory-element COS iff there exist $K(COS)$ and $I(COS)$ such that

(1) $TE(COS) = \langle K(COS), I(COS) \rangle$;
(2) $K(COS) = \langle M_p(COS), M(COS), M_{pp}(COS), C(COS), L(COS) \rangle$ is the core of $TE(COS)$;
(3) $I(COS)$ is the domain of intended applications of $K(COS)$.

Def-M$_p$(COS)

has already been introduced.

Def-M(COS)

$M(COS) := \{z_1 : z_1$ is a *model* of the theory-element COS $\}$
z_1 is a model of the theory-element COS iff

(1) $z_1 \in M_p(COS)$;
(2) $\forall s \in S\ \forall c \in AF(s)\ \forall o \in O\ \forall INT_1 \subseteq INT\ \forall v \in \mathbb{N}$:
$| \{int \in INT_1 : CO(o, s, int) = c\} | = v \longrightarrow CF(c, INT_1) = v$.

Def-M$_{pp}$(COS)
$M_{pp}(COS) = \{\langle S, CS, AF, O, INT, \leq_{int}, CO\rangle$: there exists CF such that $\langle S, CS, AF, O, INT, \leq_{int}, CO, CF\rangle \in M_p(COS)\}$.

Def-C(COS)
$C(COS) = \{Z_1 : Z_1$ satisfies the *constraint* of the theory-element COS $\}$
Z_1 satisfies the constraint of the theory-element COS iff

(1) $Z_1 \subseteq M_p(COS)$;
(2) $Z_1 \neq \emptyset$;
(3) $\mathcal{S} := \{S : \exists z_1 \in Z_1\ pr_1(z_1) = S\}$;
$\mathcal{CS} := \{CS : \exists z_1 \in Z_1\ pr_2(z_1) = CS\}$;
$\mathcal{AF} := \{AF : \exists z_1 \in Z_1\ pr_3(z_1) = AF\}$;
$\mathcal{O} := \{O : \exists z_1 \in Z_1\ pr_4(z_1) = O\}$;
$\mathcal{INT} := \{INT : \exists z_1 \in Z_1\ pr_5(z_1) = INT\}$;
$\mathcal{GG} := \{\leq_{int} : \exists z_1 \in Z_1\ pr_6(z_1) = \leq_{int}\}$;
(4) $\forall O_1, O_2 \in \mathcal{O}$ with $O_1 = \{o_1\}$ and $O_2 = \{o_2\}$ $\forall S \in \mathcal{S}$ with $S = \{s_1, .., s_i, .., s_n\}$
$\forall AF \in \mathcal{AF}$ with $AF(s_i) = \{c_{1i}, .., c_{ki}, .., c_{mi}\}$ $\forall INT_1 \subseteq INT \subseteq \mathcal{INT}$:
$NC(c_{ki}, o_2, s_i, INT_1) := \ |\{int \in INT_1 : CO(o_2, s_i, int) = c_{ki}\}|$,
$NC(c_{ki}, o_1, s_i, INT_1) := \ |\{int \in INT_1 : CO(o_1, s_i, int) = c_{ki}\}|$,
$NICo(O_1, O_2, S, INT_1) := \sum_i \mid \{int \in INT_1 : CO(o_1, s_1, int) = CO(o_2, s_i, int)\} \mid$,
$NICe(O_1, O_2, S, INT_1) :=$
$(1/|INT_1|) \sum_i \sum_{ki} (NC(c_{ki}, o_1, s_i, INT_1) \cdot NC(c_{ki}, o_2, s_i, INT_1))$.
(5) $\exists \mathcal{AGF}$ with $\mathcal{AGF} : \mathcal{O} \times \mathcal{O} \times \mathcal{S} \times \mathcal{INT} \Longrightarrow [-1, 1]$ such that
$\forall z_{11} \in Z_1$ with $z_{11} = \langle S, CS, AF, O, INT, \leq_{int}, CO, CF\rangle$ $\exists z_{12} \in Z_1$ with
$z_{12} = \langle S, CS, AF, O', INT', \leq'_{int}, CO', CF'\rangle$ and $O \neq O', \mid INT \cap INT' \mid > 5 \cdot |CS|$:
$(\exists f_5$ with $f_5 : \mathbb{N}^3 \Longrightarrow [-1, 1]$ $\forall v_1, v_2, v_3, n \in \mathbb{N} :$ $NICo(O, O', S, INT \cap INT') = v_1 \wedge$
$NICe(O, O', S, INT \cap INT') = v_2 \wedge \mid INT \cap INT' \mid = v_3\ \wedge |S| = n \longrightarrow$
$\mathcal{AGF}(O, O', S, INT \cap INT') = f_5(v_1, v_2, v_3, n)) \wedge$
$(\exists b \in [0.5, 1]\ \mathcal{AGF}(O, O', S, INT \cap INT') > b)$.

Def-I(COS)
The elements of $I(COS)$ are the assignments of categories to the behavior of subjects within time intervals by an observer, as described by the non-theoretical concepts of the theory; and $I(COS) \subseteq M_{pp}(COS)$.

Comments

Stipulation (2) of $Def\text{-}M(COS)$ asserts that the coding frequency of a category c for a set of time intervals INT_1 is derived from the number of elements of INT_1 for which the observer assigns the category to the respective person. This stipulation could lead into trouble if the codings of just any observer could form the basis for the determination of the function CF used to interpret the relative frequency function of $TE(IS)$. Therefore, only those coding structures are declared as admissible for which there are sufficiently similar coding structures from different observers. This restriction, which refers to the problem of interobserver agreement (cf. Bakeman & Gottman, 1986; Manns et al., 1987; Suen & Ary, 1989), is expressed by the constraint $C(COS)$.

Several new concepts occur in $Def\text{-}C(COS)$. In stipulation (3), several sets of sets are defined by means of the projection function explained earlier. In stipulation (4), the components of most interobserver agreement indices are introduced: $NC(c_{ki}, o_1, s_i, INT_1)$, the number of codings of category c_{ki} for person s_i and the set of time intervals INT_1 by observer o_1; $NICo(O_1, O_2, S, INT_1)$, the observed number of identical codings by observers o_1 and o_2 for the elements of S and the set of time intervals INT_1; and $NICe(O_1, O_2, S, INT_1)$, the expected number of identical codings under the same conditions. The agreement function $\mathcal{AGF}$ refers to two coding structures consisting of the same S, CS, and AF, but of different sets of observers, and of sets of time intervals having a substantial intersection. It is assumed (cf. [5]), that $\mathcal{AGF}$ is a function f_5 of four values: the observed number of identical codings; the expected number of identical codings; the number of intervals which form the basis of the agreement calculation; and the number of persons observed. The value of $\mathcal{AGF}$ is a real number out of the interval $[-1, 1]$, and it is required that this value be greater than 0.5.

The definition of $M_{pp}(COS)$ expresses that CF is a theoretical concept within the theory-element $TE(COS)$; $Def\text{-}I(COS)$ points to the subject-matter of this theory.

Function f_5 in $Def\text{-}C(COS)$ can be specified in various ways, resulting in different specializations of $TE(COS)$. House, House, and Campbell (1981), for example, list more than a dozen different indices of interobserver agreement. There are thus many possibilities for further elaboration of the theory-net. Here, only two specializations will be presented, both of which were used in the context of empirical investigations of the theory of behavior interaction.

Specialization 1 of the Theory-Element "Coding Structure"

Def-TE(COS$_1$)
$TE(COS_1)$ is the theory-element COS_1 iff there exist $K(COS_1)$ and $I(COS_1)$ such that
(1) $TE(COS_1) = \langle K(COS_1), I(COS_1)\rangle$;
(2) $K(COS_1) = \langle M_p(COS_1), M(COS_1), M_{pp}(COS_1), C(COS_1), L(COS_1)\rangle$ is the core of $TE_1(COS)$;
(3) $I(COS_1)$ is the domain of intended applications of $K(COS_1)$.

Def-M$_p$(COS$_1$)
$M_p(COS_1) = M_p(COS)$

Def-M(COS$_1$)
$M(COS_1) = M(COS)$.

Def-M$_{pp}$(COS$_1$)
$M_{pp}(COS_1) = M_{pp}(COS)$.

Def-C(COS$_1$)[5]
$C(COS_1) := \{Z_1 : Z_1$ satisfies the *specialization 1 of the constraint* $C(COS)\}$
Z_1 satisfies the specialization 1 of the constraint $C(COS)$ iff
(1) $Z_1 \in C(COS)$;

[5]In $Def\text{-}C(COS)$, f_5, b, and $|INT \cap INT'|$ are introduced as variables. To simplify the definitions of those theory-elements which are specializations of $TE(COS)$, only the additional requirements are explicitely mentioned. Therefore "f_5" in stipulation (3) of $Def\text{-}C(COS_1)$ refers to the function variable f_5, as introduced in stipulation (5) of $Def\text{-}C(COS)$; b refers to the real number variable b, as introduced in stipulation (5) of $Def\text{-}C(COS)$; etc.

(2) $| INT \cap INT' | > 10 \cdot |CS|$;
(3) $\forall v_1, v_2, v_3, n \in \mathbb{N} : f_5(v_1, v_2, v_3, n) = v_1/(n \cdot v_3)$;
(4) $b = 0.75$.

Def-I(COS$_1$)
$I(COS_1) = I(COS)$.

Comments

Def-C(COS_1) defines one of the simplest versions of an interobserver agreement index, the proportion agreement index p_0 (cf. Suen & Ary, 1989, p. 106). Its value should be greater than 0.75, and the set of time intervals which forms the basis of its computation must be large enough such that each category has a sufficient chance to occur.

Specialization 2 of the Theory-Element "Coding Structure"

Def-TE(COS$_2$)
$TE(COS_2)$ is the theory-element COS_2 iff there exist $K(COS_2)$ and $I(COS_2)$ such that
(1) $TE(COS_2) = \langle K(COS_2), I(COS_2)\rangle$;
(2) $K(COS_2) = \langle M_p(COS_2), M(COS_2), M_{pp}(COS_2), C(COS_2), L(COS_2)\rangle$ is the core of $TE(COS_2)$;
(3) $I(COS_2)$ is the domain of intended applications of $K(COS_2)$.

Def-M$_p$(COS$_2$)
$M_p(COS_2) = M_p(COS)$

Def-M(COS$_2$)
$M(COS_2) = M(COS)$.

Def-M$_{pp}$(COS$_2$)
$M_{pp}(COS_2) = M_{pp}(COS)$.

Def-C(COS$_2$)
$C(COS_2) := \{Z_1 : Z_1$ satisfies the *specialization 2 of the constraint* $C(COS)\}$
Z_1 satisfies the specialization 2 of the constraint $C(COS)$ iff
(1) $Z_1 \in C(COS)$;
(2) $| INT \cap INT' | > 10 \cdot |CS|$;
(3) $\forall v_1, v_2, v_3, n \in \mathbb{N} : f_5(v_1, v_2, v_3, n) = (v_1 - v_2)/(n \cdot v_3 - v_2)$;
(4) $b = 0.70$.

Def-I(COS$_2$)
$I(COS_2) = I(COS)$.

Comments

Def-C(COS_2) specifies function f_5 as the widely used coefficient *kappa* (cf. Cohen, 1960). The general definition of kappa is (cf. Suen & Ary, 1989, p.111):

$$\kappa = (p_o - p_e)/(1 - p_e) ,$$

where p_o is the observed proportion of agreement and p_e is the proportion of agreement expected by chance. Translated into the terms of the theory of coding structures, p_o is equal to $v_1 \,/\, (n \cdot v_3)$, and p_e is equal to $v_2 \,/ (n \cdot v_3)$. Therefore,

$$\kappa = (v_1 - v_2) \,/\, (n \cdot v_3 - v_2) \ .$$

In this case, it is reasonable to require that the value of κ be greater than 0.70.

Link to the Theory of Coding Structures

A more detailed analysis of the coding process reveals that coding structures are not yet the most basic structures which can be formulated within the present framework. Instead, the structures which are really basic to the present context are ***observation structures***; the theory of observation structures could therefore be called a "bed-rock theory-element" in the sense of Balzer et al. (1987, p. 413). As will be shown, the theory of coding structures can be related to the theory of observation structures by means of yet another intertheoretical link. Four new concepts are characteristic of this theory-element: T, $\leq_t$, OF, and HF.

T is a set of instants. Instants are the smallest time units considered. A time interval comprises several instants.

$\leq_t$ is a total ordering of the set T, i.e., $\leq_t$ is reflexive, antisymmetric, transitive, and connected in T.

OF is an observation function. An observation is defined as the assignment by an observer of a set of one or more categories to (the behavior of) a person within an instant of time. (The instant of time refers of course to the behavior of the observed person, not to the behavior of the observer.) OF expresses the basic events with which the theory is concerned; it is difficult to conceive a further interpretation of this function by other concepts. Hence, it is very basic in an empirical sense.

HF is a hierarchy function. The coding function CO assigns only one category to a person in any time interval by an observer. If a time interval comprises several instants of time, and only one category is assigned to every instant by the observation function OF, several codings per time interval are obtained. The hierarchy function HF is designed to cope with this situation. It yields, in the case of multiple potential codings, one category of primary concern to the investigator. It can also handle the frequent situations where several categories may be assigned to a single instant of time, resulting in a set of categories for this instant. Because, for every CS, the elements of HF have to be separately enumerated, it is not feasible to give an abstract characterization of HF.

The set of potential models of the theory-element "observation structure" can be defined as follows:

Def-M$_p$(OS)
$M_p(OS) = \{z_2 : z_2$ is a *potential model* of the theory-element $OS\ \}$
z_2 is a potential model of the theory-element OS iff there exist S, CS, AF, O, T, $\leq_t$, OF, HF such that

(1) $z_2 = \langle S, CS, AF, O, T, \leq_t, OF, HF\rangle$;
(2) S and CS are non-empty, finite sets;

(3) $AF : S \Longrightarrow Po(CS)$;
if $CS_i := AF(s_i)$ with $i = 1, ..., n$ and $n = |S|$, then $\{CS_1, ..., CS_n\}$ is a decomposition of CS;
(4) O is a set with $|O| = 1$;
(5) T is a non-empty, finite set ordered by $\leq_t$;
(6) $OF : O \times S \times T \Longrightarrow Po(CS)$;
if $c \in OF(o, s, t)$, then $c \in AF(s)$;
(7) $HF : Po(AF(s)) \Longrightarrow AF(s)$ for every $s \in S$.

On the basis of this definition, the link from the theory of observation structures to the theory of coding structures can be defined in the following way:

Def-L(COS)
$L(COS)$ is a *link from* $M_p(OS)$ *to* $M_p(COS)$ iff
$L(COS) \subseteq M_p(OS) \times M_p(COS)$.
$\langle z_2, z_1 \rangle \in L(COS)$ iff
(1) $z_1 = \langle S, CS, AF, O, INT, \leq_{int}, CO, CF \rangle$;
(2) $z_2 = \langle S, CS, AF, O, T, \leq_t, OF, HF \rangle$;
(3) $\exists \phi_2 : INT \Longrightarrow Po(T)$;
(4) $\forall int_1, int_2 \in INT : \langle int_1, int_2 \rangle \in \leq_{int}$ iff $\forall t_1 \in \phi_2(int_1), t_2 \in \phi_2(int_2) : \langle t_1, t_2 \rangle \in \leq_t$;

(5) $\forall o \in O \; \forall s \in S \; \forall int \in INT : CO(o, s, int) = HF(C(o, s, int))$ with
$C(o, s, int) := \{c : \exists t \in \phi_2(int)$ such that $c \in OF(o, s, t)\}$

Def-L(COS$_1$) - Def-L(COS$_2$)
$L(COS_1) = L(COS_2) = L(COS)$.

Comments

Function ϕ_2 maps the set of time intervals into the power set of the set of instants, thereby also reducing the order relation on INT to the order relation on T. In stipulation (5) of *Def-L(COS)*, the coding function of $TE(COS)$ is interpreted by the hierarchy and observation functions of $TE(OS)$. This means that the coding of a person for a time interval by an observer is interpreted as being that category which the hierarchy function yields if it is applied to the set of all categories assigned by the observer to the person for those instants of time which are elements of the image set of the time interval under ϕ_2.

Theory-Element "Observation Structure"

Def-TE(OS)
$TE(OS)$ is the theory-element OS iff there exist $K(OS)$ and $I(OS)$ such that
(1) $TE(OS) = \langle K(OS), I(OS) \rangle$;
(2) $K(OS) = \langle M_p(OS), M(OS), M_{pp}(OS), C(OS) \rangle$ is the core of $TE(OS)$;
(3) $I(OS)$ is the domain of intended applications of $K(OS)$.

Def-M$_p$(OS)
has already been introduced.

Def-M(OS)
$M(OS) := \{z_2 : z_2$ is a *model* of the theory-element $OS\}$
z_2 is a model of the theory-element OS iff
(1) $z_2 \in M_p(OS)$.

Def-M_{pp}(OS)
$M_{pp}(OS) = M_p(OS)$.

Def-C(OS)
$C(OS) = \{Z_2 : Z_2$ satisfies the *constraint* of the theory-element $OS\}$
Z_2 satisfies the constraint of the theory-element OS iff
(1) $Z_2 \subseteq M_p(OS)$;
(2) $Z_2 \neq \emptyset$;
(3) $\forall z_{21} \in Z_2$ with $z_{21} = \langle S, CS, AF, O, T, \leq_t, OF, HF\rangle$ $\forall z_{22} \in Z_2$ with $z_{22} = \langle S', CS', AF', O', T', \leq_t', OF', HF'\rangle : CS = CS' \longrightarrow HF = HF'$.

Def-I(OS)
The elements of $I(OS)$ are the assignments by an observer of categories to the behavior of subjects in instants of time; and $I(OS) \subseteq M_{pp}(OS)$.

Comments

As already mentioned, this theory-element is at the bottom of the whole complex of theory-elements defined so far. In its present form, it does not contain any special laws; therefore, it is impossible to differentiate between theoretical and non-theoretical concepts of $TE(OS)$ in the usual way. The functions OF and HF have to be specified by enumeration in each concrete case. No differences between the set of partial potential models, the set of potential models, and the set of actual models are assumed. The only restriction imposed on the set of observation structures is that expressed by the constraint $C(OS)$: If two observation structures have identical category systems, they must also agree with regard to their hierarchy functions. $Def\text{-}I(OS)$ indicates the specific subject-matter of this theory-element.

The Theory of Behavior Interaction as Part of a Theory-Holon

The set of linked theory-elements presented in this chapter forms a theory-holon as defined by Balzer, Moulines, and Sneed (1987, p. 388). As can be seen in Figure 1, there are at least five different subsets of the set of theory-elements. Four of them are specialization nets (N_1, N_2, N_3, N_5) and one consists of a single element (N_4).

N_1 is the theory of behavior interaction. It is a connected, tree-like theory-net (cf. Balzer et al., 1987, p.175) and comprises, among other theory-elements not discussed in this chapter, $TE(BI)$, $TE(BI_1)$, $TE(BISG)$, $TE(BISG_1)$, $TE(BID)$, $TE(BIT)$, $TE(BID_1)$ - $TE(BID_4)$. $TE(BI)$ is the single basic element of N_1.

N_2 is the theory of indifference structures. It is likewise a connected, tree-like theory-net and comprises, inter alia, $TE(IS)$, and $TE(IS_1)$ - $TE(IS_4)$ with $TE(IS)$ being the single basic element of N_2.

N_3 is the theory of coding structures. N_3 is a connected theory-net comprising, among many other theory-elements not dealt with in this chapter, $TE(COS)$, $TE(COS_1)$, and

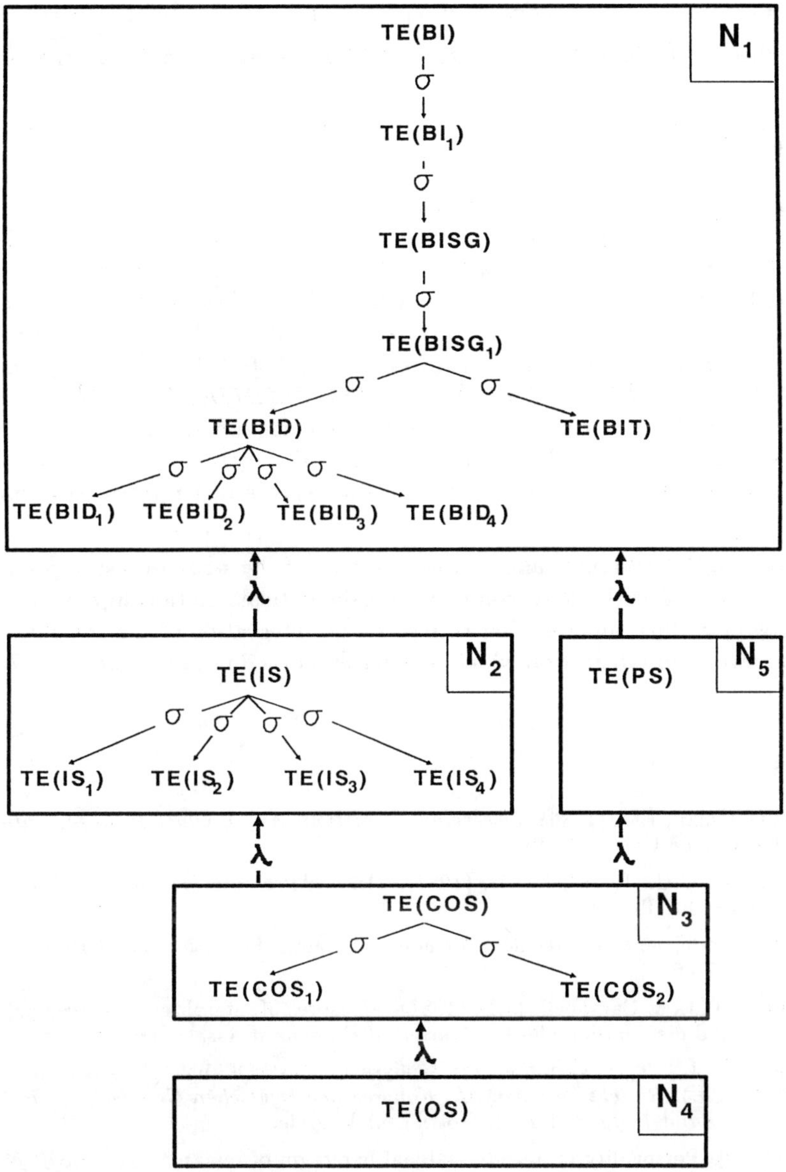

Figure 1:
The theory of behavior interaction as part of a theory-holon (*Note:* "σ" designates the specialization relation, "λ" stands for an intertheoretical link)

$TE(COS_2)$. It is likely that $TE(COS)$ is not the only basic element of N_3. If, for example, problems of intraobserver agreement (cf. Suen & Ary, 1989) are incorporated into the domain of intended applications of this theory, another basic element may be necessary.

N_4 is the theory of observation structures which, so far, consists of only one theory-element.

N_5 is the theory of probability structures. This theory-net has not been elaborated in the present chapter, but it is certainly of a rather complex nature.

All proposed links connecting theory-elements of different nets are interpreting links, i.e. links that provide interpretations for some of the non-theoretical terms of a theory-element (cf. Balzer et al., 1987, p. 396f). $TE(OS)$ is the starting point of the various interpreting paths (cf, Balzer et al., 1987, p. 402f), i.e., all these paths lead from $TE(OS)$ to the remaining theory-elements of the nets N_1, N_2, and N_3. It is easy to see that there is more than one $TE(BI)$-interpreting path from $TE(OS)$ to $TE(BI)$. The path may proceed along $TE(COS_1)$, $TE(COS)$, $TE(IS_1)$, $TE(IS)$, $TE(BID_1)$, $TE(BID)$, $TE(BISG_1)$, $TE(BISG)$, and $TE(BI_1)$; but many other variants are also possible.

Different interpretations lead to different variants of the theory, and it has been found that different variants are associated with different degrees of empirical confirmation (cf. Westmeyer, 1987).

The concept of a theory-holon, and related concepts of the structuralist approach, permit the investigator to deal with these complex intertheoretical relationships in a systematic manner, thereby providing, among other things, for an integration of the theoretical and the methodological levels, an integration which is urgently needed in psychology (cf. Westmeyer, 1988).

References

Bakeman, R., & Gottman, J.M. (1986). *Observing interaction: An introduction to sequential analysis.* London: Cambridge University Press.

Balzer, W., Moulines, C.U., & Sneed, J.D. (1987). *An architectonic for science: The structuralist program.* Dordrecht: Reidel.

Cohen,J. (1960). A coefficient of agreement for nominal scales. *Educational and Psychological Measurement*, **20**, 37-46.

House, A.E., House, B.J., & Campbell, M.B. (1981). Measures of interobserver agreement : Calculation formulas and distribution effects. *Journal of Behavioral Assessment*, **3**, 37-57.

Holling,H., & Schultze,J. (1985). Verfahren zur Analyse stochastisch abhängiger Beobachtungsdaten. In: D.Albert (Ed.), *Bericht über den 34. Kongreß der Deutschen Gesellschaft für Psychologie in Wien 1984. Band 1* (pp. 181-185). Göttingen: Hogrefe.

Magnusson,D, (1980). Personality in an interactional paradigm of research. *Zeitschrift für Differentielle und Diagnostische Psychologie*, **1**, 17-34.

Manns, M., Schultze, J., Herrmann, C., & Westmeyer,H. (1987). *Beobachtungsverfahren in der Verhaltensdiagnostik.* Salzburg: Otto Müller.

Nell, V., (1982). *Interaktives Verhalten in Situationen der Kontaktaufnahme.* München: Minerva.

Nell. V., Völkel, U., Winkelmann, K., Hannemann, J., & Westmeyer, H. (1988). Verhaltensinteraktion in Vater-Mutter-Kind-Triaden: Ein Theorie-Element und seine empirische Bewährung. *Zeitschrift für Sozialpsychologie*, **19**, 175-192.

Patterson, G.R. (1979). A performance theory for coercive family interaction. In: R.B. Cairns (Ed.), *The analysis of social interactions* (pp. 119-162). Hillsdale,N.J.: Lawrence Erlbaum Associates.

Stegmüller, W. (1986). *Theorie und Erfahrung. 3. Teilband: Die Entwicklung des neuen Strukturalismus seit 1973.* Berlin: Springer.

Suen, H.K., & Ary, D. (1989). *Analyzing quantitative behavioral observation data.* Hillsdale,N.J.: Lawrence Erlbaum Associates.

Westmeyer, H. (1987). Zum Problem des empirischen Gehalts psychologischer Theorien. In: J. Brandtstädter (Ed.), *Struktur und Erfahrung in der psychologischen Forschung* (pp. 35-70). Berlin: de Gruyter.

Westmeyer,H. (1988). Anforderungen an den psychologischen Forscher: Was dürfen wir verlangen? In: N. Groeben, W. Keil, & U. Piontkowski (Eds.), *Zukunft/ Wunsch/Gestalt/Psychologie. Zur Gestalt psychologischer Forschung nach Manfred Sader* (pp. 13-37). Münster: Aschendorff.

Westmeyer, H. (1989). Theoriebezogene Validierung diagnostischer Verfahren: eine Monotheory-Multimethod Analyse. In: H. Feger (Ed.), *Wissenschaft und Verantwortung. Festschrift zum 60. Geburtstag von K.J. Klauer* (pp. -). Göttingen:Hogrefe.

Westmeyer, H., Hannemann, J., Nell, V., Völkel, U., & Winkelmann, K. (1987). Eine Monotheory-Multimethod-Analyse: Plädoyer für einen deduktivistischen Multiplismus. *Diagnostica*, **33**, 227-242.

Westmeyer, H., & Nell, V. (1987). Psychologische Theorien aus strukturalistischer Sicht: Das Beispiel der Theorie der Verhaltensinteraktion. In: M.Amelang (Ed.), *Bericht über den 35. Kongreßder Deutschen Gesellschaft für Psychologie in Heidelberg 1986. Band 2* (pp. 179-190). Göttingen: Hogrefe.

Westmeyer, H. Winkelmann, K., & Hannemann, J. (1984). Eltern-Kind-Interaktion in natürlicher Umgebung: Darstellung einer Theorie und ihrer empirischen Bewährung. *Zeitschrift für personenzentrierte Psychologie und Psychotherapie*, **3**, 39-53.

Westmeyer, H., Winkelmann, K., & Hannemann, J. (1988). Intrasituationale dynamische Interaktion. *Zeitschrift für Differentielle und Diagnostische Psychologie*, **9**, 241-256.

Chapter 8

Interruption of Action and Stress

A Structuralist Approach

H. Holling and R. Suck

University of Osnabrück

Abstract

The interruption of action is a subject of various theories, e.g. field theory, emotion, frustration or stress theories. Following the structuralist conception of scientific theories, we first develop the basic theory element including common important components of previous theories. A theory net is built specifying the basic theory element with respect to often analyzed hypotheses within human-computer interaction. This theory-net includes several specific theory elements tested in a series of experiments.

Introduction

In many situations actions are interrupted, for example driving by car is interrupted by a red traffic light or a traffic jam, shopping by queuing at cashiers or working at the computer by system response times. Such interruptions often lead to anger, anxiety or other negative emotions, which may be summarized as stress.

Various theories deal with stress by interruptions: emotion theory by Mandler (1964, 1975), field theory by Lewin (1940) as well as frustration theories by Dollard et al. (1939) or Amsel (1962). In general these theories are nomothetic theories covering very different situations of action interruptions. Such an approach seems to be unrealistic, as will be shown with respect to one special situation, man-computer interaction.

In about 50 studies the effects of system response times on stress and performance measures have been shown. Holling (1989) and Shneiderman (1984) have recently reviewed previous studies. In nearly all studies one or both of the following hypotheses have been investigated:

(1) Variable system response times lead to more stress than constant response times given the same (mean) duration (variability hypothesis).

(2) Stress increases with increasing system response times (duration hypothesis).

The previous studies differ in many aspects. Sources of variations are

- distribution of system response times (e.g. uniform, exponential gamma or normal distributed system response times).
- kind of analyzed tasks (simple detection tasks, problem solving or programing).
- subjects (students, secretaries, programers or scientists).

- environment (field or laboratory).

Nearly all studies have a different design with respect to these dimensions. If computer novices have to solve complex problem solving tasks interrupted by system response times in a laboratory, a situation is given which is quite different from a situation where computer experienced secretaries have to write a long manuscript at their usual working places given time pressure and long system response times. Different theories are needed to explain stress by waiting times in these two situations, theories of human information processing and mental load are playing an important role in the first situation, while stress theory by Lazarus (1966) may be more appropriate in the second case.

These short examples demonstrate the important role of the analyzed situations and the necessity of specifying different theories with respect to the given context or - from a structuralist view - the intended application. The intended applications of our theory net are interruptions of computer- based working behavior. One important intended application of more specific theory elements are experiments which have stimulated the development of the theory net presented in the sequel (see also Holling, 1989).

In particular, knowledge of our experiments may help to understand the direction of the specialization of our theory net. So we first describe typical experimental designs.

Intended Applications

Our experiments (see Holling, 1989) aimed to prove the variability and duration hypothesis for typical situations given well-known tasks and interruptions (system response times). As independent variables we chose constant and approximative exponentially distributed system response times. Following the theory of stochastic processes the exponential distribution is reasonable for many situations.

We induced stress by different waiting time distributions, e.g. constant waiting times of 2 seconds (2c) and 8 seconds (8c) and approximative exponentially distributed waiting times with expectation values of two seconds (2v) and 8 seconds (8v). Subjects had to perform simple detection tasks or more complex tasks at a visual display unit given several experimental trials with different waiting time conditions.

Negative consequences of interruption were loss of money, if subjects got payment according to the number of performed tasks, or loss of time, if people had to perform a fixed number of tasks within each trial.

In some experiments subjects had to perform a series of 4 trials each representing a permutation of the 4 experimental conditions, 2c, 8c, 2v, 8v. The design of other experiments included two conditions only, e.g. 8v, 2v according to a ABAB-design for ARIMA procedures.

The dependent variable stress has been measured by different indicators: physiological indicators (heart rate, electrodermal activity, blood pressure), performance measures (speed, errors) and self-report (6 different scales, e.g. anger, anxiety).

If the variability hypothesis holds, the inequalities

$$8v > 8c \text{ and } 2v > 2c$$

must be valid.

According to the expectation hypothesis the expected values of stress must fulfill the two following inequalities:

$$8v > 2v \text{ and } 8c > 2c.$$

From our theory net further sets of inequalities can be derived (see below).

The validity of the inequalities have been proved by comparing the empirical order of the means of each stress measure with the postulated order on individual and population level. The structuralist approach may clearly show different constraints given different test procedures. A single case approach needs less constraints and is more appropriate to reveal differential validity of stress measures according to the results of modern stress theories.

Basic Theory-Element

An analysis of all previous theories dealing with stress by interruption of action leads to two important elements common to most of the different theories. These two components are

(1) psychic costs, i.e negative consequences because of the interruption,

(2) anticipation of the psychic costs.

If the interruption has no negative consequences, such as loss of money or need for more concentration, then avoidance of interruption is not important. According to some cognitive stress theories these negative consequences are called psychic costs. Often minor 'objective' costs are very high given specific circumstances such as time pressure.

We will only select interruptions of action with negative consequences, which are not decreasing during interruption. Given such psychic costs the interruptions are defined as waiting times.

Additional to psychic costs and the anticipation we have to regard the duration of the interruption as an important component of our basic theory element. Now we can specify these components within probability theory. Duration of the interruption is conceived as a probability space:

$(\mathbb{R}^+, \mathbb{R}^+ \cap \mathcal{L}, P)$, where $\mathcal{L}$ is the set of Borel sets on $\mathbb{R}$.

The monotonically non decreasing psychic costs are determined by a real valued measurable function:

C: $\mathbb{R}^+ \Longrightarrow \mathbb{R}^+$

with C P-almost-everywhere (a.e.) monotonically non decreasing.

Let T be the identity function conceived of as a random variable with distribution function $F(t) = P(0,t)$.

Stress intensity is defined as the conditional expectation:

$$SI(t) = E[C(T)|T > t] = \int_{(t,\infty)} C(s)\ P_t(ds)$$

with P_t as conditional probability measure, provided P_t exists and $SI(t)$ is finite, otherwise $SI(t)$ is not defined (see Holling, 1989).

Stress $S(t)$, i.e. accumulated stress intensity, is the sum of stress intensity:

$$S(t) = \int_{[0,t]} SI(s)\, ds.$$

In most psychological experiments only the mean stress over a time period, the expected value, can be measured:

$$E(S) = \int_{(0,\infty)} S(t)\, P(dt),$$

provided $E(S)$ exists and is finite.

If we deal with different measures in the same context, we sometimes use subscripts to identify the respective stress function and expectations, e.g. $E_P(S)$ or $E_P(S_P)$.

Now we can specify the the basic theory element in a structuralist way.

Potential Models and Models Concerning Stress by Waiting Times

Let 'stress by waiting times' be abbreviated by 'SbW'. First we specify the potential models $M_p(SbW)$.

Definition 1 : $x \in M_p(SbW)$ iff
$x = \langle (\mathbb{R}^+, \mathbb{R}^+ \cap \mathcal{L}, P), T, C, MS \rangle$
with :
1) $(\mathbb{R}^+, \mathbb{R}^+ \cap \mathcal{L}, P)$ probability space;
2) T corresponding random variable as identity function:
$T : \mathbb{R}^+ \Longrightarrow \mathbb{R}^+, \ \ T(t) = t$ for all t,
3) $C : \mathbb{R}^+ \Longrightarrow \mathbb{R}^+$;
4) MS is the mean stress empirically measured during the interruption, e.g. mean systolic blood pressure.

Definition 2: $x \in M(SbW)$ iff
(1) $x \in M_p(SbW)$;
(2) C monotonically P-a.e. non decreasing;
(3) $E(S) = MS$.

In general the equality in Condition (3) has to be analyzed within a statistical framework. One can calculate confidence intervals and regard them as a case of 'blurs' in the sense of Balzer, Moulines and Sneed (1987, p. 332).

Now we may further characterize $M(SbW)$ by the following theorems. Some of them have been already presented in Holling (1989) or Holling and Gediga (1987) and the proofs of these theorems can be inspected there. The proofs of the new theorems are given in the appendix.

Theorem 3: $t_1 > t_0 \longrightarrow SI(t_1) \geq SI(t_0)$.

Corollary 4: If $P(t_1, \infty) > 0$, $t_1 > t_0$, then $SI(t_1) > SI(t_0)$.

According to Theorem 3 and corollary 4 the stress intensity is monotonically non decreasing resp. monotonically increasing. A proof for theorem 3, which is more general than former ones (see Holling, 1989), is given in the appendix.

Furthermore stress intensity is nowhere smaller than the costs:

Theorem 5: $SI(t) \geq C(t)$ for all (feasible) t

Corollary 6: $SI(t) > C(t)$ for all $t < t_1$ with $C(t_1) > C(t)$.

Since stress intensity is a positive function and because of the monotony of the integral operator stress is monotonically increasing.

Theorem 7: $t_1 > t_0 \longrightarrow S(t_1) > S(t_0)$.

These theorems resp. corollaries provide strong empirical tests for the models of SbW, but it is difficult to get continous empirical stress measures. In nearly all cases only mean stress over a time period can be measured.

In the next section we describe a subset of $M(SbW)$ satisfying the variability hypothesis.

Variability Hypothesis

First we define a special subset of the probability measures namely those with expectation μ:

$$D(\mu) := \{P; \mu = \int t\, dP\}.$$

Let D_μ be the Dirac measure at point μ meaning constant interruption times of μ time units and let $P \in D(\mu)$. The variability hypothesis states:

$$E_{D_\mu}(S) < E_P(S).$$

Most empirical studies assume the variability hypothesis without purporting reasons. In this section we investigate conditions which single out those elements of $M(SbW)$ satisfying the variablility hypothesis.

We start by pointing out that not all models belong to this group:

Theorem 8: If for all $t \geq \mu$ $C(t) = C(\mu)$, then for all $P \in D(\mu)$

$$E_{D_\mu}(S) \geq E_P(S).$$

This theorem shows that in certain cases constant waiting times (D_μ) are worst with respect to stress. However, if costs are not constant for $t > \mu$, then measures P exist, which are worse than D_μ :

Theorem 9: If for some $t \geq \mu$ $C(t) > C(\mu)$, then there is a measure $P \in D(\mu)$ such that

$$E_P(S) > E_{D_\mu}(S).$$

The two preceding theorems motivate the following

Definition 10: $x \in M_p(SbWVH)$ iff
(1) $x \in M_p(SbW)$;
(2) $P \in D(\mu)$ for some μ and $E_{D_\mu}(S) < E_P(S)$.

Definition 11: $x \in M(SbWVH)$ iff
$x \in M_p(SbWVH) \cap M(SbW)$.

The following theorems yield sufficient conditions for the elements of $M_p(SbWVH)$.

Theorem 12: Let $x \in M_p(SbW)$ be such that the cost function is linear, i.e. $C(t) = aT + b$, $a > 0$, $b \geq 0$, then $x \in M_p(SbWVH)$.

Theorem 13: Let $x \in M_p(SbW)$ be such that the cost function is monotonic and superlinear, i.e. $C(t) \geq aT + b$, $a > 0$, $b \geq 0$, then
$$x \in M_p(SbWVH).$$

Theorem 14: Let $x \in M_p(SbW)$ be such that the cost function is a special 'shifted linear' function, i.e.
$$C(t) = \begin{cases} a(t - t_0) & \text{if } t \geq t_0 \\ 0 & \text{otherwise} \end{cases}$$
with $a > 0$, $0 \leq t_0 \leq \mu$ and $\sigma^2 \geq \mu^2 - t_0^2\,(1 - 2\,P(0, t_0])$, then $x \in M_p(SbWVH)$.

Theorem 15: Let $x \in M_p(SbW)$ with a monotonic cost function such that
$$C(t) \geq \begin{cases} a(t - t_0) & \text{if } t \geq t_0 \\ 0 & \text{otherwise} \end{cases}$$
with $0 \leq t_0 \leq \mu$ and $\sigma^2 \geq \mu^2 - t_0^2\,(1 - 2\,P(0, t_0])$, then $x \in M_p(SbWVH)$.

Theorem 16: Let $x \in M_p(SbW)$ be such that the cost function is strictly convex, i.e.
$$C\frac{(t_1 + t_2)}{2} < \frac{C(t_1) + C(t_2)}{2}$$
and probabability measure P_s has symmetric density, then $x \in M_p(SbWVH)$.

Theorem 17: Let x_1, $x_2 \in M_p(SbW)$ with cost functions C_1, C_2, resp., then there is a potential model with cost function $a\,C_1 + b\,C_2$, a and/or $b > 0$ in $M_p(SbWVH)$.

Since waiting times were exponentially distributed in our experiments, we study in the next section models with exponential distributions.

Variability Hypothesis and Exponential Distributions

Definition 18: $x \in M(SbWEX)$ iff
(1) $x \in M(SbW)$ and
(2) T is exponentially distributed.

Definition 19: $x \in M(SbWVHEX)$ iff
$x \in M(SbWEX) \cap M(SbWVH)$.

A broad class of cost functions is sufficient for the models of definition 19:

Theorem 20: Let $x \in M(SbWEX)$ with a convex cost function, then $x \in M(SbWVHEX)$.

We omit the proof of this theorem. It can be obtained by a straightforward integration or by drawing on Theorem 25 (see appendix). However, we conjecture that for convex cost functions the variability hypothesis is always true. This is investigated in a forthcoming paper.

Duration Hypothesis

We include the duration hypothesis in this theory net by the way of constraints, because it consists of a comparison of expected stress of two measures, i.e. of two different potential models. First we define

Definition 21: $Q_1 = \{\{x_1, x_2\},\ C_1, C_2$ non-decreasing, $C_1 = C_2,\ D_1 \in D(\mu_1),\ D_2 \in D(\mu_2),$ $\mu_1 < \mu_2$, and $E_{P_1}(S_{P_1}) < E_{P_2}(S_{P_2})\}$.

Q_1 is the set of all subsets of $M_p(SbW)$ consisting of two elements which have the same cost functions, their respective probability measures are P_1 and P_2 and the expected values of the corresponding stress functions show the same ordering as the expectations.

If we set

$Q := Q_1 \cup \{\{x\} : x \in M_p(SbW)\}$,

Q satisfies the conditions of constraints according to Stegmüller (1986, p.98).

Two models of SbW which are in Q are said to satisfy the duration hypothesis. The following theorems give sufficient criteria for the validity of this hypothesis.

Theorem 22: If $x_1,\ x_2 \in M_p(SbW)$ have Dirac measures with unequal μ_i, $i = 1,2$, then $\{x_1,\ x_2\} \in Q$, i.e. the duration hypothesis is satisfied.

Theorem 23: Let $x_1,\ x_2 \in M_p(SbW)$ have the same continous cost functions C and probability measures P_1, P_2, resp. and if $P_1([0,x)) > P_2([0,x))$ for all $x > 0$, then $\{x_1,\ x_2\} \in Q$.

Corollary 24: In Theorem 22, C can have discontinuities, provided the corresponding distribution functions of P_1 and P_2 are continous at these points.

From Theorem 23 and Corollary 24 it is easy to derive many special distributions fulfilling the duration hypothesis, e.g. exponential distributions with different expectations and distributions, which are invariant with respect to translation (see Bauer, 1978). So the duration hypothesis is valid, if waiting times are exponentially distributed.

Theoreticity and Statistical Testing

The clarification of the theoreticity of the specific terms our potential models consist of is important because the empirical content and the empirical claim of the theory elements depend upon this concept. If this problem has been solved satisfactorily an empirical content can be determined just by applying Definition 2.4 of Stegmüller (1986) or an approximate weakening. The intended applications stem from the experiments above or from Holling (1989).

There is especially one term which may be theoretical, the term 'psychic costs'. We have to deal with the theoreticity of this term, before we can develop statistical tests to evaluate the equality $E(S) = MS$, the variability and duration hypothesis.

Considering our experiments we can distinguish three cases:

(1) No negative consequences because of the interruption, such as loss of money are given in the experiment. It is, however, possible, that subjects have 'subjective' costs, e.g. time during interruption could be better used for other concerns. If we make such an assumption and specify this assumption in terms of a feasible cost function, costs are a theoretical term.

(2) If 'objective' negative consequences according to feasible cost functions are introduced and these 'objective' costs are equated with subjective costs, costs are, of course, not a theoretical term. But this assumption may be as critical as the first assumption.

(3) Perhaps, the best way is to introduce a link to utility theory (see the contribution of Stephan in this book). If we measure the utility of time during interruption (with or without 'objective' costs), we can determine psychic costs by a suitable function. Following this procedure psychic costs are not a theoretical term and E(S) can be computed given a probability space for the waiting times.

If psychic costs are not a theoretical term, $E(S)$ can be computed as described above. Thus the equality $E_P(S) = MS$ can be evaluated after measuring stress empirically, e.g. in an experiment. Evaluation of duration and variability hypothesis only implies testing the equality $E_P(S) = MS$ for different probability measures P. But no comparisons of MS measured under different conditions are needed.

However, when psychic costs are theoretical terms, we can only determine sufficient conditions for the variability and duration hypothesis, since $E_P(S)$ cannot be computed. Given the experimental conditions outlined above, constant waiting times of 2 and 8 seconds ($2c$, $8c$) and exponentially distributed waiting times with expectancies of 2 and 8 seconds ($2v$, $8v$), necessary conditions for the variability hypothesis are the validity of the inequalities:

$$8v > 8c, \quad 2v > 2c$$

for the mean of stress (MS) measured under the respective conditions.

According to the duration hypothesis the inequalities

$$8v > 2v, \quad 8c > 2c$$

have to be fulfilled by the mean stress.

Further inequality sets may be derived as necessary conditions (see Holling, 1989), e.g a model SbW has to fulfill the inequality $8c > 2c$ according to theorem 22, while models $SbWEX$ imply inequalities

$$8v > 2v, \quad 8c > 2c$$

because of theorem 23.

It is not realistic to assume empirical stress measures with perfect reliability. So we have to perform statistical tests to evaluate the inequalities or the equality $E_P(S) = MS$. Selection of applicable tests depends upon special characteristics of the stress measure. To avoid distributional assumptions the equality $E_P(S) = MS$ can be tested by the Chebycheff inequality. However, independently identically distributed random variables are required, which are seldom encountered in stress measurement. If autocorrelations occur ARIMA-modelling seems to be more adequate, with the drawback that normality of errors is presupposed.

Even if continous physiological stress indicators, e.g. electrodermal activity are used, we do not have enough points of measurement during one interruption. Several identical interruptions are needed to get 'good' estimations of MS. Regarding several trials requires an extension of our models as n-tupels of the previous structure and the introduction of constraints with respect to the implications of the statistical tests.

Up to now we had a single case approach. Use of analysis of variance leads to the necessity of the introduction of further constraints, such as identical cost function for all subjects and identically distributed MS, which are crucial assumptions. These further complications will be considered in a subsequent paper.

Appendix. Proofs of the Theorems 3, 8, 9, 14, 15, and 25

Theorem 3: $G_1, G_2 \in \mathcal{L}$, $P(G_1)$, $P(G_2) > 0$, $\underset{t \in G_1}{inf}\ C(t) \geq \underset{t \in G_2 - G_1}{sup}\ C(t)$,
then $SI_1(G_1) \geq SI_1(G_2)$, where $SI_1 := E(C(T)|T \in G)$

Proof: $Z(s,t) := (C(t) - C(s)) I_{G_1 \times G_2}(s,t)$,
$= (C(t) - C(s)) I_{G_1 \times (G_2 - G_1)}(s,t) + (C(t) - C(s))\ I_{G_1 \times G_1}(s,t)$,
where I_A is the indicator function.
$E(Z \mid G_1 \times G_2) = E((C(t) - C(s))\ I_{G_1 \times G_2 - G_1} \mid G_1 \times G_2)$
$+\ E(C(t) - C(s))\ I_{G_1 \times G_2} \mid G_1 \times G_2$.
Since $C(t) - C(s)$ is symmetric on $G_1 \times G_2$, the second integral on the right is zero. Thus,

$$E(Z|G_1 \times G_2) = \frac{1}{P(G_1)\,P(G_2)} \int\limits_{G_1 \times G_2 - G_1} (C(t) - C(s))\, dP^2 \geq 0.$$

On the other hand

$$E(Z \mid G_1 \times G_2) = \frac{1}{P(G_1)\,P(G_2)} \int\limits_{G_1 \times G_2} (C(t) - C(s))\, dP^2$$

$$= \frac{1}{P(G_1)\,P(G_2)}((\int\limits_{G_1} C(t)\, dP)\ P(G_2) - (\int\limits_{G_2} C(s) dP)\ P(G_1))$$

$$= \frac{1}{P(G_1)} \int\limits_{G_1} C(t)\, dP - \frac{1}{P(G_2)} \int\limits_{G_2} C(s)\, dP$$

$$= SI(G_1) - SI(G_2).$$

Thus $SI(G_1) \geq SI(G_2)$.

Lemma 8.1 and 8.2 prepare Theorem 8.

Lemma 8.1: If for all $t \geq \mu = E_P(T)$ $C(t) = C(\mu)$ then
$SI(t) \leq C(\mu)$ for $t \leq \mu$ and $SI(t) = C(\mu)$ for $t > \mu$ (if $P(t,\infty) > 0$).

Proof: $SI(t) = \frac{1}{P(t,\infty)} \int_{(t,\infty)} C(t)\, dP$

Since C non-decreasing and constant for $\tau > \mu : C(t) \leq C(\mu)$ for all t. Thus, if $t \leq \mu$

$$SI(t) \leq \frac{C(\mu)}{P(t,\infty)} \int_{(t,\infty)} P\,(dt) \;=\; C(\mu)$$

If $t > \mu$ then

$$SI(t) = \int_{(t,\infty)} C(\tau)\, dP_t = C(\mu) \int_{(t,\infty)} dP_t = C(\mu).$$

Lemma 8.2: Given the assumptions of Lemma 8.1, then $S(t) \leq t\; C(\mu)$.

Proof: For $P = D(\mu)$ we have

$$SI(t) = \begin{cases} C(\mu) & t \leq \mu \\ 0 & t > \mu \;. \end{cases}$$

Thus, for this special measure we conclude

$$S(t) = \int_{[0,t)} SI(\tau)\, d\tau = \begin{cases} t \cdot C(\mu) & t \leq \mu \\ \mu \cdot C(\mu) & t > \mu \end{cases}$$

and $S(t) \leq t\; C(\mu)$ is satisfied.

Let P be an arbitrary measure and t such that $P(t,\infty) > 0$.
Then by Lemma 8.1
$SI(\tau) \leq C(\mu)$ for all τ

$$S(t) = \int_{[0,t)} SI(\tau)\, d\tau \leq t \cdot C(\mu) \;.$$

Theorem 8: If, for all $t \geq \mu = E_P(T)$, $C(t) = C(\mu)$ then
$E_P(S) \leq E_{D_\mu}(S)$ $(= \mu \cdot C(\mu))$.

Proof: Because $S(t) \leq t \cdot C(\mu)$ by Lemma 8.2

$$E_P(S) = \int_{[0,\infty)} S(t)\, dP \leq C(\mu) \int_{[0,\infty)} t\, dP$$

$$= \mu\, C(\mu) = E_{D_\mu}(S).$$

Lemma 9.1: Let P be a two-point-distribution $P(x) = p$, $P(y) = 1 - p$
then $E_P(S) = x \cdot C(x) \cdot p + y \cdot C(y) \cdot (1 - p)$.

Proof:

$$SI(t) = \begin{cases} C(x) \cdot p + C(y)(1-p) & \text{for } 0 < t < x \\ C(y) & \text{for } x \le t \le y \\ 0 & \text{for } t \ge y \end{cases}$$

$$S(t) = \begin{cases} t \cdot (C(x) \cdot p + C(y)(1-p)) & \text{for } 0 < t < x \\ x \cdot (C(x) \cdot p + C(y)(1-p)) + (t-x)C(y) & \text{for } x \le t < y \\ x \cdot (C(x) \cdot p + C(y)(1-p)) + (y-x)C(y) & \text{for } t \ge y \end{cases}$$

$$\begin{aligned} E_P(S) &= x \cdot (C(x) \cdot p + C(y)(1-p)) + (y-x)C(y)(1-p) \\ &= x \cdot C(x) \cdot p + y \cdot C(y) \cdot (1-p) \end{aligned}$$

Theorem 9: If for some $t > \mu$ $C(t) > C(\mu)$ then there is a measure $P \in D(\mu)$ such that $E_P(S) > E_{D_\mu}(S)$.

Proof: We construct a two-point measure P and evaluate $E_P(S)$ by Lemma 9.1 . Let t be a fixed value satisfying the condition of the theorem.

Let $p := 1 - \frac{\mu}{t} + \epsilon$ for $0 < \epsilon < min\{1 - \frac{C(\mu)}{C(t)}, \frac{\mu}{t}\}$

$s := \frac{1}{p}(\mu - t(1-\mu))$.

Since $t > \mu$ and $\epsilon > 0$, we have

$0 < s \le \frac{\mu}{p}(1 - 1 + p) = \mu$.

Now we define P:

$$P(x) = \begin{cases} p & \text{for } x = s \\ 1-p & \text{for } x = t \\ 0 & \text{otherwise .} \end{cases}$$

We apply Lemma 9.1 to P and obtain

$$\begin{aligned} E_P(S) &= s\,C(s) \cdot p + tC(t)(1-p) \\ &\ge t\,C(t)(1-p) \;=\; t\,C(t)(\tfrac{\mu}{t} - \epsilon) \\ &= (\mu - t\,\epsilon)\,C(t). \end{aligned}$$

From this estimation we see that $E_P(S) > \mu\; C(\mu) = E_{D_\mu}(S)$, if we choose ϵ sufficiently small.

Any choice satisfying

$p = 1 - \frac{\mu}{t} + \epsilon$ for $0 < \epsilon < min\{1 - \frac{C(\mu)}{C(t)}, \frac{\mu}{t}\}$

is feasible and yields $E_P(S) > E_{D_\mu}(S)$

Lemma 14.1 and 14.2 are auxiliary results, which are useful for the proofs of Theorems 14, 15 and 25.

Lemma 14.1: Let $Q(u,v)$ denote the quotient, defined for $0 < u \leq v$, u such that $P(u,\infty) > 0$

$$Q(u,v) := \frac{P(u,v]}{P(u,\infty)}$$

and let $x(t)$ be a monotonic function of time satisfying $x(t) \geq t$. Then

$$E(S) \geq E(\int_{[0,T)} C(x(s))(1 - Q(s, x(s))\, ds) + E(\int_{[0,T)} C(s)\, Q(s, x(s))\, ds)$$

and

$$E(S) \geq E(\int_{[0,T)} C(x(s))\, ds) - E(\int_{[0,T)} C(x(s)) - C(s))\, Q(s, x(s))\, ds).$$

Note that $0 \leq Q(u,v) \leq 1$ and $C(x(s)) - C(s) \geq 0$.

Proof: Let t be such that $P(t,\infty) > 0$. For $x \geq t$ we split the interval (t,∞) into the parts $(t,x]$ and (x,∞); thus by the monotonicity of C

$$SI(t) = \frac{1}{P(t,\infty)}(\int_{(t,x]} C(s)\, P(ds) + \int_{(x,\infty)} C(s)\, P(ds))$$

$$\geq C(t) \cdot \frac{P(t,x]}{P(t,\infty)} + C(x) \cdot \frac{P(x,\infty)}{P(t,\infty)}\,.$$

Since $x \geq t$ we can evaluate the second term

$$\frac{P(x,\infty)}{P(t,\infty)} = 1 - \frac{P(t,x]}{P(t,\infty)} = 1 - Q(t,x)$$

yielding

$$SI(t) \geq C(t)\, Q(t,x) + C(x)(1 - Q(t,x)).$$

If we now think of x as a function of t we obtain by integration

$$S(t) = \int_{[0,t)} SI(s)\, ds$$

$$\geq \int_{[0,t)} C(s)\, Q(s, x(s))\, ds + \int_{[0,t)} C(x(s))(1 - Q(s, x(s))\, ds\ .$$

Computing the expectation yields the lemma. The second estimation is easily obtained by a few algebraic transformations.

Lemma 14.2: Let

$$A(t) := \int_{[0,t)} C(s)\, ds \quad \text{denote the area under the cost function.}$$

Then $E(S) \geq E(A)$.

Proof: We use the second estimation in Lemma 9.1 choosing $x(s) = s$.

Theorem 14: Let $C(t)$ be the cost function

$$C(t) = \begin{cases} a(t-t_0) & t \geq t_0 \\ 0 & \text{otherwise} \end{cases}$$

with $a > 0$, $t_0 \geq 0$, and P be a measure such that $VAR(T) = \sigma^2$ exists and $\sigma^2 \geq \mu^2 - t_0^2\,(1 - 2\,P(0,t_0])$.
Then the variabilty hypothesis is satisfied.

Proof: We use the estimation of Lemma 13.2

$$\int_{[0,T)} C(t)\,dt = a \int_{[t_0,T)} (t-t_0)\,dt \;=\; \frac{a}{2}(T^2 - t_0^2) - at_0\,(T - t_0)$$

Thus

$$E(S) \geq \frac{a}{2} \int_{(t_0,\infty)} t^2\,P(dt) - a\,t_0 \int_{(t_0,\infty)} t\,P(dt) - \frac{a}{2} t_0^2\,P(t_0,\infty) + a\,t_0^2\,P(t_0,\infty)$$

$$\geq \frac{a}{2}(\sigma^2 + \mu^2) - \frac{a}{2} \int_{(0,t_0]} t^2\,P(dt) - a\,t_0\,\mu + \frac{a}{2} t_0^2\,P(t_0,\infty)$$

where we used the fact that $\sigma^2 + \mu^2$ equals the second moment of a distribution. Inserting in the last inequality the estimation

$$\int_{(0,t_0]} t^2\,P(dt) \leq t_0^2\,P(0,t_0]$$

we obtain

$$E(S) \geq a\{\frac{\sigma^2 + \mu^2}{2} - \frac{t_0^2}{2}(P(0,t_0] - P(t_0,\infty)) - t_0\}$$

or, if we introduce the abbreviation $p_0 = P(0,t_0]$ which implies $1 - p_0 = P(t_0,\infty)$,

$$E(S) \geq a\,\mu\,\{\frac{\sigma^2 + \mu^2}{2\,\mu} - \frac{t_0^2}{2\,\mu}(2p_0 - 1) - t_0\}$$

$$= a\,\mu\,\{\frac{\sigma^2 + \mu^2}{2\,\mu} + \frac{t_0^2}{2\,\mu} - t_0 - \frac{t_0^2}{\mu}\,p_0\}.$$

However, from $\sigma^2 \geq \mu^2 - t_0^2\,(1 - 2p_0)$ we derive

$$E(S) \geq a\,\mu\,\{\frac{2\,\mu^2 - t_0^2\,(1 - 2p_0)}{2\,\mu} + \frac{t_0^2}{2\,\mu} - t_0 - \frac{t_0^2}{\mu}\,p_0\}$$

$$= a\,\mu\,(\mu - t_0).$$

Thus the proof of Theorem 14 is finished.

Lemma 15.1: Let C_1 and C_2 be two cost functions and let S_1 and S_2 be the stress functions calculated with C_1 and C_2 respectively. Then, for all distributions, if $C_1(t) \geq C_2(t)$ then $E(S_1) \geq E(S_2)$

Proof: Since integration is a monotonic operation the lemma is obvious.

Theorem 15: Let the cost function C be supershift linear, i.e. satisfy

$$C(t) \geq \begin{cases} a(t-t_0) & \text{for } t \geq t_0 \\ 0 & \text{for } 0 \leq t < t_0 \end{cases}$$

and P be a measure for which expectation μ and variance σ^2 exist and satisfy $\mu > t_0$

$C(\mu) = a\,(\mu - t_0)$

$\sigma^2 \geq \mu^2 - t_0^2\,(1 - 2\,p(0, t_0])$

Then the variability hypothesis is satisfied, i.e.

$E_P(S) \geq a\,\mu\,(\mu - t_0) = \mu\,C(\mu)$.

Proof: Let $K(t)$ denote the shifted linear cost function, i.e.

$$K(t) \geq \begin{cases} a(t-t_0) & \text{for } t \geq t_0 \\ 0 & \text{for } 0 \leq t < t_0 \end{cases}$$

Then $C(\mu) = K(\mu)$ and $C(t) \geq K(t)$.
Let S_0 be the stress function pertaining to K. Then by Lemma 15.1
$E_p(S) \geq E_p(S_0)$.
From Theorem 14 we know $E_p(S_0) \geq \mu\,D(\mu)$. Since $C(\mu) = D(\mu)$, the theorem follows.

Theorem 25: Let C be a convex cost function, i.e.

$$C(\frac{t+s}{2}) \leq \frac{C(t)+C(s)}{2} \text{ for all } s,\, t \geq 0,$$

and let P be a probability measure for which μ and σ^2 exist.
If $C(\mu) > 0$ then

$$\lim_{n\to\infty} \frac{C(t_n) - C(\mu)}{t_n - \mu} := a$$

exists and satisfies $a > 0$ for all decreasing sequences $t_n \to \mu$, $t_n > \mu$; and if $t_0 := \mu - \dfrac{C(\mu)}{a}$

and

$\sigma^2 \geq \mu - t_0^2\,(1 - 2\,P(0, t_0])$

then the variability hypothesis is satisfied.

Remark. If $C(\mu) = 0$ the limit a may be zero and t_0 is not defined. However in this case, the variability hypothesis holds trivially true. Furthermore a can be replaced by any limit point of $(C(t_n) - C(\mu))/(t_n - \mu)$ for arbitrary sequences (t_n) converging to μ. However, the a given in the theorem is the largest possible value and therefore yields the biggest t_0, which in turn allows for more distributions than a smaller t_0. The boundary given for σ^2 can be lowered, possibly down to zero, which would imply that all distributions fulfil the variability hypothesis provided the cost function is convex.

Proof: We want to draw on Theorem 14. Thus, we have to demonstrate that C can be estimated below by a shifted linear function $a(t - t_0)$ with $C(\mu) = a(\mu - t_0)$. The case $C(\mu) = 0$ is trivial, so we can assume $C(\mu) > 0$ whence $0 \leq t_0 < \mu$ provided $a > 0$. Furthermore the convexity and monotony of C together with $C(0) = 0 < C(\mu)$ implies that $C(t)$ is strictly increasing for $t > \mu$.
Our first aim is to show that the limit defined in the theorem exists. Let (t_n) be a sequence $t_n \geq t_{n+1} \geq ... > \mu$ such that $t_n \to \mu$. We define

$$\frac{C(t_n) - C(\mu)}{t_n - \mu} =: c_n.$$

First we show that (c_n) decreases monotonically. The straight line $g_n(t) = c_n t_n + C(\mu)$ satisfies $g_n(\mu) = C(\mu)$, $g_n(t_n) = c_n(t - \mu) + C(\mu) = C(t_n)$.
Consequently by the convexity of C we have $C(t) \leq g_n(t)$ for all $t \in (\mu, t_n)$. In particular $C(t_{n+1}) \leq g_n(t_{n+1})$. Thus $C(t_{n+1}) \leq c_n(t_{n+1} - \mu) + C(\mu)$ or, equivalently,

$$c_n \geq \frac{C(t_{n+1}) - C(\mu)}{t_{n+1} - \mu} = c_{n+1}.$$

Second we observe that (c_n) is bounded below. This is obvious, since by the monotony of C each $c_n \geq 0$. Thus the sequence (c_n) converges. Let us denote the limit by a. We know already $a \geq 0$. However, the case $a = 0$ can be ruled out in the following way: the line $g_n(t)$ has an inclination of c_n. If $c_n \to 0$ then, for sufficiently large n, $C(\mu) - c_n \mu > 0$. However, again by the convexity we have
$C(t) \geq g_n(t)$ for $t \notin (\mu, t_\mu)$.
Thus $C(0) \geq g_n(0) = C(\mu) - c_n \mu > 0$ in contradiction to $C(0) = 0$. From $C(t) \geq g_n(t)$ for $t \notin (\mu, t_\mu)$ we conclude: for all $t \geq 0$ $C(t) \geq \lim_{n\to\infty} g_n(t) = a(t - \mu) + C(\mu) = a(t - t_0)$ with the definition of t_0 given in the theorem. Since for $t \leq t_0$ $a(t - t_0) \leq 0$ we can estimate $C(t)$ below by

$$K(t) \geq \begin{cases} a(t - t_0) & \text{for } t \geq t_0 \\ 0 & \text{otherwise} \end{cases}$$

and now the theorem follows from Theorem 14.

References

Amsel, A. (1962). Frustrative nonreward in partial reinforcement and discrimination learning. *Psychological Review*, **69**, 306-328.

Balzer, W., Moulines, C.U., Sneed, J.D. (1987). *An architectonic for science*. Dodrecht: D. Reidel Publishing Company.

Bauer, H. (1978). *Wahrscheinlichkeitstheorie und Grundzüge der Maßtheorie*. Berlin: de Gruyter.

Dollard, J., Doob, L., Miller, N., Mowrer, O., & Sears, R. (1939). *Frustration and aggression*. New Haven: Yale University Press.

Holling, H. (1989). *Psychische Beanspruchung durch Wartezeiten bei computergestützten Tätigkeiten*. Springer: Heidelberg.

Holling, H., & Gediga, G. (1987). Stress in waiting situations – Predictions from a mathematical model. In E.E. Roskam & R. Suck (Eds.), *Progress in Mathematical Psychology*. Amsterdam: North-Holland.

Lazarus, R. S. (1966). *Psycholgical stress and the coping process*. New York: McGraw-Hill.

Lewin, K. (1940). Formalization and progress in psychology. *University of Iowa studies in child welfare*. 16, 3, 9-42.

Mandler, G. (1964). The interrution of behavior. In Levine, R. (Ed.), *Comments on Dr. Schachter's and Dr. Latané's paper*. Lincoln: University of Nebraska Press.

Mandler, G. (1975). *Mind and Emotion*. New York: Wiley.

Shneiderman, B. (1984). Response time and display rate in human performance with computers. *Computing Surveys*, 16, 3, 265-285.

Stegmüller, W. (1986). *Theorie und Erfahrung: Dritter Teilband. Die Entwicklung des neuen Strukturalismus seit 1973*. Berlin: Springer.

Author Index

W

XYZ

Subject Index

List of Contributors

Prof. Dr. Wolfgang Balzer; Seminar for Philosophy, Logic, and Philosophy of Science; University of Munich; Ludwigstraße 31; D - 8000 München; FRG

Dipl.-Psych. Elke Heise; Institute of Psychology; University of Göttingen; Goßlerstraße 14; D - 3400 Göttingen; FRG

PD Dr. Heinz Holling; Department of Psychology; University of Osnabrück; Knollstraße 15; D - 4500 Osnabrück; FRG

Dr. Martti Kuokkanen; Department of Philosophy; University of Helsinki; Unioninkatu 40B; 00170 Helsinki; Finland

Dipl.-Math. Phillio Marcou; Poste Restante; GR - N.Karlovassi-Samos; Greece

Dr. Ekkehard Stephan; Institute of Social Psychology; University of Cologne; Herbert-Lewin-Straße 2; D - 5000 Köln; FRG

Dr. Reinhard Suck; Department of Psychology; University of Osnabrück; Heger-Tor-Wall 12; D - 4500 Osnabrück; FRG

PD Dr. Rainer Westermann; Institute of Psychology; University of Göttingen; Goßlerstraße 31; D - 3400 Göttingen; FRG

Prof. Dr. Hans Westmeyer; Institute of Psychology; Free University of Berlin; Habelschwerdter Allee 45; D - 1000 Berlin 33; FRG

List of Contributors